NELSON

BY
CLENNELL WILKINSON
Author of *Dampier*

GEORGE G. HARRAP & CO. LTD.
LONDON · BOMBAY · SYDNEY

First published 1931
by GEORGE G. HARRAP & CO. LTD.
39–41 *Parker Street, Kingsway, London, W.C.*2

PRINTED IN GREAT BRITAIN AT THE PITMAN PRESS, BATH

TO

MY WIFE

WHO WROTE DOWN THIS BOOK FROM DICTATION
AND GREATLY IMPROVED IT IN THE PROCESS
BY HER SUGGESTIONS

CONTENTS

ILLUSTRATIONS

NELSON

CHAPTER I

THE ARTIST IN ACTION

IT IS an extraordinary fact — from the biographer's point of view a rather irritating and disconcerting fact — that it seems quite impossible to discuss the character of Lord Nelson without comparing it at almost every point with that of his great contemporary the Duke of Wellington. An essay on Nelson becomes, almost before you are aware of it, as much an essay on Wellington. Modern critics seldom mention one without the other; it has become with us a fixed habit of mind.

Nor is it difficult to find the cause. You have here one of those dramatic oppositions of character and method that occur only two or three times in a nation's history. We think of Cæsar and Pompey, or — to descend the scale a little abruptly — Disraeli and Gladstone. In all these cases two violently contrasted temperaments serve to illustrate as nothing else could the opposing tendencies of the age they lived in, the apparently irreconcilable attitudes of mind which went to make up the national character. It is only by looking at them both together that we can see the picture whole. And in the same way it is by looking at them both that we can most easily understand either of them. In the case of Nelson and Wellington the contrast is curiously, almost humorously, complete. In every little detail they differed. Nelson has been called theatrical by comparison with Wellington — and theatrical, of course, he was; it was one of his leading characteristics. But this is not simply a question of manners. His whole career unfolds itself before our eyes like a stage play.

It begins in the quiet Norfolk rectory at Burnham Thorpe, and works up slowly, with the inevitability of a Greek tragedy, to its final magnificent "curtain." There never was so *complete* a life. Wellington's, on the other hand, faded out dismally in political failure and dyspepsia. Nelson died as he would have wished to die, at the hour of victory; Wellington died in his bed, and one of his last memories must have been the sound of the breaking of the windows of Apsley House by an English mob.

Wellington never mentioned those broken windows. Nelson, perhaps, would have said too much about them; they would have broken his heart. We remember the feminine strain in Nelson's character, as compared with Wellington's uncompromising masculinity. Nelson was always delicate, but neglected his health; Wellington was robust, but was careful of his. "Do not give the stomach too much to do," was the rather uninspiring slogan of his declining years. Nelson loved medals and magnificence, but dressed very carelessly; Wellington despised medals, but dressed with scrupulous care. Small things, but significant. Nelson, as a young man, fell frequently in love, and he remained a romantic lover to the end. Wellington (without putting too high a value on the ill-natured gossip of Harriette Wilson) seems to have taken women as he found them, and gone to them when he felt inclined, as much for the good of his health as anything; the cynicism of Napoleon and the raptures of Nelson were equally foreign to him.

And as in love so in war. Wellington, the realist, disliked the bloody business; Nelson saw it as a crusade. Nelson loved and idealized his men; Wellington despised his, and said so. Compare their opinions of their great antagonist — Wellington's "the fellow isn't a gentleman," and Nelson's passionate cry "I hate everything French." And, as the final and most striking contrast, there is the well-known difference in their methods of fighting. Nelson always attacked. He attacked in column against a French or a Spanish fleet in line, breaking that line, and making the issue certain within an hour or two of the firing of the first shot. Wellington, in his most characteristic actions, precisely reversed these tactics. He preferred to stand

on the defensive — his long red line of British infantry waiting quietly on the hill-top for the attack of the French
columns, who came storming up from the valley with their
flags flying, "huzza-ing like mad" — as Rifleman Harris says,
who saw them.

Thus these two great commanders expressed themselves in
battle — in attack and defence, in the column and the line. And
thus have they stamped for ever on England's fighting services
the impress of their strangely divergent temperaments. We
have never lost the tradition that a British army is at its best in
defence — or even in retreat. We have "Mons heroes," but not
"Marne heroes." We even extend the idea to foreign armies,
and hastily assume, in our newspapers, that every besieged
general — the incompetent Russian, for instance, who surrendered Port Arthur to the Japanese — has put up a gallant
defence. Undoubtedly that tradition has much to be said for
it. It is firmly founded in the national psychology. But England's sea tradition, it need hardly be pointed out, is all the
other way. There exists no kind of prejudice in favour of
rearguard actions by the British Navy. There is instead the
tradition of the "Nelson touch."

There is a well-known passage in Mr George Bernard
Shaw's introduction to his play *John Bull's Other Island* in
which the author, caught by this fascinating subject, as so
many lesser men have been, proceeds to compare the characters of Nelson and Wellington at some length. He takes
Nelson as the typical Englishman and Wellington as the typical Irishman — and it is true, of course, that the former was
born in Norfolk and the latter in Ireland — and points out,
with malicious delight, that the real Irishman is the Englishman of tradition, while the real Englishman is the traditional
theatrical foreigner. He refers to the famous story, resting
solely on the rather doubtful authority of Croker, of the one
and only meeting which ever took place between the two
men. Wellington's contemptuous disgust at Nelson's theatricality as "a professed hero, patriot, and rhapsode" — "a theatricality," says Mr Shaw, "which in an Irishman would have

been an insufferably vulgar affectation" — was quite natural and inevitable. Wellington's formula for that sort of thing was the well-known Irish one: "Sir, don't be a damned fool." It is, Mr Shaw assures us, the formula of all Irishmen for all Englishmen to this day. Nelson's genius, he argues, instead of producing intellectual keenness and scrupulousness, produced mere delirium. He was "drunk with glory, exalted by his fervent faith in the sound British patriotism of the Almighty." Getting the bit between his teeth, Mr Shaw rushes on to say that Nelson "never had to fight a technically capable and properly equipped enemy except on land where he had never been successful."

We may pause here to take a breath, and remind ourselves, first, that Nelson was often successful on land, for instance at Corsica; secondly, that the French admirals, as a matter of fact, were "technically capable" in a very high degree (they *had* to be with their tip-and-run tactics); and thirdly, that in the matter of equipment they nearly always had the advantage. In most of Nelson's actions the British ships had been at sea for weeks, or even months, whereas the French had but just emerged from harbour in apple-pie order. Their rigging, sails, and so forth, their food supplies would be better than ours. Or perhaps Mr Shaw means the guns? The French artillery, it is now generally admitted, was excellent, and their shooting often as accurate as our own. What *was* different was the man behind the gun — and the admiral behind the gunner — and the national spirit behind the admiral — which made it a rule in the British Navy to seek close action at once, and to fire always at your enemy's hull; whereas the French fired at the masts and rigging, with the object of doing what damage they could, and then getting hastily out of reach.

I cannot resist making one more quotation from Mr Shaw (it is the Mr Shaw of the nineties, and perhaps I ought to apologise to him for digging it all up):

Compare Wellington, who had to fight Napoleon's armies, Napoleon's marshals, and finally Napoleon himself, without one moment of illusion as to the human material he had to command, without one gush of the "Kiss me, Hardy" emotion which enabled Nelson to idolize his crews and his staff, without forgetting even in his dreams that the normal British officer of that time was an incapable amateur (as he still is) and the normal British soldier a never-do-well (he is now a depressed and respectable young man). No wonder Wellington became an accomplished comedian in the art of anti-climax, scandalizing the unfortunate Croker, responding to the demand for glorious sentiments by the most disenchanting touches of realism, and, generally, pricking the English windbag at its most explosive crises of distention. Nelson, intensely nervous and theatrical, made an enormous fuss about victories so cheap that he would have deserved shooting if he had lost them, and, not content with lavishing splendid fighting on helpless adversaries like the heroic De Brueys or Villeneuve (who had not even the illusion of heroism when he went like a lamb to the slaughter), got himself killed by his passion for exposing himself to death in that sublime defiance of it which was perhaps the supreme tribute of the exquisite coward to the King of Terrors (for, believe me, you cannot be a hero without being a coward: supersense cuts both ways), the result being a tremendous effect on the gallery. Wellington, most capable of captains, was neither a hero nor a patriot: perhaps not even a coward; and had it not been for the Nelsonic anecdotes invented for him — "Up guards, and at 'em" and so forth — and the fact that the antagonist with whom he finally closed was such a master of theatrical effect that Wellington could not fight him without getting into his limelight, nor overthrow him (most unfortunately for us all) without drawing the eyes of the whole world to the catastrophe, the Iron Duke would have been almost forgotten by this time.

This is all wrong. I am not concerned with the wider implication — what may be called the international aspect of the matter — which so much interests Mr Shaw, and I do not think we need waste any time over the suggestion that Nelson must have been at heart a coward, simply because he behaved like an unusually brave man. Mr Shaw's weakness — his typical Irish weakness — is that he can appreciate only the more obvious kind of stage effect; which may be one explanation of his resounding success as a playwright. He does not allow enough for the dramatic value of mere reticence (when one comes to think of it, silences are rare in his plays). Yet there is a theatricality of reticence, which the English as a nation have commonly preferred, and which is exemplified in their two military heroes Wellington and Kitchener. But Wellington's occasional "goddams" are accepted by Mr Shaw as a proof of Wellington's naturalness, whereas Nelson's "Kiss me, Hardy" is dismissed as a piece of studied stage emotionalism. In fact, both of them were natural, instinctive. Great men, it may even be argued, are always theatrical figures (is there not a touch of it in Mr Shaw?). They cannot help themselves. Wellington was every bit as theatrical as Nelson, and his "goddams" produced the same "tremendous effect on the gallery" as Nelson's "Kiss me," — as the Iron Duke must very well have known. The difference is that while the gallery admired Wellington, it loved Nelson. I am trying not to take a side in this Nelson *versus* Wellington controversy — a question which will continue to divide mankind into two camps as long as we are able to sit up and argue. Each of us has his preference; it is a question of temperament, not of facts. But I do protest against the assumption that Nelson was any more of a mountebank than Wellington, or Napoleon, or Metternich, or Blücher. Like all of these, he had the great man's gift of expressing himself completely — in battle, in death, in whatever he was doing. He expressed that, and nothing else, with perfect simplicity and sincerity.

It is important that we should try to deal simply with great and simple men. It is one of the virtues of the Duke of Wellington, from a historian's point of view, that he never seems to have done or said a single thing out of character. Nelson is a little more complicated than that. He was fond of attitudinizing. His mental attitudes, indeed, were almost as remarkable as those more famous attitudes of Lady Hamilton's, which her contemporaries loved to paint. They were his own, as hers were, and as unaffected; and they all meant the same thing. But they do make it possible to argue about his psychology, and dissect it, in a way in which it would be absurd to dissect Wellington. Moreover, the very fact that

Nelson was so much beloved led to his being credited with all sorts of virtues which he never possessed, while his obvious faults—his vanity, for instance—were ignored.

Adam Collingwood, writing in 1806, said with truth of Nelson that he "was attentive to and gentle in delivering his orders; he was mild without effeminacy; of an expanded heart; he was complacent to his inferiors; compassionate to the afflicted; considerate to, and consequently loved by everyone" —and then went on to spoil it all by asserting that his hero was also "unambitious." Could a more absurd claim be put forward on behalf of a commander who, on two occasions, is reported to have gone into action exclaiming: "A peerage or Westminster Abbey!" It is true that his ambition had a fanatical quality, which was inspired by love of country, not of self; it is true that he was one of the greatest patriots that ever lived; but it is also true that he was always determined to make his own "niche," and boasted that he would one day have a "Gazette" all to himself. Yet the petty meannesses of ambition were unknown to him: he was utterly without jealousy; he was ready to take every one to his heart, and seems never to have known a man well without liking him. In the same way attempts have been made to defend his treatment of Lady Nelson, whereas it is painfully obvious that he was an unusually susceptible young man (even for a sailor), ready to throw himself at the feet of the first good-looking woman he met, and that he married Mrs Nisbet (as she then was) without ever being really in love with her, and threw her over without hesitating when the right woman came along. He would not have been Nelson if his heart had not ruled his head. In the same way we can make nothing very noble of his childish, fantastical hatred of Buonaparte. It was out of all reason. "That vile fellow Buonaparte," he writes to a friend, "I have long known him to be a Thief, Lyer, and Murdurer." And he appeared to extend this feeling to the whole French nation. Yet Southey and his other admirers have represented these characteristic exuberances as no more than a proper patriotism. The modern biographer, in fact, will find that

B

one of his first duties to Nelson is to save him from his friends.

We must see Nelson for what he was — a poet and an artist in temperament. It has been said of Napoleon that he, also, was an artist, and that men were the material he happened to work in. As for Nelson, he was always composing lyrics of action and setting them to the music of his naval guns. Nelson, for the first time, made sea warfare beautiful, a thing not only of majesty and self-sacrifice and colour, but of a swift and certain rhythm, like a movement by Brahms. He would stand on the deck of his flagship in a kind of ecstasy, watching the long columns of his battleships bearing down upon the enemy line, breaking it or encircling it, exactly as he had planned — exactly as he had explained so eagerly to his captains the night before round the table in the great cabin — each ship arriving punctually at its proper station, carrying the flag of England triumphant through the smoke. That was the "Nelson touch," and it was the touch of an artist.

He was as tender-hearted as a woman (his men were his "children" to him), but he had also an artist's ruthlessness; in his pictures the red is not left out. He had an incredible swiftness, too, the swiftness of the hawk, which appeared not only in battle, but in everything he did. Five minutes, he used to declare, makes the difference between a victory and a defeat. "Whatever Lord Nelson might have to do," says one who knew him, "he did it instantly — it was his habit." * And this sensitive, theatrical, passionate temperament was allied to an irresistible personal charm which is plainly one of the first necessities for an artist who would work in human material. Napoleon understood this; it was Wellington's weakness (not his strength) that he did not. Nelson was the kind of man who, if he had been employed in a modern business office (with the motto "Do it now!" hanging, no doubt, on the wall!), would have been known in twentieth-century slang as a "professional charmer." Yet his friends would have agreed that, like all the most successful of that type, he was

---

* *Farrington Diary*, December 10, 1820.

quite unaware of his own power. He behaved as he did instinctively, laying siege to the affections of every one he met; and, whatever the Duke may have thought of him, it is amusing and delightful to observe how quickly he won the hearts of all kinds of sailormen, from hard-bitten old admirals, who had never been accused of sentimentality, down to the pressed men, escaped criminals, and goodness knows what else, who populated the lower decks. His rise in his profession was meteoric for those days, yet I do not suppose that there has ever been a successful career which aroused less jealousy.

I have mentioned the Duke again — one cannot help it. Has anyone ever pointed out that that famous meeting with Wellington gave us, as a matter of fact, an outstanding example of Nelson's powers of fascination? Here is Wellington's account of it:

> I went to the Colonial Office in Downing Street, and there I was shown into the little waiting room on the right hand, where I found, also waiting to see the Secretary of State, a gentleman whom, from his likeness to his pictures and the loss of an arm, I immediately recognised as Lord Nelson. He could not know who I was, but he entered at once into conversation with me, if I can call it conversation, for it was almost all on his side, and all about himself; and in, really, a style so vain and silly as to surprise and almost disgust me. I suppose something that I happened to say may have made him guess that I was somebody, and he went out of the room for a moment, I have no doubt to ask the office-keeper who I was, for when he came back he was altogether a different man, both in manner and matter. All that I had thought a charlatan style had vanished, and he talked of the state of this country and of the aspect and probabilities of affairs on the Continent with a good sense and a knowledge of subjects both at home and abroad that surprised me equally and more agreeably than the first part of our interview had done: in fact, he talked like an officer and a statesman. The Secretary of State kept us long waiting, and certainly for the last half or three quarters of an hour, I don't know that I ever had a conversation that interested me more.

Is it not perfectly obvious that Nelson, scenting something hostile in his companion's demeanour, walked out of the room, ascertained who, and what kind of man, he was, came back and made his usual conquest? It is a tribute to the force of character of Sir Arthur Wellesley (as he then was) that it was necessary for Nelson to make this tentative approach. It was indeed a historic encounter. But the attack in column won.

We have said that he was ambitious. He thirsted for glory. But he did not thirst for wealth; and that was something exceptional in his — and perhaps any — age. In Nelson's time bribery and corruption were rampant everywhere, and the Navy seems to have given its employees more and bigger opportunities than those of almost any other profession. The tapping of Government stores alone cost the country about half a million a year — a colossal sum for those days. Soon after Nelson was given his first command, a Parliamentary Committee reported that in the year 1780 there was deficient in Portsmouth alone: "278,042 lbs. of bread; 9672 bags of bread; 11,162 pieces of beef; 4649 pieces of pork; 3748 lbs. of flour and 2798 lbs. of suet; besides considerable deficiencies in other species of victually stores." * And we all know Marryat's entertaining description in *Peter Simple* of the post-captain who habitually used both his stores and his men for domestic purposes at his house on shore. That case is plainly intended to be taken as typical. As to bribery, every one was underpaid, and it was a recognized thing that they should make up for it by charging "fees," which was generally done quite openly and at a fixed rate. A man might make £2750 with a salary of only £250. Yet Nelson remained a poor man until he reached the very top of the tree and was voted money by Parliament. His ambition was quite otherwise. We remember the last words he ever spoke — "Thank God I have done my Duty." That was his favourite word, and by it he simply meant living up to his ideal. It is given to few men on their death-beds to see their ambition so completely fulfilled.

Now it is undoubtedly true that Nelson, without thinking about it, schooled and trained himself for his chosen part in

---

* Sir J. K. Laughton in the *United Services Magazine*, 1895.

life — that of a national hero. And included in the "make-up"
for such a part is a kind of innocent vanity, which is not so
much a personal vanity as a vanity in his achievements. Nelson always "played up." For instance, he welcomed the acclamations of the mob, except when he had sea business to attend to, when he quietly and quickly evaded them. And we
may take it that he liked having his portrait painted; it is one
of the principal duties of a hero. In a dozen different portraits we have been shown that slight, one-armed figure, and
can guess the quick movements and the eager way of speaking. Unfortunately he never sat to a painter of the very first
rank; none of these portraits shows real intellectual understanding. The death-masks, one of which may be seen in the
museum at Portsmouth Dockyard, are more eloquent. The
physical suffering, which he knew so well in life and was not
spared in death, has left strangely little mark upon that calm
face. Nelson is at peace, his duty done. His eyes — which were
not like other sailors' eyes, for instead of seeming to be fixed
upon some distant horizon they concentrated brightly on the
person to whom he spoke — are closed. And because so much
of the animation has gone from the poet's face, we are able
to notice the large, sensitive mouth and the jutting, determined underlip — the mark of a man of action.*

It is easy, with these portraits and with all his letters before
us—those miles of letters which Sir N. Harris Nicolas has preserved, in which Nelson poured out his simple soul to all and
sundry, proving once again that the least literary of men are
often the best letter-writers — it is easy to produce some kind of
mental reconstruction of this heroic and lovable figure. We
see him taking his ease in the garden at Burnham Thorpe, or
at Merton, quietly reading a book, but with one eye cocked at
the garden gate, where at any moment his friend Captain
Collingwood may appear, with news that war is declared and
the fleet ordered to sea; we see him hurrying about the streets
of Portsmouth or Plymouth, past the bow-windowed houses

* See Appendix II.

and the delightful early nineteenth-century inns, where the original John Bull drank beer at the tap; and we see him at sea again, in his real home, on the deck of a man-of-war, happy and confident, hastening to his next victory; and we feel that there is no personality in the whole of our history that we can hope to know as intimately as his.

It is impossible, of course, to say anything new about Nelson. If that is to be a *sine qua non,* there will never be another book written about one of the most interesting and attractive figures in the annals of the sea, and perhaps the greatest of all naval captains. We shall never get beyond Southey — who wrote a model short biography, but by no means a model life of Nelson. Although he realized the great truth that, in his own words, "the best eulogy of Nelson is the faithful history of his actions," Southey slurred over many things which would be frankly stated nowadays, and he inserted all kinds of doubtful anecdotes without telling us where he got them. In point of fact they were all lifted from Harrison, or Clarke and MacArthur, or some other authority. (No one can be accused of lifting facts from Southey; there is no Southey to lift from.)

Nelson, I suggest, should be written about freely and often — not only as an exponent of naval tactics, or as the lover of Lady Hamilton, but for his own sake. He should be a favourite subject with English writers, even if they are aware (as I am) that they can make no new contribution to history. He should be written about for modern readers in the modern way. He should not be taken too desperately seriously. I think it was Mr Chesterton who once said — how many years ago! — that no one could love the Church of England properly who did not see the humour of it.

Those are the considerations which have led me to undertake the task of writing these succeeding chapters — those, and a passionate interest in the subject, which every Englishman must surely feel who has attempted, even in the most amateurish way, to investigate it.

CHAPTER II

THE MIDSHIPMEN'S BERTH

IT IS sad that we have not Nelson's own account of his boy-
hood, for he was evidently an extraordinary child. In the
short *Sketch of My Life* which he wrote for MacArthur he
merely states briefly that he was born on September 29, 1758,
in the parsonage house at Burnham Thorpe, and was put to
school first at "The High School at Norwich," and afterward
at North Walsham, and went to sea at the age of twelve.

In the absence of any autobiographical information about
those first twelve years it was left to Nelson's early biographers
to fill in the details themselves. They approached the task
with enthusiasm. Few careers of great men have been more
generously furnished with those flattering, if unconvincing,
anecdotes of childhood which were so dear to our ancestors'
hearts. Even Washington's famous cherry-tree must acknowledge a rival in the pear-tree in a schoolmaster's garden which
Nelson climbed, not — it need hardly be said — with any intention of eating the pears, but merely to show his greedier but
more cowardly playmates that the thing could be done. And
Washington's "I cannot lie" is paralleled by Nelson's question
when his grandmother asked him if he had not been overcome by fear when he lost his way in the dark and was out
all night. "Fear, Grandmamma!" he asked. "I never saw fear;
what is it?"

The old parsonage house has gone, but its site is known, and
the general appearance of the pretty little village of Burnham
Thorpe and of the parsonage garden cannot have been greatly
altered since the fair-haired, fragile little boy played there
with his brothers and sisters. The villagers will show you a

tree in the old churchyard where Nelson is said to have spent an entire night because some one dared him to face the ghosts which were believed to haunt the place. The most that can be said of such stories is that they do seem to indicate that young Horace, as he was then called,* made a strong impression upon his contemporaries. He was obviously a bold and enterprising boy, ready for any kind of venture, and we can guess that he must have been a source of considerable anxiety to his parents. Years afterwards he wrote of himself, "I require nursing like a child; my mind carries me beyond my strength, and will do me up; but such is my nature."

He never seems to have shown any special inclination for the sea. And, owing to his delicate physique, that was certainly not the profession that his guardians would have selected for him in the ordinary course of things. The headaches and pains in the chest of which he was a victim in later life may not have troubled him at this stage, but we know that he was considered a "weak" child. "His health had been much impaired by an agueish complaint." † Moreover, he never in his life went to sea in a small ship without suffering terribly from sea-sickness. Yet it is generally agreed that it was on his own initiative that a letter was written to his uncle Captain Maurice Suckling, then commanding the *Raisonnable* (64). His mother was dead (leaving the widower with eight children), and perhaps he was bored with school. Anyhow, the letter was written, and Captain Suckling's reply was to send for the boy to join his ship, then lying in the Medway.

Southey (as usual paraphrasing Harrison) has given us an admirable little account of Nelson's introduction to the British Navy — how he arrived at Chatham on the coach from London, where his father had left him, and wandered about in the cold, trying to find his ship; and of how, when at last he

---

* The name Horatio came into the Nelson family from the Walpoles — rich relations to whom Mr Nelson owed the three livings he held. Young Horatio Nelson was Horace Walpole's first cousin, thrice removed.
† Clarke and MacArthur.

THE MIDSHIPMAN'S INTRODUCTION TO HIS BERTH

From a sketch by Captain Marryat in the British Museum.

midshipmen's berth would probably be surrounded with canvas screens, which could easily be removed when the ship was cleared for action — as, indeed, were most of the wooden bulkheads — and it would be situated in any convenient corner of the orlop, or lowest deck above the hold. The atmosphere in this part of the ship, below the water-line, must have been stifling. Even the common sailors, who slept and ate their meals between the guns on the deck above packed together like sardines, breathed a purer air. In this corner of the orlop deck the midshipmen's hammocks were slung, and the chests stowed beneath them, and there would be a rough table for meals. When the ship was cleared for action, and all the canvas screens, chests, hammocks, and other movables were swept away, and the cockpit filled with wounded, these mess tables, which were permanent fixtures, would be used by the surgeon for his rough-and-ready operations. (Blood stains and gravy stains mixed!)

A hurricane lamp and a few candles supplied the only light. The food was terrible, consisting mainly of salt beef and pork with biscuits; the biscuits were full of weevils, and one of the first things a midshipman learned was that weevils were of two kinds, one of which tasted bitter and caused a dryness of the throat, while the other — which was, properly speaking, a maggot, not a weevil, and was nicknamed "the bargeman" — slipped down easily enough if you shut your eyes and did not allow your appetite to be spoiled by the sight of his ugly black head. Sometimes they supplemented this menu with roast rats, caught in the storerooms; Rear-Admiral Raigersfeld * relates that there was a regular trade in these animals, the price of which went up and down according to the state of the other provisions. He has also a ghastly story of a completely bald mouse found dead at the bottom of a jar of butter which had been inexplicably full of hairs.

But the classic description of an officers' mess on the orlop

---

* *The Life of a Sea Officer*, privately printed 1830. Modern edition: the Seafarers' Library, edited by G. E. Manwaring, London, 1929.

deck is, of course, in *Roderick Random*. Smollett describes
it as "a square of about six feet," formed by the officers' chests
and by pieces of canvas nailed round to the beams of the
ship. There was a locker for food above the table in the centre. Three such messes, those of the quartermasters, the surgeons, and the midshipmen, had been rigged up side by side
within the cable tiers. He adds a lurid description of the eating and sleeping arrangements. The hammocks were slung
close together, and during rough weather it was impossible to
sleep owing to "a most horrible din, occasioned by the play of
the gun-carriages upon the deck above, the cracking of cabins,
the howling of the winds through the shrouds, the confused
noise of the ship's crew, the pipes of the boatswain and his
mates, the trumpets of the lieutenants, and the clanking of
the chain pumps." And now that we are quoting Smollett,
one further inconvenience of life on board ship may be mentioned. The space between decks was insufficient to allow a
tall man to walk upright, so that Smollett represents Commodore Trunnion as having "contracted a habit of stooping by
living so long aboard"; and the same habit may be noted
among the sailors depicted in the naval art of the period.

We do not know what may have been Nelson's feelings as
he peered into this gloomy hole — whether, for instance, he
would have agreed with the great Mr Easy's description of a
similar berth as "infinitely inferior to the dog kennels which
received his father's pointers." The sight of it possibly acted
as an additional spur to his ambition by displaying the practical advantages of an early promotion to the gunroom. He
did not know that he was to pass the last hour of his life beside the midshipmen's berth in the cockpit of the *Victory*. At
the moment, probably, his principal sensation was one of acute
depression. As he assayed the unaccustomed task of climbing
into his hammock on that first night of his great career he
must have felt a very lonely little boy, and nothing more.

Then his messmates arrived. There would be one or two
youngsters like himself, a few older midshipmen, and perhaps a middle-aged mate, a man of forty or fifty, who would

act as a president of the mess. What is quite certain is that, however this mess was composed, young Horatio must have been one of the most popular members of it from the start. Contemporary authorities are agreed that there was a great deal of bullying and brutality among the midshipmen at this period, and perhaps even more of it later. The most trivial arguments were settled by a resort to fisticuffs, and it was a constant preoccupation of naval commanders to prevent their young officers from going ashore and fighting duels about nothing in particular. Nelson must have been worse than useless in a rough-and-tumble, and in later life he always expressed the strongest objection to duelling. Yet we feel with absolute certainty that he was liked from the beginning, and early accepted as a leading spirit.

It is a fact, however, and it may possibly be traced to this moment, that Nelson as a commander was always especially kind to his midshipmen — his "children." There is a good story of how Nelson, then a captain, went out of his way to encourage a timid little middy, with the sporting challenge, "Well, Sir, I am going a race to the mast-head, and beg I may meet you there." We may be sure he did. Or again, upon introducing a midshipman to the Governor of the Barbadoes, "Your Excellency, I make it a rule to introduce them to all the good company I can, as they have few to look up to beside myself during the time they are at sea."

A few days later Captain Suckling came aboard. He was a man of some distinction, and with a talent for getting on, which later procured for him the post of Comptroller for the Navy, in which he was able to assist his nephew's career materially. At this time, however, he was known only for his share in a gallant little exploit at sea in the year 1757, which, as it turned out, was to be his single adventure of the kind. This action, by an odd coincidence, took place on October 21, later to be known all over the English-speaking world as Trafalgar Day. Captain Forrest in the *Princess Augusta,* with the *Dreadnought* (Captain Suckling) and *Edinburgh* (Captain Langdon), all 60-gun ships, was detailed by the admiral at Jamaica to intercept a French convoy homeward bound. He did so, but found that he had caught a Tartar, for the convoy had an escort of four ships of the line and three frigates. On the quarterdeck of the *Princess Augusta* the three English captains met, and held one of the briefest consultations on record.

"Well," said Forrest, "you see they are come out to engage us." Suckling replied, "I think it would be a pity to disappoint them." Langdon agreed; and a few minutes later the three ships formed line and ran down to attack the seven. The engagement lasted three hours, when the French drew off, the English being too badly damaged to follow them. Indeed, it was all they could do to get back to Jamaica. So the French won the trick, for their convoy was saved; but the honours were distinctly with the English.

Nelson was always very fond of his uncle Suckling, and can seldom have been more pleased to see him than on this occasion. As for Suckling, he had been shocked at the suggestion that this delicate little boy should be sent to sea. "What," he wrote, "has poor Horatio done . . . that he, above all the rest, should be sent to rough it out at sea?" However, since they insisted, "let him come," and perhaps, in the first action, "a cannon ball may knock off his head and provide for him at once." He was evidently sorry for the child, and would be correspondingly kind to him now.

Nothing more is known of Nelson's life on the *Raisonnable* except that it was very brief. The ship had been commissioned for service against the Spaniards, in connexion with a dispute about the Falkland Islands; but the Dons, finding that the French were unwilling to support them, very wisely evacuated the islands and withdrew all their claims. So the *Raisonnable,* with many other British ships, was paid off, and Captain Suckling found himself transferred to the guardship in the Medway, the *Triumph.* He took his young nephew with him; but it is interesting to note that he changed the boy's rating, entering him on the books of the *Triumph* not as midshipman, but as captain's servant. Now this, again,

CAPTAIN MAURICE SUCKLING

From the painting by T. Bardwell in the National Portrait Gallery.

was a common practice; it was, indeed, a recognized method
by which the sons of gentlemen might enter the Navy. They
were not, of course, expected to perform any menial duties,
but were supposed to go through a practical apprenticeship in
their profession. Meantime their parents paid for their up-
keep, while the captain pocketed their pay as servants. Everybody did it. Even the lieutenants and the master might have
one such "servant" each, and the captain was always allowed
several, according to the size of the ship's company.

But Captain Suckling now took a step which, though well
conceived from the point of view of Nelson's education, was
obviously a flagrant breach of the regulations. While keeping
his name in the muster-book of the *Triumph* (and continuing
to draw his pay and victuals), he sent him off on a voyage to
the West Indies in a merchant ship to learn something about
sailoring. Nelson's father would raise no objection, but it was
plain that the public funds were being defrauded. Such prac-
tices as this were not put a stop to until the trial by court-
martial in 1788 of a certain Captain Coffin, who had four boys
who had never been on board entered in his muster-book as
his servants. Sometimes children of five or six, or younger,
were so entered with the idea of gaining seniority. In the
present case, however, Suckling might argue that his nephew
was better employed, from the point of view of his future use-
fulness to his country, than if he had remained on the guardship. And indeed there can be no manner of doubt that this
early voyage laid the foundation of Nelson's practical seamanship.

But it had another and rather startling effect which Captain
Suckling never contemplated. The lad came back with a
strong aversion for the Royal Navy and its whole system of
discipline. He has told us himself that he had a "horror" of
it, and would go about quoting a saying then common among
seamen, "Aft the most honour, forward the better man." The
commander of the trader in which Nelson had sailed was a
certain John Rathbone, who had served under Suckling on
the *Dreadnought* as a master's mate, but, though he had

passed his examination, could never get promotion, nor latterly even employment, in the Navy, and had joined the Merchant Service in disgust. We may infer that he had no love for the Navy, and had spoon-fed the boy with sentimental stories of the brutal discipline on a man-of-war — which, as he was getting Nelson's services for nothing, was rather a shabby return.

Captain Suckling must have been a little startled and amused to discover these Bolshevist sentiments in the breast of the budding admiral, but he appears to have taken it goodnaturedly, and to have adopted the most sensible measures to counteract it. Nelson says that his uncle held out to him as a reward that "if I attended well to my navigation I should go in the cutter and decked long-boat, which was attached to the Commanding Officer's ship at Chatham." What boy would have refused such an offer! It meant many trips up and down the river, and by means of it he soon became a good pilot from Chatham to the Tower of London, down the Swin and to the North Foreland. He learned, thus early, to be confident of himself among rocks and sands, "which has many times since been of the very greatest comfort to me." And we may take it, amid these new excitements, he soon forgot John Rathbone's grouse against the Navy.

Taking into consideration all that is known about the lives of young naval officers of that time, and the manner in which some rudimentary knowledge of seamanship was hammered into them, and bearing in mind also that there was no war on, and no chance of active service, it may be said that young Nelson had made a lucky start.

CHAPTER III

THE FIRST COMMAND

NELSON was still only a boy when, in the spring of 1773, an expedition was being fitted out of a kind which seems to make a special appeal to the boyish imagination. It was proposed to send the *Carcase* and the *Racehorse,* two stoutly built vessels of the type known as "bombs," on a voyage of discovery in the Arctic Seas. The expedition was fitted out with great care, and the First Lord of the Admiralty, Lord Sandwich, took a personal interest in the equipment and manning of the ships. Every member of the crew was specially selected, and, unfortunately for Nelson's hopes, it was laid down as a rule from the beginning that no boys were to be employed. But here we get one of our first glimpses of his quality when he had set his heart on anything. He once said of himself in another connexion: "I know it is my disposition that difficulties and dangers do but increase my desire of attempting them." There was likely to be plenty of both on this expedition. In command of the *Carcase* was a certain Captain Lutwidge, and it was to him that Nelson turned, "using every influence," he tells us, to induce the Captain to get round the regulations by rating him as his coxswain. It was a cool suggestion from a slip of a boy of fifteen, but the "interest" (presumably Suckling's) won in the end, and when the expedition left the Nore on June 4, young Nelson was on board. Perhaps they had kept him out of sight of the First Lord of the Admiralty when the great man came down to bid them farewell.

This was not a particularly distinguished Arctic expedition; indeed, if Captain Lutwidge's coxswain had not been present, few ordinary readers would ever have heard of it. On July 30 they had reached the latitude of 80° 13' — nothing very remarkable if studied in a modern map — and found themselves becalmed in a large bay with the ice rapidly increasing behind them. The situation was not without danger; but in the meantime there were tempting opportunities for sport on shore. Polar bears would come down close to the ship, for they had not yet learned to be afraid of man (the penguins of the Antarctic have not learned it yet), and, of course, there was great keenness to pursue them. Here was the occasion of the most celebrated of all the anecdotes of Nelson's youth. One night he and a comrade slipped off the ship, entirely against orders, and went in pursuit of bears. Their absence was discovered and caused some anxiety, but at dawn they were seen, in the dim light, at some distance from the ship, furiously engaged with a large bear. Their ammunition had given out, and Nelson was seen striking at the bear with the butt-end of his musket across a chasm in the ice which happily divided them. He was encouraging his companion, crying out that they would yet get the "devil."

There is a famous picture by Benjamin Westall, R.A., in which this Homeric contest is depicted with much unconscious humour. Nelson, who appears extremely small for his years, aims his futile blows at a bear of incredible size and ferocity, which does nothing in reply. Polar bears are not usually of a temper to allow boys to bully them, but this one was probably subdued by the hero's flashing eye, which the painter has strongly emphasized. Captain Lutwidge saved the animal from further humiliation by firing a signal of recall, and when the two truants returned to the *Carcase,* he sent for them and demanded an explanation of their conduct. Nelson, "pouting his lips as he was wont to do when agitated," could only reply that he had wanted to get the animal's skin to take home to his father. This story, which modern writers find it so hard to believe, seems to have been widely accepted as early as 1806, and, as the longest version appears in Harrison, it may be that it has Lady Hamilton's authority.

"On another occasion," says Harrison, "two officers in a boat belonging to the *Racehorse* having fired at and wounded one of these animals [walruses], it immediately dived and brought up a number of others, which all joined in an attack on the boat, wresting an oar from one of the men, and were with difficulty prevented from staving or over-setting the boat. But a boat from the *Carcase* guided by the intrepid young coxswain soon arrived and effectually dispersed them." The Arctic seemed to have suited Nelson. Neither the cold grey monotony of the surrounding landscape nor the unpleasantness of the situation in which the expedition now found itself could affect his health or his spirits. It was at this point that Captain Phipps of the *Racehorse,* who led the expedition, began to doubt whether he could extricate his ships before the winter set in. A winter in the Arctic was, in those days, almost unthinkable, and he therefore provisioned his boats and sent them off with parties to man-haul them across the ice in the bay until they found more open water, where the rest of the ships' companies might join them. Nelson was in charge of the four-oared cutter; he must have been proud of his command, for he tells us that he had "exerted himself" to get it, and it is easy to believe that he thoroughly enjoyed this journey across the ice at a time when his health was probably better than at any other period of his life. As it happens, however, a favourable wind sprang up, the ships were able to break through and overtake the boats, which they took on board, and the whole expedition sailed comfortably home to England, where the *Racehorse* and the *Carcase* were paid off on October 14, 1773.

Within a fortnight, thanks to Suckling's "interest," Nelson was transferred to the *Seahorse* frigate, then fitting out for the East Indies in Sir Edward Hughes's squadron. Having just spent four months in the coldest part of the world, he was now going to the hottest. He was at first rated as a midshipman, and he sailed as such when the squadron left England in November 1773. After reaching the East Indies his rating

was changed to that of able seaman, not through any fault
of his own, but to make room among the midshipmen for one
of the captain's sons. As an able seaman, stationed in the
foretop, he attracted the notice of the master, Surridge, and,
at his intercession, was again rated midshipman and transferred to the quarterdeck. In the *Colonial Magazine* for
July 1841 there was published a curious letter addressed by one
Mr Bentham, of the Navy Office, to a Mr Kee, a Navy agent,
who "he understands is agent to Mr Surridge, the master of
the *Seahorse*," and "should be obliged to him for a recommendation in favour of Horatio Nelson, a young lad, nephew
to Captain Suckling, who was going in that ship." The
writer adds that "the master is a necessary man for a young
lad to be introduced to," and certainly Nelson made few more
useful friends than Surridge. Another acquaintance first
made on this voyage was that of Thomas Troubridge, then a
youngster not much older than himself. But apart from
these friendships there was little to enliven the tedium of one
of the least eventful voyages he ever made.

The description of Nelson's personal appearance at this
time, as given by Surridge, is almost startlingly different from
all previous accounts. Evidently the Arctic had made a new
man of him. He was now "a boy with a florid countenance,
rather stout and athletic." It is not easy to believe this, and
anyhow the climate of the East Indies soon restored the old
flimsiness. He had a severe attack of malaria which came
near to ending his life, and did reduce him to a "mere skeleton." As the modern Englishman knows well enough, seventeen is a dangerous age in which to transfer suddenly from
the Polar regions to the fever-stricken Indies. Nelson was so
ill that for some time he "entirely lost the use of his limbs";
and on March 14, 1776, he was discharged sick and put on
board the *Dolphin* for a passage to England. It was none too
soon. For the first and perhaps the last time in his life his
courage entirely deserted him. As he swung in his hammock
on the *Dolphin* he almost gave himself up to despair. Many
years later he described his sensations:

I felt impressed with a feeling that I should never rise in my profession. My mind was staggered with a view of the difficulties I had to surmount, and the little interest I possessed. I could discover no means of reaching the object of my ambition. After a long and gloomy reverie, in which I almost wished myself overboard, a sudden glow of patriotism was kindled within me, and presented my King and Country as my patron. "Well, then," I exclaimed, "I will be a hero, and confiding in Providence, I will brave every danger."

Quite a change from the days when he despised the King's service and objected to its discipline! In the meantime he tells us himself that he owed his life to the kind attentions of Captain Pigot of the *Dolphin,* who seems to have looked after him like a father until the ship reached England.

On October 8, just a fortnight after the *Dolphin* was paid off, Nelson was well enough to join his new ship, the *Worcester,* as acting lieutenant. This rapid promotion was no doubt due to the influence of his uncle, the Comptroller, who also gave him a letter of introduction to Captain Mark Robinson of the *Worcester,* who, in his turn, introduced him to the Commander-in-Chief at Portsmouth. But what particularly gratified Nelson was that when the *Worcester* was sent to sea in very bad weather in charge of a convoy to Gibraltar, the captain paid him the compliment of giving him a watch. "Although," says Nelson, "my age [he was nineteen] might have been a sufficient cause for not entrusting me with the charge of a watch, yet Captain Robinson used to say, 'he felt as easy when I was upon deck as any officer in the ship'."

The return of the *Worcester* to England marks an important point in Nelson's history. Several things happened. In the first place he passed his examination for lieutenant. Captain Suckling was himself on the board of examiners, and a pretty story is told to the effect that he concealed his nephew's identity until all the questions had been triumphantly answered, when he rose from his seat and introduced him to the other examiners. He did more, for he secured Nelson's appointment the very next day (April 10, 1777) as lieutenant of the 32-gun frigate *Lowestoft,* then fitting for the West Indies; and the *Lowestoft* was commanded by Captain William Locker, who, when Suckling died, was to take his place as Nelson's great friend and helper throughout his life. Locker was a capable and conscientious officer, and a man of ideas, who in his youth had been a *protégé* and close friend of Hawke's. As Sir J. K. Laughton has pointed out, "the great debt which Nelson owed to Locker, and through Locker to Hawke, has perhaps not been sufficiently recognised."

The other event of this period was the writing of the first of those letters of Nelson's which have been brought together in Nicolas's great collection, and have formed the basis of every later study of his career and character. It is just a simple little letter to his brother in Norfolk, the Rev. William Nelson, announcing that he has passed his examination and received his first commission as lieutenant: "So I am now left in the world to think for myself, which I hope I shall do so as to bring credit to myself and friends." Nothing important in itself, but highly characteristic and interesting to the biographer as opening one of the most remarkable series of letters ever left behind him by a great man. Nicolas's dispatches and letters have since been supplemented by many letters addressed to Nelson and, in particular, by his correspondence with Lady Hamilton; but they remain the best of all authorities, not only for the bare facts of his life, but still more for any study of his psychology.

Up to the moment we have now arrived at Nelson has not heard a shot fired in anger. His promotion has been due partly to the influence of his uncle, but mainly to his own exertions and the force of his personality. In naval affairs, apart from the bickering with Spain and the rebellion of the American Colonies, there was literally nothing doing. But when the *Lowestoft* sailed for Jamaica, American privateers, assisted unobtrusively by Frenchmen flying the American flag, were doing considerable damage to English trade in those waters, and it was the task of his Majesty's frigates to retaliate. Nelson, therefore, had a lively voyage, and gained much useful experience, since he was always the first to volunteer to go in one of the *Lowestoft's* tenders or command a prize.

He himself has told one story of this cruise, which it seems impossible to omit from any account of his career, since he tells us that it "has often occurred to my mind," and evidently means to suggest that it was one of the significant events of his life — an opportunity seized at the right moment. The frigate had overhauled an American privateer and compelled her to surrender. The first lieutenant was ordered to board her, but did not immediately do so, Nelson says, because there was "a very high sea," which fully justified his hesitation. It has since been explained (by Harrison) that the officer was only searching for his hanger, which had somehow been mislaid among the cabins! Anyhow, Captain Locker became impatient and demanded to know, "Have I no officer in the ship who can board the prize?" Immediately the master volunteered, but Nelson, as his senior, insisted that it was his turn, and sprang into the boat. He succeeded in boarding the privateer, which was so waterlogged that at the first attempt his boat was washed on to the deck and off again before his men could lay hold.

In the meantime he had used his opportunity as commander of the *Lowestoft's* tender to make himself "a complete pilot for all the passages through the islands situated on the North side of Hispaniola." But he was not getting on fast enough, and he must have been delighted when, in 1778, he was transferred to the Admiral's flagship, and in Sir Peter Parker found a new and powerful friend. Further promotion was now assured. In December of this very same year he was in command of the brig *Badger*.

Nelson got his first command at the age of twenty, and it has been pointed out, with some justice, that he got it largely through interest. There had been few opportunities of distinguishing himself, and though Captain Locker liked him and would no doubt speak in his favour, the Admiral, when he took him on board the flagship, knew almost nothing about him except the important fact that he was the nephew of the Comptroller of the Navy. Now the system of promotion on foreign stations in those days was that when vacancies occurred on any ships of the squadron, they were filled from the Admiral's flagship. If a captain died or was sent home, the first lieutenant of the flagship would get his place, and so on. Most of the officers on the flagship were there simply because the Admiral was interesting himself in their careers. Heavy losses in action or through some epidemic disease might lead to a certain number of promotions on merit alone, but at ordinary times it was simply an elaborate system of favouritism based on interest.

It sounds a thoroughly rotten arrangement, and, as every one knows, it gave way during the nineteenth century to a system of promotion by seniority, which, at any rate, had the appearance of being more equitable. But Sir J. K. Laughton, writing in 1895, has pointed out that under the later system Nelson could not possibly have risen higher than the rank of captain at the date of Trafalgar! In Victorian times few captains were under the age of fifty. The old system, while quite indefensible in theory, did have the advantage, in practice, of giving openings to young men of genius. In fact, if young Nelson got his promotion through a "job," we may conclude with W. S. Gilbert that it was a "good job too." But in Nelson's case there is another point to make. His excellent uncle, the Comptroller, died in July 1778, and Nelson was not given his command until December of that year; so that the Admiral must have known when he promoted him that there was no further interest to be made in England by so doing. The truth is that Nelson, apart from his professional zeal, which impressed every one at this time, had completely won the hearts of Sir Peter and (what was perhaps even more important) Lady Parker. He was on terms of the closest friendship with them. Lady Parker was genuinely fond of him; it was to her kindness he probably owed his life two years later, when she nursed him through a severe attack of fever.

Walking his own quarterdeck now, for the first time, Nelson was sent with the *Badger* to the Bay of Honduras, to protect the settlers there against the American privateers. From the naval point of view the work was easy enough; but the episode is of some importance in his career, because he was now called upon, at this early age, to show his powers of diplomacy in dealing with the people on shore. In one of the little boasts which he allows himself in the sketch of his life, which we have quoted elsewhere, he records that he "gained so much the affections of the settlers that they unanimously voted me their thanks, and expressed their regret on my leaving them." They also entrusted to this youth of twenty the duty of reporting to Sir Peter Parker and the general in command at Jamaica in regard to their situation in the event of a war with Spain.

Another event of this cruise which left a strong impression on his mind was the tragic loss of H.M.S. *Glasgow*. This 20-gun ship was in Montego Harbour, Jamaica, when one of her stewards, going down into the afterhold with a light in order to steal the rum, contrived to set fire to the ship. The flames spread rapidly; but the *Badger* happened to be lying near, and Nelson at once sent out his boats, and, with their assistance, the whole of the *Glasgow's* crew were saved. Nelson sent his story of the affair to England, entrusting his letter to the lieutenant of the *Glasgow,* whom he recommends personally to Locker. "He is a very good young man, I believe, and has not saved a rag but what was on his back." Nelson himself was then twenty! His appearance at this time, owing to his delicate health and diminutive figure, was very different from that of the sturdy young midshipman whom we met on the *Seahorse* only two years before. There was nothing of the typical British sailor about him. What people seem chiefly to have noticed was "his temperance and simplicity of manners." On professional subjects he would talk eagerly, but when other topics were introduced, "he seemed to retire within himself, and to care but little for the refined courtesies of polished life." In his dress "he had all the cleanliness of an Englishman, though his manner of wearing it gave him an air of negligence." Yet of this absent-minded, rather eccentric, unsailorly-looking young man it was as true then, as through-out his life, that "when he wished to please" he "possessed a charm that was irresistible." *

On June 11, 1779, Nelson was further promoted to be Captain of the *Hinchinbroke,* a French prize. She was away on a cruise, and Nelson went ashore at Port Royal to wait for her. He found Jamaica in a state of high excitement — in fact, as he put it, "turned upside down," owing to the general expectation that the powerful French fleet, then at sea under Admiral d'Estaing, was about to attack the colony. It was believed that D'Estaing had a hundred and twenty-five sail with him, and that his transports were preparing to take on board twenty thousand men at the Cape, and another five thousand at Port au Prince, for the invasion of Jamaica. Nelson hastened to offer his services to Sir Peter Parker and Governor Dalling, who was in command on shore. He states that he was "entrusted with the command of the batteries at Port Royal," and also that he had five hundred men under him in Fort Charles. Another six or seven thousand troops were available; Parker's ships lined the entrance to the harbour, and every one waited with the best hopes they could muster for the arrival of the French armada. Nelson, generally such a confirmed optimist, wrote significantly to his brother, "I think you must not be surprised of my learning to speak French."

In the end nothing happened. D'Estaing, that singularly ineffective commander, instead of attempting the easy prize within reach, went off to North America to try to help the rebel colonists, was repulsed as usual, and returned ignominiously to France. Meantime the *Hinchinbroke* had returned, and Nelson was glad to see her. He was not feeling fit and wrote, grumbling, to Locker: "I am never well in port." He started immediately on a two months' cruise, in the course of which the *Hinchinbroke* took four prizes, which meant a very welcome windfall of about £800 to the young Captain. Through-

---

* Clarke and MacArthur.

out his career Nelson made remarkably little money out of prizes, partly because he was always looking for glory rather than wealth, but partly also because he was unlucky. For instance, he now learned that soon after he left the *Lowestoft* his old shipmates had suddenly found themselves rich through the capture of a fort in the Bay of Honduras, in which was found a treasure of two hundred and fifty quintals of quicksilver and three millions of piastres.

Spain had now entered the war, and Governor Dalling, relieved of the menace of the French fleet, conceived the unhappy idea of attempting one of those combined military and naval operations for which, as Sir John Fortescue has pointed out, England was peculiarly well equipped, but which she nearly always mismanaged. It is true that Nelson, who promptly volunteered for, and secured, the naval command, broke all the rules by keeping on most cordial terms with the soldiers; but even his exertions could not make a success of such a scatter-brained expedition as this. The idea was to seize the Spanish forts in the San Juan river in Nicaragua, and force a way up the river to the Lake of Nicaragua, upon the shores of which the wealthy city of Granada lay open to attack. In this way Spanish Central America would be cut in half, and a way opened into the Pacific. It was one of the dreams of the old buccaneers brought to life again. But it is doubtful if even those hardy warriors would have attempted such an exploit with only five hundred troops and a single ship — Nelson's *Hinchinbroke*. It is certain that they would have been careful not to arrive at the wrong time of year — which is what Dalling did. The attempt was made in April, three months too late, when the rainy season had set in. Twenty-three years later Nelson wrote a note on the affair for Dr Moseley's *Treatise on Tropical Diseases,* in which he points out that it was inevitable, at that time of the year, that the men should be constantly getting wet, and so contracting fevers; while the violent exertions that were required of them, owing to the flooded state of the countryside, increased their liability to disease. He had to carry troops in boats a hundred miles up a river which no one had navigated, except Spaniards, since the times of the buccaneers.

On April 9 they reached the fortified island of Il Bartolomeo, and Nelson, leaping ashore at the head of his seamen, lost his shoes in the mud and advanced barefoot against the battery, which was quickly taken. The next objective was the castle of San Juan, sixteen miles farther up the river. Nelson wanted to attack it immediately, but it was decided to proceed by regular siege. Nelson himself slept on shore, slinging his hammock between two trees. One night he was awakened by a poisonous lizard crawling over his face. Starting up and thrusting back the blankets, he found a snake coiled up at his feet. On another occasion he and several others quenched their thirst at a spring which was subsequently discovered to have been poisoned, apparently by the same root which the Indians used for their arrows. All were taken ill, and Nelson suffered severely from its effects. Clarke and MacArthur, who give this story on the authority of Prince William (afterwards William IV), Nelson's friend, add that His Royal Highness was always of opinion "that the delicate health of his friend thus experienced a severe and lasting injury." But the whole circumstances of this expedition were enough to undermine a much stronger constitution than Nelson's. For instance, the besieging force now ran so short of food that they were reduced to living on broth made by boiling the monkeys they shot. But Nelson could never touch it "after seeing their appearance in the pot."

San Juan surrendered on the 24th, but the delay had been fatal to the health of the army, and when they entered the crowded inconvenient little fort, dysentery and fever had their own way with them. Nelson tells us that of the *Hinchinbroke's* crew eighty-seven took to their beds in one night; of the total strength of two hundred they buried a hundred and forty-five, and he does not believe that more than ten survived the adventure. In fact it became apparent that the expedition had shot its bolt — yet it is extraordinary that they managed to find a small garrison to leave in the fort when they eventually retired down the river.

Nelson had gone before this. Fortunately for him he had been recalled to Jamaica on appointment to command the 44-gun ship *Janus*. Otherwise he must have died, for his health had gone to pieces. Throughout the expedition he had worked like a galley-slave. He himself claims to have been "a principle cause of our success — such as it was." This characteristic swagger is fully borne out by the report of Colonel Polson, who was in command of the troops. "I want words," he wrote, "to express the obligations I owe that gentleman; he was the first on every service, whether by night or by day; there was scarcely a gun but was pointed by him or by Lieutenant Despard." But for that appointment to the *Janus* Captain Nelson would undoubtedly have killed himself in this service. As it was he arrived in Jamaica so ill that he had to be carried ashore and remained there for some time, nursed by Lady Parker. He was a thoroughly bad patient and would not take his medicines, until Lady Parker hit upon the device of sending them in by her little daughter; he could not refuse the child. In later life he always remembered this, and spoke of Miss Parker as his little nurse. This was his second serious illness, and though he was presently able to get about again he was obviously in no condition to take the *Janus* out to sea. He was therefore compelled to resign his command and seek a passage to England. He sailed in the *Lion,* commanded by Captain (afterwards Admiral) Cornwallis, with whom he had shared lodgings in Jamaica, and he afterwards declared that it was Cornwallis's care and attention on the voyage that saved his life. In the meantime he had been succeeded on the *Hinchinbroke* by another friend of his, Cuthbert Collingwood, the "Dear Coll" of so many of his letters.

The *Lion* reached Portsmouth on November 24, 1780, and we next hear of Nelson at Bath, industriously taking the waters.

CHAPTER IV

ILL HEALTH

It is tempting to write a whole chapter on Nelson's health. An essay on this subject, written with authority — which I do not possess — and in the light of modern medical knowledge, would make an interesting addition to existing Nelsoniana. Throughout his life he was constantly falling ill, and it was the exception rather than the rule for his doctors to be able to say exactly what was the matter with him. His headaches, "agues," and "pains in the breast" were always with him; he caught cold easily and dreaded the damp, so that it is not surprising to hear that on one occasion "the doctor thought I was in a consumption and gave me quite up." Undoubtedly the malaria remained in his blood for years. His own view of the matter has already been indicated — "my activity of mind is too much for my puny constitution"; but the truth more probably is that he had to thank this same activity of mind for the fact that he did not die in his bed.

At Bath, during this winter of 1780-81, his symptoms were so varied and distressing that merely to attend to him must have been a liberal education for his doctor. In addition to the weakness left by the fever he suffered from what sounds like gout down his left side, and also from "that cursed bile." By January 23, however, he was a little better and wrote to Captain Locker:

> I have been so ill since I have been here, that I was obliged to be carried to and from bed in the most excruciating tortures. But, thank God, I am now upon the mending hand. I drink the waters three times a day, and bathe every other night; besides (not) drinking wine, which I think the worst of all.

I pause to defend that "not." Nelson must have meant it. This was the eighteenth century. Besides, he concludes another letter, also from Bath, with the jocular remark: "I must now wish you a good night, and drink your health in a draught of my physician's cordial, and a bolus."

One does not altogether envy his medical attendant. "As you will suppose," wrote Nelson on January 28, "I do not sit very easy under the hands of a doctor; although I give myself credit this once for having done everything and taken every medicine ordered by the doctor; so that Dr Woodward, who is my physician, says he never had a better patient." This time we refuse to believe the boast! The truth is that Dr Woodward was both a long suffering and a very patriotic man, and felt it an honour to do the best he could for Nelson. The latter, when his cure was completed, and he was leaving Bath, was astonished at the smallness of the Doctor's bill, and told him so. "Pray, Captain Nelson, allow me to follow what I consider to be my professional duty," replied Woodward. "Your illness, Sir, has been brought on by serving your King and country, and believe me, I love both too well to be able to receive any more." It is extraordinary that, even at this early stage of his career, people who could know nothing of his professional standing seemed to look upon Nelson as one of England's rising hopes.

In the meantime he was distinctly better. He liked the mild climate of Bath. "This is like Jamaica to any other part of England." On February 15 he wrote that his health was "very nearly perfectly restored" — though it was true he was still unable to use his left arm, which, "from the shoulder to my fingers' ends," seemed "half dead" — and was already beginning to talk about getting another ship. On March 5 "I never was so well in health that I can remember"; and a week or two later he went up to London. Of course, it was too soon, and in May he was ill again, having entirely lost the use of his left arm "and very near of my left leg and thigh." He then went to Norfolk and lived quietly with his family for a while, which was certainly the best thing he could have done.

Nelson's next active employment was about the worst that could have been contrived from the point of view of his health. He was appointed to command the 28-gun frigate *Albemarle,* and convoy the Baltic fleet of merchantmen from Elsinore. Here was precisely one of those "cold damp voyages" that he dreaded. But anything was better than kicking his heels at Burnham Thorpe. He went down to Woolwich in August to take over his new command, and, as usual, was delighted both with the ship and the ship's company. "I am perfectly satisfied with her"; "my quarterdeck is filled, much to my satisfaction, with very genteel young men and seamen"; "not a man or officer in her I would wish to change"; "they are, in my opinion, as good a set of men as I ever saw." That was Nelson all over. And the best of it was that under his leadership nearly every one turned out to be as good as he thought.

It is fair to add that, before they sailed for Elsinore, he did have to get rid of one member of this wonderful ship's company — a midshipman who could not pay his mess bills. It was a curious incident, unimportant in itself and neglected by the biographers, but not without interest for the light it throws on the financial arrangements in the midshipmen's messes. We know of it only because this discharged midshipman spread the story on shore that Nelson had told him that he could not remain on the *Albemarle* unless he had £30 a year of his own. Nelson hears of this, on his return from Elsinore, and writes indignantly to Captain Locker:

What in the name of God could it be to me whether a midshipman in my ship had not a farthing or fifty pounds a year? When he came on board I sent him in to Mr Bromwich's mess, where he was two or three days. In that time they spoke to me, that they hoped I would not take it amiss, but they could not think of keeping that young man (I forget his name) in their mess, as he could not pay his part of their small expenses. I am sure that you will not think I should attempt to force any person upon people who were behaving exceedingly well in the ship . . . I told him of what the mess had said. He then said he could not live in a mess that cost anything . . . he pressed me much to discharge him as he could not live in any of the mid-messes.

Much against my inclination I did discharge him. Where he took the idea of thirty pounds a year from I know not; for I declare I never opened my lips to him on the subject. A youngster in the ship, whose friends are Norfolk people, who had not made an allowance to their son, I took upon me to allow twenty pounds.

And he adds, with some bitterness, "had I in the least suspected the story he has told he should have stayed on board and might have lived as he pleased." The Mr Bromwich referred to was a lieutenant, described elsewhere by Nelson as "a very good officer."

The *Albemarle* reached Elsinore on November 4, and found about fifty sail there waiting for convoy, while a hundred more were expected shortly. That meant waiting another two or three weeks in an unamiable climate. Nelson did not like it. He complains in his letter that he was "almost froze," and in the *Sketch of My Life* suggests that the Government must have kept him there in mid-winter on purpose to "try my constitution." It tried his temper, too, for the Danes were at that time pursuing a policy of armed neutrality, and when Nelson anchored off Elsinore they sent an officer on board to ask who he was and what was his strength. "The *Albemarle*," he replied "is one of his Britannic Majesty's ships; you are at liberty, sir, to count the guns as you go down the side; and you may assure the Danish Admiral that, if necessary, they shall all be well served." That was Nelson's first encounter with the Danes.

He was disappointed, too, in the *Albemarle*. She had unsuspected faults; for instance, her masts were dangerously overlong and had to be cut down when they got back to England. Soon after they started on the homeward journey a French privateer got among the fleet; Nelson chased her for an hour, but could not come up with her and had to return. The spell of bad luck continued; they reached Yarmouth on December 17, but were kept there by adverse winds, and did not arrive in the Downs until New Year's Day 1782. There they waited three weeks without orders, but were finally in-

D

structed to proceed to Portsmouth and take in eight months' provisions. This put new heart into Nelson, for he assumed that it must mean that he was to join Sir Richard Bickerton's squadron, then under orders for the East Indies — a nice, warm voyage. And so probably it did; but on the morning of January 28 a gale sprang up in the Downs, and a large East India store-ship drove from her anchors and came on board the *Albemarle,* causing her to lose her foremast and bowsprit, and otherwise damaging her considerably. She had to go into dock for repair, and so lost her chance of the Indies.

Nelson was as near disgust with life as he ever was. At the same time he was worried about the affairs of his elder brother, the Rev. William Nelson, a dissatisfied curate, who had set his heart upon going to sea as a naval chaplain — a post for which his younger brother knew him to be totally unfitted. It was probably Horatio's own fault. While convalescent at Burnham Thorpe he had talked so much about the adventurous, care-free life at sea that even his more phlegmatic brother had been stirred by a desire which is never far from the hearts of Englishmen. Even before the *Albemarle* sailed for Elsinore we find Horatio writing:

> I have talked with Mr. Suckling [William Suckling, the late Comptroller's brother], about your going chaplain in the Navy, and he thinks, as I do, that fifty pounds where you are is much more than equal to what you can get at sea; but in that I know you will please yourself, therefore shall not attempt to state any argument to dissuade you from it. As to my real opinion, whether or no you will like it, I say, as I always did, that it is five to one you will not. If you get with a good man, or a gentleman, it will be tolerable; if not, you will soon detest it.

And now, while the *Albemarle* is in dock, he hears that his brother has got a living, and seizes the opportunity to make another attempt to frighten him off the sea:

> I wish I could congratulate you upon a rectory instead of a vicarage: it is rather awkward wishing the poor man dead, but we all rise by deaths. I got my rank by a shot killing a post-

CAPTAIN NELSON IN 1781

From the painting by J. F. Rigaud in the possession of Earl Nelson.

captain, and I most sincerely hope I shall, when I go, go out of the world the same way; then we go all in the line of our profession — a parson praying, a captain fighting.

But nothing could damp brother William's ardour. Many years later, when Nelson was starting for the West Indies in command of the *Boreas,* he returned to the charge and induced his brother to take him with him. He never tried it again.

In April fell what seemed to be the heaviest blow of all. The *Albemarle* was ordered to Cork to join the *Dædalus* and sail with a convoy to Quebec — "where, worse than all to tell, I understand I am to winter." Nelson dreaded the prospect — "I want much to get off from this damned voyage" — "Mr Adair [his doctor] has told me that if I was sent to a cold damp climate it would make me worse than ever — cold weather is death to me." He could probably have got out of it, if he had cared to pull the strings. There was Admiral Keppel, for instance, who was being attended by this same Dr Adair, and might have taken a hint from him. And there was Admiral Barrington, who had made friends with Nelson in Portsmouth and would have helped him — a man after his own heart, for "he gets amongst all the youngsters here, and leaves out the old boys." But he had received his orders from Lord Sandwich direct, and he would not shirk them.

They arrived in the St Lawrence with the convoy on July 1, and three days later the *Albemarle* sailed alone on a two months' cruise, which was to be more exciting and more valuable, from the point of view of professional experience, than any of Nelson's previous voyages. It must be remembered that this was one of the most sought-after stations the Navy had to offer, for there were rich prizes to be picked up off the North American coast and much less danger of retaliation by hostile fleets than in the stations further south; so that anyone but a Nelson would all this time have been rejoicing at the prospect of easily acquired wealth. Luck, however, was still against him. They took several prizes, but, by ill health, he came late to an aspect of life in which sailors are not usually behindhand. But he soon made up for lost time.

There was an "amiable American lady" then resident in Quebec (she afterwards married some one else and came to live in England). And there was also, rather fortunately, a cool and candid friend, in the person of Alexander Davison, who afterwards became Nelson's banker and agent. Obviously it was from Davison that Clarke and MacArthur, who are the authorities for this romantic affair, derived their information. (Harrison, as representing Lady Hamilton, knows nothing about it!) It appears that Nelson kept his head pretty well, until the day when he was ordered to leave Quebec. Even then he managed to say good-bye without committing himself fatally, and hastened on board his ship in that desperate frame of mind common to lovers on such occasion.

But the next morning, shortly before the ship was due to sail, his friend Davison was astonished to see Nelson returning to the shore in a boat. Scenting danger, he hastened down to the landing-stage and met him there. Asked what he was doing, Nelson declared passionately that he was about to return to his lady-love and throw himself and his fortunes at her feet. Davison laid a soothing hand upon his arm, and led him gently up the street towards his own house while they discussed the matter. He pointed out to Nelson that such a match would be the very height of imprudence, since neither of the parties had any money. It could only mean one thing — debt; and after that, said Davison, "ruin must follow." "Then let it follow," exclaimed Nelson majestically, "for I am resolved to do it." "And I," replied Davison, "positively declare that you shall not." Is it necessary to add that Davison won, or that Nelson felt a grateful affection for him ever after?

Now, all this happened, no doubt, as Davison says, though he may have exaggerated the importance of his own share in the work of rescue. But it is quite impossible to take it seriously after reading Nelson's letters written at the time. He is so serenely cheerful, so full of himself and his career, and, above all, so delighted at getting away from Quebec! He hopes that presently "we shall go to the *grand theatre* of Actions, the West Indies." Not a word about the girl! And when the orders come he writes (October 19):

When I was at Quebec with no other expectations or desires than to return to England, arrives the *Drake* sloop, and *Cockatrice* cutter, with orders for the transports to be fitted for the reception of troops, and to be sent to New York; in consequence whereof old Worth [a disrespectful reference to his senior officer, Captain Worth, of the *Assistance*] has given me orders to carry the fleet to New York — a very pretty job at this late season of the year, for our sails are at this moment frozen to the yards.

This was written only four days after that tragic parting. The truth is that at this stage of his career Nelson was a young man who found it very easy to fall in and out of love.

So he sailed for New York, without much enthusiasm — not knowing that here was to be one of the great opportunities of his career — and arrived at Sandy Hook on November 11, to find the harbour full of British ships, sixty-fours and even larger line-of-battle ships, with frigates like his own, and much smaller fry, making an animated and inspiring scene, delightful to the professional eye. Nelson cast anchor, had himself rowed across to the flagship, and interviewed Admiral Digby. "You are come on a fine station for making prize money," said the Admiral. "Yes, sir," replied Nelson, "but the West Indies is the station for honour." * As he spoke his eye wandered across the blue waters to where a group of twelve sail of the line were riding at anchor, a little apart, a detachment from Rodney's fleet, fresh from the scorching South,

---

* Yet he could be keen enough about prizes where his friends were concerned. Speaking of a certain Captain Pole, he writes home to mutual acquaintances: "He has been pretty successful since he came upon this station, and will be very much so if a neutral which he sent in is given to him. She is condemned in Jamaica, but they have appealed, and in England we are afraid of the cursed neutral flag"— an unintentional but none the less impressive tribute to the honesty of those wonderful British prize courts.

fresh from the resounding victory of April 12, when Rodney had scattered a powerful French force under the Comte de Grasse. They were commanded by Admiral Lord Hood.

Nelson had arrived with all his transports safe, "which is a very fortunate thing at this season of the year," so that his interview with Admiral Digby was, no doubt, a pleasant one. Moreover, it is by this time obvious that his reputation for energy and professional efficiency has got about, and that there is a certain amount of competition for his services. In his own mind, however, he knew exactly what he wanted to do. At the first opportunity after leaving Digby he paid a visit to those twelve battered ships from the South and went on board the *Barfleur*, Hood's flagship. It was in many ways a memorable visit — one of the decisive acts in his career. Not only did it decide his immediate movements; it also gave him two influential and life-long friends, in the persons of Lord Hood himself and a certain sturdy, full-bodied youth among his midshipmen; and it gave to posterity by far the best pen-picture of Nelson as he appeared at that time, written by this same midshipman, who never wrote anything else memorable in his life. The midshipman was H.R.H. Prince William Henry, afterwards King William IV. He writes:

I was then a midshipman on board the *Barfleur*, lying in the Narrows off Staten Island, and had the watch on deck, when Captain Nelson, of the *Albemarle*, came in his barge alongside, who appeared to be the merest boy of a captain I ever beheld, and his dress was worthy of attention. He had on a full-fledged uniform, his lank, unpowdered hair was tied in a stiff Hessian tail of an extraordinary length; the old-fashioned flaps of his waistcoat added to the general quaintness of his figure, and produced an appearance which particularly attracted my notice; for I had never seen anything like it before, nor could I imagine who he was or what he came about. My doubts were, however, removed when Lord Hood introduced me to him. There was something irresistibly pleasing in his address and conversation; and an enthusiasm when speaking on professional subjects that showed he was no common being. Nelson afterwards went with us to the West Indies, and served under Lord Hood's flag during his indefatigable cruise off Cape François. Throughout the whole of the American War, the height of Nelson's ambition was to command a line-of-battle ship; as for prize money, it never entered his thoughts.

A genuine friendship sprang up between these two men of such different temperaments. Nelson's passionate loyalty, of course, made it impossible for him to see any fault in the Prince. "He is a *seaman,*" he writes, using the highest praise he could think of — though he frankly adds, "which you would hardly suppose." Moreover, "he will be a *disciplinarian,* and a strong one." A few years later he was to prove the truth of this last prophecy rather inconveniently for Nelson.* As for the Prince, there is a certain unconscious humour in his attitude towards this impulsive, eccentric new friend of his. Himself slow and cautious by nature, he seems to have been half afraid of the flimsy fire-eater. There are in existence certain letters exchanged between them in 1796, shortly before the battle of St Vincent, which may suitably be quoted here as illustrating, rather amusingly, the difference in their characters. Nelson writes (Spain being then about to declare war and add her fleet to that of France):

As to our Fleet, under such a Commander-in-Chief as Sir John Jervis, nobody has any fears ... We are now twenty-two Sail of the Line, the combined fleet will not be above thirty-five Sail of the Line, supposing the Dons detach to the West Indies. I will venture my life Sir John Jervis defeats them; I do not mean by a regular battle, but by the skill of the Admiral, and the activities and spirit of our officers and seamen. This country is the most favourable possible for skill with an inferior fleet; for the winds are so variable that some one time in twenty-four hours you must be able to attack a part of a large Fleet, and the other will be becalmed or have a contrary wind; therefore I hope Government will not be alarmed for our safety — I mean more than is proper.

* See p. 73.

This naïve communication, evidently dashed off in a hurry in Nelson's cabin, frankly scared William Henry, who replied:

> It is a pleasant circumstance to every Englishman, and particularly to professional men [which he always liked to be considered], to see the navy of this country ride triumphant in all quarters of the globe. Still, dear Nelson, I never wish to hear of twenty-two British Sail of the Line being opposed to thirty-five of the enemy, though a combined fleet. I venerate and esteem Jervis' abilities as high as any man, and I am fully acquainted with the intrepidity and valour of the English sailor, and the knowledge and experience of their officers; and, as a seaman myself, I can easily understand the advantages to be taken from variable winds and calms. However, the risk, believe me, between two such unequal forces, is too great.

It was the ambition of William Henry, which he confesses over and over again in letters to his friend, to be put in charge of the "executive management of the Admiralty." He would have been a "safe" man as First Lord; he would have worked hard and risked nothing.

But we must return to the decks of the *Barfleur* off New York, on November 11, 1782. The upshot of the interview with the Admiral was that Nelson became "a candidate with Lord Hood for a line of battle ship." It was more than could be obtained at the moment; but Hood, who, like William Henry, had taken to the young captain, immediately succeeded in persuading Digby to let the *Albemarle* go. It was a considerable concession, because, apart from Nelson's personal value, every admiral hated to lose a frigate, one of the "eyes of the fleet." So the *Albemarle* sailed south with Hood's twelve ships, and we may be sure that no one in the detachment was happier than the commander. "My situation in Lord Hood's fleet," he writes, "must be in the highest degree flattering to any young man." Hood treated him "as if I was his son"; and it appears that he told Prince William Henry in Nelson's presence — "indeed I cannot make use of expressions strong enough to describe what I felt" — that if

WILLIAM IV AS DUKE OF CLARENCE
National Portrait Gallery.

48

he wished to ask any questions about naval tactics, Nelson was the man to go to. Which is extraordinary when we consider that he had never yet been in a fleet action, whereas every other captain in that squadron had.

On the way south the *Albemarle* chased and captured a French prize, worth £20,000, but as the rest of the fleet were in sight at the time, they all had a right to share in her — which was bad luck again. The squadron of the defeated French fleet which Hood was looking for having slipped away, he went on to Jamaica, dispatching the *Albemarle* to find out where the enemy had gone. Nelson found them in Porto Cavallo, and reported accordingly. It was during this independent reconnaissance that Nelson made the unsuccessful attack on Turk Island, which his biographers, including even Mahan, have so strangely ignored, and which he himself fails to mention in his *Sketch of My Life*. Yet there was nothing disgraceful about the defeat, nor did it shake Lord Hood's good opinion of Nelson. It was while he was returning from Cavallo (in the Gulf of Mexico) to Jamaica that he fell in with H.M.S. *Resistance* and learned that the French had recently seized Turk Island, in the Bahamas, with a force of one hundred and fifty regular soldiers and three vessels of war. Nelson had with him the *Drake* and the *Tartar,* which had recently joined company, and these four, with the *La Coquette,* a French ship-of-war, prize to the *Resistance,* made, as he says in a letter, "a tolerable outward show." So he anchored at the island and sent a flag of truce ashore, demanding surrender, which the French refused. Next morning it was found that the *Tartar* had departed, for no ascertainable reason; but Nelson landed a hundred and sixty-seven seamen and marines, and sent them against the town. Unfortunately the enemy were much stronger in artillery than had been supposed, and, although another English ship, the *Admiral Barrington,* arrived at the last moment and assisted in the attack, it was plain that the place could not be taken, and Nelson drew off his men rather than suffer heavy loss. Hood was probably pleased to hear that he was capable of so much caution. That was his last opportunity of active service for some time to come. Peace had been signed between England, on the one hand, and France, Spain, and America, on the other, and when the news reached Jamaica, there came with it orders for Lord Hood to return home with his fleet. Nelson, before leaving, had one more peaceful duty to perform. He was detailed to escort the *Fortunée* with Prince William Henry on board on a visit to Havana, and there is no reason to doubt that he did it very well. He returned to England in June 1783.

"After all my tossing about into various climates, here at least I am arrived, safe and sound." So wrote Nelson from Portsmouth to Locker. He adds that he has brought home twelve dozen of rum for him, and will warehouse it if it can be slipped past the customs. If not, the customs may keep it, as he does not think that rum is worth the duty. It got through.

CHAPTER V

THE PARSON'S DAUGHTER

"SALT SEA," says Nelson, somewhere in his correspondence, "is a wonderful specific for love." Certainly he had succeeded in forgetting his "amiable American" with surprising rapidity. No doubt he now regarded himself as a complete cure. But he was to find that this new malady, which had assailed him, shared one feature in common with his old enemy malaria — that it had a way of getting into a man's system so that it might break out again unexpectedly at any time. Certain well-recognized precautions, however, do exist — at any rate, certain things to be avoided — and we can only ascribe to the temerity of youth Nelson's next step, which was to apply for leave to visit a French holiday resort.

It had been very pleasant getting home again, and in such good fettle. It is true that there had been some trouble at landing, owing to a stupid official mistake in paying off the seamen at the wrong port, and then Nelson was kept busy for weeks trying to recover wages due to them. "The disgust of the seamen to the navy," he writes, "is all owing to the infernal plan of turning them over from ship to ship, so that men cannot be attached to their officers, or the officers care twopence about them." He might have mentioned the still more infernal plan of transferring men from homeward- to outward-bound vessels, just when their time was nearly up. Indeed the British tar of those days had ample cause for complaint and but little incitement to loyalty. Yet as soon as the *Albemarle* made port the ship's company came to Nelson in a body and offered, "if he could get another ship, to enter for her immediately." And this was to be a common experience throughout his career.

At the moment he had other plans. He went to London, and there, for the first time in his life, found himself mildly lionized — and seemed to take to it naturally. Lord Hood presented him to the King at St James's Palace, and a few days later he was at Windsor, by command, to say good-bye to his friend Prince William Henry, who was about to depart for a tour of the Continent. His friend Davison, from Quebec, was in London, and it is recorded that, after being presented at Court, Nelson went to dine with Davison at Lincoln's Inn. On arrival in his friend's chambers he immediately threw off his "iron-bound coat" — a formidable affair, as any contemporary portrait of a post-captain in full dress uniform will show — and, slipping on a dressing-gown, lolled at his ease, while the two friends talked over all that had happened to them since they parted that day by the landing-stage at Quebec, including no doubt a full account by Davison of the subsequent demeanour of the "amiable American." Did they laugh? Surely not — that was never a fault of Nelson's.

Nelson, as he says, "closed the war without a fortune"; but he must have had the satisfaction of feeling that he was now generally regarded as a coming man and a person of some account. He had no intention of applying for another ship; in fact, he felt that he deserved a holiday, and, like many other British officers at this time, he decided to take advantage of the peace and pay a visit to France. The idea was to combine business with pleasure by learning to speak the language, a useful but rare accomplishment in the Navy. His travelling companion was a Captain Macnamara, who had been his messmate on Sir Peter Parker's flagship in the West Indies five years before. They set out on October 21, 1783, and, after spending a night with Captain Locker at Malling, went on to Dover and made the crossing on the following morning, with a fine northwest wind which got them to Calais in three and a half hours. From Calais they started off by post, aiming vaguely at Saint-Omer (which had been recommended to

Macnamara, though Nelson had heard that it was a "dirty, nasty town"), but prepared to stop at any likely place where suitable lodgings and French lessons might be obtained.

Nelson gives a delightful description of the tour, in some of the best letters he ever wrote. He compares it with Sterne's *Sentimental Journey*, little anticipating how very sentimental it would be before the end. The change of scene fascinated him:

> I was highly diverted with looking what a curious figure the postilions in their jack boots, and their rats of horses, made together. Their chaises have no springs, and the roads generally paved like London streets; therefore you will naturally suppose we were pretty well shook together by the time we had travelled two posts and a half, which is fifteen miles, to Marquise. Here we were shown into an inn — they called it — I should have called it a pig-stye; we were shown into a room with two straw beds, and, with great difficulty, they mustered up clean sheets; and gave us two pigeons for supper, upon a dirty cloth, and wooden-handled knives — O what a transition from happy England!

At Boulogne, next day, they found the place full of English, "I suppose because wine is so very cheap"; and at Montreuil, where they dined and slept, "we put up at the same house and with the same jolly landlord that recommended Le Fleur to Sterne." They would have liked to stop here, for partridges cost "twopence halfpenny a couple, pheasants and woodcocks in proportion, and in short, every species of poultry." But "poultry" do not talk French, and there was no prospect of teachers, so they pushed on, reaching Abbeville at eight o'clock at night. Unfortunately two Englishmen, one of whom called himself Lord Kingsland, and the other a Mr Bullock, had decamped from Abbeville that very afternoon "in debt to every shopkeeper in the place"; so that "we found the town in an uproar," and English visitors not specially popular. Macnamara now once more urged the claims of Saint-Omer, and Nelson, after these many disappointments, could hardly resist. So they turned and travelled due north again, and, on reaching their destination, found a pleasant, well-kept town, with plenty of convenient lodgings and French teachers to choose from.

Captains Nelson and Macnamara went to lodge with a respectable French family, in which there were two "agreeable daughters." One daughter served their breakfast and the other their tea, and both would honour them with their company after dinner, and, since neither knew a word of English, Nelson found that both duty and inclination drove him on to learn French, "if 'tis only for the pleasure of talking to them." He remarks that "French ladies make full as much use of their tongues as our English ones." It would be hard to imagine more auspicious circumstances for the study of a foreign language — it is, indeed, a widely practised method today — and what with the girls, and the teacher, and his own native intelligence, one would have expected Nelson, after a month or two at Saint-Omer, to have been chattering French like a "darned mounseer."

That he did nothing of the kind requires some explanation. As a matter of fact, there were too many English at Saint-Omer — not tourists, for the most part, but residents. Nelson and Macnamara had made a self-denying ordinance not to visit more than two English families ("for if I did I should never speak French"), and now, having looked them over, they seem to have begun by rejecting the tourists — in particular two naval captains who annoyed Nelson by wearing epaulettes, which was still regarded as a Frenchified trick, and was no part of the official English uniform.* But two English families were more than enough for his peace of mind. He was at the time of life when every girl appeared beautiful. "I must take care of my heart," he says, but the truth is that no craft was ever more recklessly piloted among the Saint-Omer shoals. If he avoided the bright eyes of the landlady's daughters, it was only to fall the more easily before

---

* Eleven years later epaulettes were officially adopted in the English Navy. Captain Alexander John Ball, one of these epauletted officers, afterwards became a close friend of Nelson's.

the demure charms of a Miss Andrews, one of a largish family
resident at Saint-Omer. He makes his brother his confidant:

> My heart is quite secured against the French beauties; I almost
> wish I could say as much for an English young lady, the
> daughter of a clergyman, with whom I am just going to dine,
> and spend the day. She has such accomplishments that had I
> a million of money, I am sure I should at this moment make
> her an offer of them: my income at present is far too small to
> think of marriage, and she has no fortune.

And again, a month later:

> I must conclude as I am engaged to tea and spend the evening
> with the most accomplished woman my eyes ever beheld; and
> when a lady's in the case, all other things they must give way.

It appears that Miss Andrews and her sister used to "play
and sing to us" when Nelson and Macnamara called. To
Locker again he writes: "I must take care of my heart, I
assure you." No wonder "the French goes on but slowly."

These girls were about twenty years old. It is not to be
supposed that their father could do anything much for them
when they married, though Nelson's Miss Andrews had
£1000 of her own. Nelson's income was at this time just
£130 a year. But, in spite of his disclaimer of serious inten-
tions, he wrote to his uncle Mr William Suckling on
January 14, 1784, asking him to make him an allowance of
£100 a year in order that he might marry the girl. He even
hinted at some desperate action if refused. "Life is not worth
preserving without happiness," he exclaims theatrically, "and
I care not where I may linger out a miserable existence." He
concludes with the hope that his uncle "may never know the
pangs which at this instant tear my heart."

Mr Suckling, like a wise man, seems to have responded
sympathetically to this appeal. He agreed to make the allowance if the marriage took place. No doubt he felt that time
was on his side.

In the meantime there were two other incidents worth
E

recording during Nelson's stay at Saint-Omer. First, he was much upset by hearing of the death of his sister Anne, which took place at Bath in November. Secondly, he received an invitation from a certain Comte de Deux Ponts, whom he had met in the West Indies in somewhat unusual circumstances. After the *Albemarle* had located the French squadron in Porto Cavallo (as recorded on p. 49) Nelson was cruising in the neighbourhood in the hope of picking up further information, when he met a Spanish launch carrying a number of French officers and men of science who were engaged in a peaceful mission in search of natural history specimens. It seems extraordinary that such an expedition should have been organized in wartime, but so it was.* Some one on the *Albemarle* hailed the Spaniard in French, and she came alongside unsuspectingly, and no one could have been more astonished than these scientific gentlemen when they found themselves prisoners of war. But Nelson treated them with great hospitality, though several, like the Comte de Deux Ponts, held rank in the French Army, and finally let them go, only taking their promise that they would return to captivity should Lord Hood object to what he had done. The Comte de Deux Ponts who, though Nelson did not know it at the time, was a Prince of the Empire and Heir-Apparent to the Electorate of Bavaria, never forgot this kindness; and now, hearing that Nelson was in France, he wrote urgently inviting him to Paris. Nelson was unable to accept, for reasons which will appear in a moment; but he notes, with some complacency, that he seems to have had the honour of taking prisoner "a man who will be a sovereign Prince of Europe and brings into the field near a hundred thousand men." As a matter of fact the Comte, by the death of his brother, became in 1806 not only a prince, but King of Bavaria.

To return to Miss Andrews, the affair came to nothing after all. We have no precise information, but it seems hard to

---

* It will be remembered that the famous Captain Cook started on his third voyage of discovery when England was at war with France, Spain and America.

resist the conclusion that Nelson was refused — which, at any rate, provides this Miss Andrews with an interesting little niche in history all to herself. He took it well, and did not break with the family; one of her innumerable brothers, Captain George Andrews of the Navy, afterwards became his faithful follower. And, when he had been given his dismissal, he retreated in reasonably good order to London, setting up a smoke-screen of excuses to explain this unexpected return. For he had told every one that in no circumstances would he apply for another ship during the peace; he could not afford it. Now he wrote to Locker that, "some little matters in my account obliged me to come over." To his brother William he said: "My health is not very stout this cold weather; I must come over to get a little good advice from some of the London physicians."

That last excuse was prophetic, for as soon as he landed, no doubt in very low spirits, he did catch a violent cold, and afterwards made it worse by being "fool enough to dance attendance at St James's," which brought on a fever. He was in a bitter mood, and applied immediately for a ship, expecting to remain in England only two or three weeks. No one but Macnamara (still at Saint-Omer) knew the cause of his gloom, though some of Nelson's letters to his brother, about this time, suggest that he may also have confided in him.

But gradually there is a change. He begins to notice the march of events around him. He takes an interest in politics. He even talks of returning to France and making another attack upon that impossible language. "I return to many charming women," he writes sadly to his brother, "but no charming woman will return to me." It was only the language he wanted — "I hate their country and their manners." But he never went. He was caught up in the whirl of London life — which was probably the best thing that could happen to him. He was invited to dinner with Lord Hood, who was at that time thinking of standing for Parliament in the event of a dissolution. How far Nelson ever harboured a similar ambition it is difficult to say. He certainly flirted with the idea

about this time, though in later life he was accustomed to
assert his contempt for the political game. His personal difficulty at the moment was that, whereas all his family traditions
were Whig (owing to the Walpole connexion), he himself
had no use whatever for any group even remotely allied with
Fox and the "defeatists." He was all for Mr Pitt and loyalty
and the vigorous prosecution of the war; while at the same
time his sympathy with the working classes, as we shall see
later, went a good deal further than either Whigs or Tories
at that time were prepared to go. Fox and his party are "a
turbulent faction who are striving to ruin their country.
Mr Pitt, depend on it, will stand up against all opposition;
an honest man must always in time get the better of a *villain.*"
All this to his brother, to whom he also remarked "as to your
having enlisted under the banners of the Walpoles, you
might as well have enlisted under those of my grandmother."
He adds that he hopes his brother will "vote for Mr Pitt"
(who was duly elected for Cambridge, William Nelson being
a Christ's man), and that he and his friends in London expect
to "unkennel Fox at Westminster." (They did not — he was
re-elected.) Yet ten years later, when Nelson is definitely
approached on this subject by some of his friends, he replies
that he "will not attempt to come into Parliament but in support of the real Whig interest — I mean the Portland interest"
— in other words, the Walpoles! The fact is that these political excursions were of no importance except as indications of
his frame of mind. Perhaps, in the familiar phrase, he was
just "trying to forget."

On March 18, 1784, Nelson was appointed to the *Boreas,* a
28-gun frigate, then under orders to the Leeward Islands.
Before we follow him on this voyage it may be noted at once
that, as the result of Miss Andrews's behaviour, he evidently
went to the West Indies more than usually determined not to
be put upon—at any rate by his own sex. If this interpretation
is accepted, it explains a good deal of his subsequent conduct,
which otherwise is not easy to account for. He shows a touchi-
ness, and a readiness to stand on his dignity and by the strict

letter of the law, which we do not observe at any other stage of his career.

The voyage began badly. Several things happened which might have ruffled the temper even of one who had not recently been crossed in love. In the first place, on the very day of his appointment, he had an attack of malaria ("ague and fever") which lasted for a week, and "pulled me down most astonishingly." Then his brother, hearing the news, wrote immediately to raise the old vexed question of a naval chaplaincy for himself, ending his letter with a tactless inquiry as to what "interest" had helped Nelson to his new ship. Horatio answered stiffly that the fact of "having served with credit" was his only recommendation to the Admiralty. But he agreed at last to take his brother with him — not indeed as a chaplain, for no such rating was allowed on a ship of this size, but as an indeterminate member of the ship's company who might be asked by the Captain to conduct the services on Sundays. It was a generous action; the more so as this stout, self-indulgent relative might easily have died on Nelson's hands, as a result of the sudden change of climate and diet. It doubtless gave the Reverend William something to talk about for the rest of his life.

And then there was Lady Hughes! And her daughter! Lady Hughes was the wife of Admiral Sir Richard Hughes, commanding at the Leeward Islands. We can guess that young Nelson, even in his most amiable mood, would be the sort of officer who would object to women on board ship. Least of all would he want them on a voyage which he had undertaken with the express purpose of forgetting the very existence of their sex. Moreover, he thought the whole thing a piece of cheek. He writes to Locker, with one of his rare attempts at sarcasm: "I am asked to carry out Lady Hughes and her family — a very modest request, I think, but I cannot refuse, so I must put up with the inconvenience and expense. Also the ship is full of young midshipmen and everybody is asking me to take someone or other." And to his brother, quite savagely, "I am asked to carry out Lady Hughes and her daughter, so that I shall be pretty well filled with *lumber.*" In fact the whole world seemed in league to try and impose upon him, and he was in no mood to stand it. He really had a grievance too, for he was expected to pay Lady Hughes's expenses, and these came to "nearly two hundred pounds" — a serious matter for a hard-up young post-captain. In return, at the end of the voyage, Lady Hughes presented him with a silver tea-caddy, "which could hardly be worth more than five shillings." (All this comes from Harrison, who says he got it on the "most respectable authority," which no doubt means Lady Hamilton.)

We must not exaggerate this picture of gloom and misogyny, for it happens that we can convict Nelson of riding about the streets of Portsmouth in company with a young lady — no doubt trying to forget his sorrow. Alas, even this diversion turned to ashes in his mouth! Sailors are but clumsy horsemen, both animals bolted through a narrow place, Nelson saved his life by throwing himself off and hurting his back on the cobblestones, and some anonymous landlubber intervened to rescue the girl by seizing her horse's bridle. And, as if that were not sufficiently exasperating, there was a series of misadventures when the ship put to sea. First the pilot. "The damned pilot — it makes me swear to think of it — ran the ship aground where she lay, with so little water that the people could walk around her till next high water." Now Nelson — unlike a great contemporary with whom I have already compared him at perhaps undue length — was not in the habit of scattering "damns" about; if he swore, it meant that he was really angry. A day or two later, when the *Boreas* was waiting in the Downs, he got into a quarrel with a Dutchman, who had sixteen Englishmen on board, employees of the Dutch East India Company, who had served out their time and now wished to go home. But the Dutch skipper said they were in debt to his ship and refused to let them remove their chests. Nelson was informed, and at once took a high line. He sent a cutter to anchor beside the Dutchman and prevent any boats from leaving or approaching her until the skipper gave way — which he did in the end, but not without complaining to the Admiralty of Nelson's conduct. Last of all he wrote to his brother: "Come when you please . . . bring your canonicals and sermons . . . I have a fine, talkative lady for you to converse with."

That was the trouble with poor Lady Hughes. A strong-minded, aggressive, opinionated sort of woman, who had probably been very popular in her youth, she chattered her way through life, never listening to anyone else, serenely confident in that charm of manner which had once been so irresistible, and totally unaware of the hatred which she was arousing in the breasts of anyone compelled to listen to her for a prolonged period (say, on a sea voyage), and particularly if that person was paying for the privilege at the rate of about a hundred pounds a month. It is impossible not to feel sorry for her; but we feel sorrier for Nelson. "She has an eternal clack," he cries in despair. As for the daughter, she was apparently going to the West Indies to find a husband. We shall hear more of her later on.

Lady Hughes — who, as I have said, was quite unaware of Nelson's feeling towards her — afterwards put the whole world in her debt by supplying Clarke and MacArthur with a gushing little description of Nelson's relations with his midshipmen, of whom there were no less than thirty on board. This was just the feature of life on board ship which would naturally attract a woman passenger's attention. "Captain Nelson," she says, "every day went into the schoolroom and saw the mode in which they [the midshipmen] pursued their nautical acquirements." On ceremonial occasions he would take no less than ten midshipmen with him in his barge — "so that nothing could have a more respectable appearance." To her, also, we owe the story (quoted on p. 19) of how Nelson encouraged a timid little middy by offering to race him to the mast-head. He treated his "young gentlemen" exceptionally well, and, himself not much of a society man, always made a point of introducing them to the leading English inhabitants at every port. He even urged them to learn dancing.

As his views on the education of midshipmen are of some interest, it may be worth while to quote a letter which he addressed to the father of one of them at the end of this very voyage:

> In the first place, it is necessary that he should be made complete in his navigation; and if the peace continues, French is absolutely necessary. Dancing is an accomplishment that probably a sea-officer may require. You will see almost the necessity of it, when employed in foreign countries; indeed, the honour of the nation is so often entrusted to sea-officers that there is no accomplishment which will not shine with peculiar lustre in them.

On arrival at Antigua in the Leeward Islands he met his Admiral, and liked him no better than he had liked Lady Hughes. He "bows and scrapes too much for me." In truth he was a good-natured, easy-going man, only anxious to avoid trouble, who would be certain at any time to rub Nelson up the wrong way. "The Admiral and all about him are ninnies." As for the other captains on the station, Collingwood, his friend, is "an amiable good man," but "all the rest are geese." Little Sandys, Captain of the *Latona,* is "a goodnatured laughing creature"; but "I am sorry to say he goes through a regular course of claret every day," and he keeps his ship just anyhow. And later: "What a pity he should have that failing: there is not a better heart in the world." He does not think the Admiral lives on shore in a manner befitting his dignity; in general he is disgusted at the slack way in which things are done; and, to sum up, "the longer I am upon this station, the worse I like it." Nor can we put all the blame for this upon Miss Andrews.

But there were two major questions, altogether more important than mere private irritations, on which Nelson presently found himself at issue with his chief, and since the attitude which he took up in these disputes — though he was technically right in both of them — undoubtedly led the authorities to mark him down as a man likely to be a nuisance in peace time through excess of zeal, and so kept him out of employment for several years, it is necessary to state briefly what happened. In the first place, the inhabitants of the United States, having declared their independence, pulled down the Union Jack, exiled their loyalists and confiscated their goods, were continuing to trade with the British islands in the West Indies as though they were loyal British subjects — that is, without being subjected to the restrictions imposed upon foreign trade. In fact they were getting things both ways — as they sometimes still do. But they calculated that English officials would allow themselves to be hoodwinked — as they sometimes still are — and they knew that they would have the hearty support of the inhabitants of the islands, most of whom stood to gain by this illicit trade. And — until the arrival of young Captain Nelson — these calculations were fully justified. This illegal trade was not proclaimed from the housetops, of course, but there was hardly a decent pretence of concealment. American ships putting into port would pretend they had sprung a leak, or needed a surgeon or some other form of assistance commonly accorded at sea; but, once tied up to the quay, they would buy and sell as they liked, and depart at their leisure. Of course every one knew all about it, including the Admiral, good easy man; and every one was happy, and getting his little perquisite, if he was not actually in the deal; and no one was being cheated except England, whose fleet was always there to defend them the next time America declared war; and, in short, all was for the best in the best of dishonest worlds. That is, until Captain Nelson arrived with his unimportant little frigate.

We can understand his fiery indignation when he discovered what was going on. He could do nothing for the moment, being directly under the Admiral's orders, but when he and Collingwood (in the *Minotaur*) were sent away on an independent cruise to St Kitts and Nevis, they turned back every American ship they could see and captured five of them which were found in port. Immediately a storm broke loose. Protests poured in to Hughes, who wrote to Nelson ordering him never to interfere with a ship which the island authorities had admitted to their harbours. Nelson refused point-blank. He and Collingwood, and Collingwood's brother, Winifred, on the *Rattler,* continued to arrest ships. When he interviewed General Sir Thomas Shirley, Governor of the Leeward Islands, and explained his point of view to him, no doubt at some length and with some animation, that personage gruffly observed that "old generals were not in the habit of taking advice from young gentlemen." "Sir," replied Nelson, "I am as old as the Prime Minister of England, and think myself as capable of commanding one of His Majesty's ships as that minister is of governing the State." In a letter to Locker he boasts that he soon had the Governor "trimmed up and silenced."

Hughes, now really angry, was for trying him by court-martial, but dropped the idea upon finding that nearly all his captains (from among whom such a court must be formed) were strongly on Nelson's side. Then the colonists raised a subscription for the American captains, who sued Nelson for damages to the extent of £40,000. To avoid arrest he was compelled to remain a prisoner on his own ship. The Admiral did absolutely nothing. But Nelson had sent an explanation of his conduct to the Admiralty, and orders now came out that he was to be defended at the cost of the Treasury. At the same time the Admiralty conveyed its congratulations upon this zealous action — to Admiral Hughes!

While this controversy was still in progress there was a still more serious clash between Nelson and his senior officer. It was the custom to appoint half-pay officers as commissioners, or superintendents, of the various ports; and — simply as a matter of convenience — Sir Richard Hughes had ordered the commissioner at the busy port of Antigua (a certain Captain Moutray) to hoist a broad pennant as commodore, and to act as senior officer in the port. But no authority except the Admiralty could raise an officer from half-pay to full pay, and Nelson, coming into port and finding himself the senior captain there, promptly ordered the broad pennant to be struck, and told Moutray to take orders from him. The mild little

Sandys had the unpleasant task of seeing that this was carried out. Hughes saw his opportunity. He reported the matter to the Admiralty, who reprimanded Nelson for having taken such high-handed action without first addressing himself to his Commander-in-Chief.

Finally, he unearthed a first-class scandal — an elaborate system of cooking accounts by which, according to his two informants, the Government in the Leeward Islands had been swindled out of thousands of pounds in customs dues in the last few years. But, as these facts were not made public, nor any inquiry held, until after his return to England, we may postpone our review of the sordid story till then.

Nelson was to remain two further years on this station, and — mainly for reasons which will appear in the next chapter — they were to be a good deal happier than the former two. Twelve months after the Moutray incident Sir Richard Hughes returned to England, leaving Nelson the senior officer on the station for the time being. In December of that year his friend Prince William Henry arrived in command of the *Pegasus,* and there was a pleasant re-union. There was no more talk of arresting him now. He made friends with some of the colonists and even (as we shall see) found a wife among them. In the early summer of 1787 the *Boreas* set sail for England — a little earlier than had been expected, but Nelson wrote to the Admiralty that she was in such a leaky condition that she would not be able to make the voyage at all if it was left till after the hurricane season. So he turned his back on the Leeward Islands. He had done his duty as he saw it. He had not enjoyed it. "I want not — I wish not — to be a Custom House Officer," he protests in one of his letters home. He had not been particularly tactful, nor set a particularly good example to younger officers in the matter of prompt and unquestioning obedience to an admiral's orders. But, as usual, he had refused to be deflected by a single inch from what seemed to him the right and proper course. And, for the first and last time in his career, he had made himself thoroughly unpopular.

CHAPTER VI

MARRIAGE

NELSON had gone to the West Indies to forget. There is no doubt that he had been badly hurt. But while he nursed his wounded heart, sitting many nights alone in the great cabin of the *Boreas,* perhaps staring gloomily out through the stern windows across the blue waters, waiting for some impudent Yankee skipper upon whom he might vent his spleen, wishing that he had never met Miss Andrews, wishing her sex did not exist, he nevertheless, like so many disappointed lovers before and after him, found his first solace in the companionship and sympathy of another woman. To her he poured out his woes, and in a deep, warm friendship — which he, at any rate, supposed to be entirely Platonic — he quickly learned to forget, and to recover his old breezy attitude towards life.

The surprising thing is that the lady selected for this honour was none other than the wife of that Commissioner Moutray of Antigua who was so brusquely treated by Nelson and compelled to haul down his pennant, as recorded in the last chapter. But, although Admiral Hughes had used this occasion to get Nelson into trouble with the Admiralty, it would appear that Moutray himself never took offence. Indeed, Nelson rather forestalled anything of the kind, for, with a characteristically impulsive gesture, he went ashore that same evening to see the Commissioner, and assure him that there was no personal feeling in the matter, with the result that they dined together most amicably. Of the personality of Mrs Moutray, Nelson's friend, we can gather little, though he often refers to her in his letters. Not very long after this dinner party she went home to England. Nelson sorrows over her

66

departure almost in accents of despair. "My sweet amiable
friend," he writes in March 1785, "I took leave of her with a
heavy heart. What a *treasure* of a woman! God bless her."
And in May of the same year:

> This country appears now intolerable, my dear friend being
> absent; not all the Rosys [we will explain poor Rosy presently]
> can give a spark of joy to me. English Harbour I hate the sight
> of, and Windsor I detest. I went once up to the Hill to look at
> the spot where I spent more happy days than in any one spot in
> the world. E'en the trees drooped their heads and the tamarind
> tree died — all was melancholy; the road is covered with thistles;
> let them grow. I shall never pull one of them up. By this time
> I hope she is safe in England. Heaven's choicest blessing go
> with her.

It was, perhaps, what the French call an *amitié amoureuse*.
What Commissioner Moutray thought of it we do not know.
Nelson had a marvellous way with husbands.

It is clear, at any rate, that his friendship with Mrs Moutray
had the best possible effect upon Nelson. She cheered him up
and shook him out of himself, so that the whole tone of his
private letters alters about this time. The querulous note entirely disappears; he begins to notice pretty women again, and
describes with malicious humour the many love affairs of the
Admiral's daughter ("Rosy"), who, with her mother, Lady
Hughes, was probably the only woman he ever disliked. He
could not forget that miserable voyage, with their clacking
tongues and their silver tea-caddy. Nelson seems to have been
fitter too: in one letter he gives us an entertaining picture of
his morning bath on the *Boreas,* a sailor tipping six pails of
water over the naked hero.

The jocularities about the ladies are mostly contained in
letters addressed to his brother, after the latter's return to
England. The Reverend William had seen enough of the
station before his health broke down to be amused by such
gossip. Indeed, it is pretty clear, from some of Horatio's remarks, that William himself had carried on a mild flirtation

with Miss Hughes. Here is a typical effusion dated February
1785:

> Come, I must carry you to our love scenes. Captain Sandys
> [he of the claret] has asked Miss Eliot — *refused*. Captain
> Sterling was attentive to Miss Elizabeth E; but never having
> asked the question, Captain Berkley is, I hear, to be the happy
> man. Captain Kelly is attached to a lady at Nevis, so he says:
> I don't much think it . . . Rosy has had no offers: I fancy she
> seems hurt at it. Poor girl! You should have offered. I have
> not gallantry enough. A niece of Governor Parry's has come
> out. She goes to Nevis in the *Boreas;* they trust any young lady
> with me, being an old-fashioned fellow.

Seven months later Rosy finds a husband after all:

> Rosy — your Rose — is very unwell, and is obliged to apply to
> an Irish physician to cure her disorder, which is what the world
> calls Love. A bold Major Browne of the 67th Regiment is the
> man, and the Admiral sails on Tuesday in the *Latona* to join
> them together. God help the poor man: has he taken leave of
> his senses? The mother will be in a few years the handsomest
> of the two.

And we hear more of the doings of poor little Sandys, who
between "Bacchus and Venus is scarcely ever thoroughly in
his senses." Nelson is "very sorry for him, for his heart is
good; but he is not fit to command a man-of-war." Indeed
"such men hurt the service more than it is in the power of
ten good ones to bring back." Nelson doubts if he will ever
reform. "I never knew any of these grog drinkers quit it."
Soon after this Sandys was sent home ill.

Nelson was often at Nevis and St Kitts about this time. Of
his famous visit to St Kitts in company with Collingwood (in
the *Minotaur*) when the American hare was started, we have
spoken in the previous chapter. It is important to remember,
while we read his foolish letters to his brother (he was only
twenty-eight), that he was at this time going through one of
the busiest and most anxious periods of his whole life. He
was unpopular with the colonists everywhere, as we have seen,

but nowhere more than at Nevis and St Kitts, where the trouble had begun. Yet it was at Nevis that he made his best and stoutest friend among them — the wealthy Mr Herbert, "president," or governor, of the island. When Nelson, as related in the last chapter, was afraid to go ashore lest he should be arrested at the instance of the American skippers who were making fantastic monetary claims against him, it was Herbert, the president, than whom no colonist stood to lose more by the suppression of the American trade, who went bail for the young Captain and saved him from personal indignity. We get the impression of an irascible, proud, good-hearted nabob, quick to take offence, but quick also to detect genius and driving-power in a man of a very different type from his, and broadminded enough to respond to it without regard to his own interests.

But Mr Herbert had a niece. She was then twenty-four years of age,* but was already a widow with a child (Josiah) aged three, of whom we shall hear more. In 1779 she had married a Dr Nisbet, who shortly afterwards went out of his mind and died. For some time that kind of whimsical fate which governs the movements of young men and maidens prevented Nelson and Mrs Nisbet from meeting each other, though at the same time it arranged that Fanny Nisbet should continually be hearing of the great deeds and the forceful personality of young Captain Nelson. He was, of course, a frequent visitor to her uncle's house. "Good God!" exclaimed Mr Herbert on one occasion, after being called out of his dressing-room to greet Nelson, whose ship had unexpectedly arrived at Nevis, "Good God, if I did not find that great little man, of whom everybody is so afraid, playing in the next room under the dining table with Mrs Nisbet's child." The whole colony must have been talking about him, if not usually in very complimentary terms. There is a letter to Fanny, then at Nevis, from a girl friend at St Kitts, which contains

---

* Southey, for some reason, asserts that she was only seventeen at this time, which would make her married at thirteen and a mother at fourteen!

the best description (after Prince William Henry's) of Nelson at this period of his life. This young lady writes:

We have at last seen the Captain of the *Boreas,* of whom so much has been said. He came up just before dinner, much heated, and was very silent, yet seemed, according to the old adage, to think the more. He declined drinking any wine; but after dinner, when the President, as usual, gave the following toasts, "The King," "The Queen and Royal Family," and "Lord Hood"; this strange man regularly filled his glass, and observed that these were always bumper toasts with him; which having drunk, he uniformly passed the bottle, and relapsed into his former taciturnity. It was impossible, during this visit, for any of us to make out his real character; there was such a reserve and sternness in his behaviour, with occasional sallies, though very transient, of a superior mind. Being placed by him, I endeavoured to rouse his attention by showing him all the civilities in my power; but I drew out little more than "yes" and "no." If you, Fanny, had been there, we think you would have made something of him; for you have been in the habit of attending to these odd sort of people.

All this must have excited Fanny's interest in Nelson. Without accusing her of setting her cap at him we may remember the learned opinion of Mr Weller senior to the effect that "vidders" are the worst. And it is fair to point out that he was generally regarded as a rising young officer, and that, in his present mood, he was easy game.

We do not know when or how they met; but the result was a foregone conclusion. Fanny was a quiet, cool, sensible girl. She appealed to that side of Nelson which derived from the country parsonage; and he was yet too young to understand that this was the unessential part of his character. She was before everything a lady. We can imagine her laying a cool, competent white hand on his fevered brow, and helping him to forget all his worries. He surrendered eagerly. He thought this was the real thing — so much better and more lasting than his gusty passion for the parson's daughter. He began to write her letters, and we — wise after the event — notice at once that their whole tone of voice was utterly and hopelessly wrong. Nowhere in the two stout volumes of correspondence edited by Nicolas do we find such flat, conventional, unconvincing epistles as these. "My greatest wish is to be united to you." "The foundation of all conjugal happiness, real love, and esteem, is, I trust, what you believe I possess in the strongest degree towards you. My whole life will ever be devoted to make you completely happy, whatever whims may sometimes take me" — there is surely a kind of cautious hedging here. Another remark, "Salt water and absence always wash away love," seems, to put it mildly, a little out of place in a letter to his *fiancée*.

There is no doubt whatever of the sincerity of his affection for Fanny Nisbet. There is equally no doubt that he was never really in love with her. He was convinced that every man ought to be married; promiscuity in the relations of the sexes was a thing disgusting to him. Some months later, when he heard that his uncle had been married, he wrote to his brother William: "I am truly happy to hear Mr Suckling is married; it will add to his felicity, for had he not done that he must have kept a woman, which you will allow would have been very disagreeable." That is a plain, unequivocal statement of Nelson's attitude to these matters — though whether he meant that it would be more disagreeable to Mr Suckling or to his nephews is not quite clear. But it is an illuminating remark, and we can only conclude that, coming to the West Indies in the circumstances that we have seen, and in the frame of mind of a rejected lover, he was bound to marry somebody, and that — leaving poor Fanny's interests out of account, for the moment — he might have gone farther and fared worse.

We get a somewhat unexpected confirmation of this view of Nelson's marriage from that observant friend of his Prince William Henry. The Prince came out to join the station in November 1786, and found Nelson already engaged, but with no intention of marrying "till near the time of our sailing for England." The old friendly relations were quickly re-established. The Prince insisted that, when the happy day arrived,

F

he should give away the bride. But he seems to have detected in the affair some of the unromantic atmosphere of a marriage of state, such as he himself was doomed to; for we find Nelson writing to Fanny only a few weeks after his arrival:

> His Royal Highness often tells me he believes I am married; for he never saw a lover so easy or say so little of the object he has a regard for. When I tell him I certainly am not, he says, "Then he is sure I must have a great esteem for you, and that is not what is (vulgarly), I do not much like the use of that word, called love." He is right: my love is founded on esteem, the only foundation that . . .

How many millions of lesser men have made the same silly mistake! Nelson was free enough with the word "love" in all his other affairs. It was not in his nature to shirk any word if he meant it.

But in the meantime Mr Suckling had to be written to again. Fanny was Herbert's favourite niece (he preferred her to his own daughter); she was promised £20,000 when he died, and it seemed certain — he had as good as said so to Nelson — that he would make her an allowance of two or three hundred a year on her marriage. But Nelson needed that hundred a year, already promised by his uncle, if only for his self-respect. "When I open my business," he writes bashfully to Mr Suckling, "you will perhaps smile in the first instance, and say, 'this Horatio is for ever in love.'" He goes on to make a manly, straightforward statement of his position, and to repeat his earlier appeal. It appears that Mr Suckling (who was still a bachelor when he received this letter, though both he and William Nelson were married before Horatio in the end) again came up to scratch.

So that the joyful consummation of this rather tepid, Victorian sort of courtship was now only a matter of time. Early in 1787 — two or three months after the arrival of Prince William Henry and more than a year since he wrote to his uncle — Nelson saw that, owing to the leaky condition of the *Boreas*, it would be necessary for him to leave for England that summer, and he therefore hastened forward the arrangements for his marriage. On March 12, 1787, he was formally united to Fanny Nisbet, the Prince giving the bride away, as arranged. In July the newly married pair returned to England, taking young Josiah with them.

While this happy pair are being wafted home to England upon "aerial and rose clouded paths not indicated on the map," enjoying, we may suppose, a kind of second honeymoon (for they had seen little enough of each other since their marriage in March), we may pause to record a curious and rather disconcerting incident which occurred soon after Prince William Henry's arrival at the Leeward Islands, and in which he was the principal figure. It may be conveniently referred to as the "Schomberg incident." The Prince, as we have already seen, was a strict disciplinarian. He was in command of the *Pegasus,* Nelson, in the *Boreas,* being his senior officer. Schomberg was First Lieutenant of the *Pegasus.* The Prince gave (or thought he gave) an order that no boat was to leave the ship without his permission. The First Lieutenant either never saw the order or did not suppose it applied to him. He took a boat; whereupon he was publicly reprimanded. He replied by demanding a court-martial, addressing himself to Nelson as senior officer of the fleet. Nelson promptly put him under arrest to await trial; and at the same time he issued a strong general order to the fleet, stating that he should in future regard it as an offence against the Articles of War for officers to demand a court-martial at such a time, "thereby depriving His Majesty of their services," and that if anyone did it again he would be put on trial for *that* offence as well as for the one that was to be the subject of the court-martial.

In the meantime the fleet was so actively engaged in chasing Yankee traders that for months no court-martial could be assembled. Schomberg remained under arrest. An appeal to Nelson brought a curt reply. In a letter to Commodore Alan Gardner, who was coming out from England to take command, Nelson argued that if officers demanded a court-martial every time they were reprimanded by a superior then "farewell discipline, the Service is ruined, His Majesty may be deprived of the services of his officers, and the best-laid schemes may be frustrated by the malignity of individuals or pique against their commanders." This letter was sent to Jamaica by the *Pegasus* to await Gardner's arrival. That was in May, and when Nelson himself got back to England, two months later, he was asked by the Admiralty what he meant by sending the ship away from the station, and was briefly informed that he would be "answerable for the consequences if the Crown should be put to any needless expense upon that account."

There can be no doubt that in his somewhat severe conduct of this affair Nelson was influenced by his loyal devotion to the Prince, whose qualities he doubtless exaggerated. Indeed, in a letter to Captain Locker, in which he praises William Henry to the skies, he is constrained to admit that "some others, I have heard, will tell another story." But the important point to notice is that as soon as he heard (being then in England) that his successor, Gardner, had succeeded in settling the matter without a court-martial, he sat down and wrote to his friend the Prince a letter which shows him at his very best. In the course of it he says:

If to be truly great is to be truly good (as we are taught to believe), it never was stronger verified than in your Royal Highness, in the instance of Mr. Schomberg. You have supported your character, yet, at the same time, by an amiable condescension, have saved an officer from appearing before a court-martial, which ever must hurt him. Resentment I know your Royal Highness never had, or I am sure ever will bear anyone; it is a passion incompatible with the character of a man of honour. Schomberg was too hasty certainly in writing his letter; but now you are parted, pardon me, my Prince, when I presume to recommend that Schomberg may stand in your Royal Favour, as if he had never sailed with you; and that at some future day you will serve him. There only wants this to place your character in the highest point of view. None of us are without failings; Schomberg's was being rather too hasty; but that, put in competition with his being a good Officer, will not, I am bold to say, be taken in the scale against him.

To return to Nelson's homecoming with his bride. It was not particularly auspicious. He must have been conscious of a distinct change of temperature — not only in the climate, which promptly drove him to bed with a sore throat and "slow fever," but also in the official atmosphere. For instance, the *Boreas,* instead of being paid off immediately, was left at the Nore from July to the end of November, serving as a slop- and receiving-ship. A Nelson in command of a slop-ship! Clarke and MacArthur give us a fancy picture of the hero carrying on these menial duties with "strict and sullen attention"; and Southey, copying from them, says that when the *Boreas* was eventually paid off, Nelson loudly proclaimed his "firm and unalterable determination never again to set foot on board a King's ship." There is no reason to suppose that he behaved so childishly. There is nothing in his letters to suggest it, and his biographers, as usual, fail to give their authorities. But it is quite likely that, having his wife with him, he was inconvenienced and perhaps vexed at the delay.

At any rate, he seems to have used some fairly strong language to the senior officer commanding his Majesty's ships in the river Medway, and may even have talked about resigning his commission, as soon as he could get to London and see the First Lord of the Admiralty. The senior officer, however, had the sense to get in touch with Lord Howe and explain the situation, so that when Nelson's gloomy face eventually appeared in the doorway, he was received by the First Lord with a heartiness he could not resist, assured of the Admiralty's support against the claims of the Yankee skippers, and carried off to be presented to the King at the next levee.

But they would not give him a ship. Nor can they be blamed for it. They had recognized him, quite accurately, as the sort of "live wire" who would always be likely to cause trouble in peace time, simply through excess of zeal. He would always be right, of course, and they would always have to back him, often against his superior officers; but wherever he was these awkward questions would be sure to turn up. A first-class man on active service, no doubt; but, as the sergeant-major said of the drunken V.C. in the late War, "You'll never make a *soldier* of him, sir." That was probably the feeling about Nelson. At any rate, they did not give him a ship.

He could not leave London immediately. The scandal which he had unearthed in the Leeward Islands about the cooking of accounts in regard to the victualling of the fleet and so forth had now assumed vast proportions. Prince William Henry had been informed of it, and the papers had been forced upon the attention of the Admiralty. Nelson was continually getting letters from his two informants in the Leeward Islands, Messrs Higgins and Wilkinson, who not unnaturally feared for their liberty now that their names were known to the colonists (and with good cause, as it turned out, for they were both clapped in gaol). He did his best for them. Hearing that the matter had been referred to the Treasury, he went and called upon a Mr Rose, who agreed to see him in the morning, if it could be early. Nelson at once suggested six o'clock, and it is a sober fact that these two hardy ancestors of ours met at that hour and talked till nine, when Nelson stayed to breakfast. But nothing ever seems to have been done about these disgraceful charges against the not particularly loyal colonists of the Leeward Islands. Nobody seems to have suffered except the informers, to whom Nelson had to explain, in response to their appeals, that he had not the same authority in England as he had when senior naval officer on the station.

These things worried him so much that he left London and went to his beloved Bath by way of Plymouth, where he visited Prince William Henry, the *Pegasus* being then in harbour. At Bath his health and spirits quickly improved ("never was I so well"), and he took the opportunity of introducing his wife to some of his relations in the west country. His aged father, too, had to spend every winter there. He suffered from paralysis, which had grown upon him to such an extent that he could not speak in the mornings for some hours after he got up. It was here, no doubt, that he offered to lend his son and daughter-in-law the parsonage house at

Burnham Thorpe. Nelson, after one more futile attempt to stir the Admiralty into giving him a ship (it was about this time that he decided, quite wrongly, that even Lord Hood must be his personal enemy), agreed to the proposal and departed to East Anglia with his wife. There he "did not disdain to cultivate a few acres of glebe land annexed to the rectory"; and there he remained, clumsily striving to adapt himself to bucolic pursuits, for the next five years.

At first he had contemplated only a short stay, and had even talked of crossing the Channel with Mrs Nelson to have another go at that obstinate French language (which she already understood). He studied charts and naval plans, just to keep his hand in; but gradually he was falling into a rut; he went coursing, like Parson James Woodforde; and he even tried partridge-shooting; but "the manner in which he carried his gun, always cocked as if he were going to board an enemy, and his custom of firing immediately when any birds appeared, without even putting the fowling piece to his shoulder, rendered any attendance on him a service of considerable danger." It is further said that he often went birds'-nesting, no doubt taking young Josiah with him, along the hedgerows of that pleasant Norfolk countryside, and that he cultivated the garden with zeal, digging violently, "as it were for the sake of being wearied."

Then one day he went into the nearest town to buy a pony, and in his absence a writ was served upon his wife, on the part of the American captains, who laid their damages at £20,000. Naturally Mrs Nelson was upset. "This affront I did not deserve," exclaims Nelson indignantly, and he wrote a strong letter to the Treasury, saying bluntly that if such invitations could not otherwise be avoided, he should go into voluntary exile in France. What is more, he made all his plans to do so, his wife to follow ten days later under his brother's charge; but the prompt and cordial reply of the Treasury, assuring him of their support, prevented any such action.

So the dreary years of enforced inactivity crawled on. He tried once again to take an interest in politics, and his attitude

towards current affairs is not without interest to the student
of his character. France is breaking out into revolution. He
is horrified at the disloyal "societies" which are being formed
all over East Anglia in imitation of the Jacobin clubs, societies
"of which our dissenters are the head, and in this country they
have great riches." He cannot understand why orators like
the famous Dr Priestley are not arrested; he puts the question
to a local magistrate, and is answered, to his disgust, that "no
one dared to do it for fear of the mob." He writes indignantly of this to Prince William Henry (now Duke of Clarence) on December 10, 1792, but adds characteristically:

> That the poor labourers should have been seduced by promises
> and hopes of better times, your Royal Highness will not wonder
> at when I assure you that they are really in want of everything
> to make life comfortable. Part of their wants, perhaps, were
> unavoidable, from the dearness of every article of life; but much
> has arose from the neglect of the country gentlemen in not
> making the farmers raise their wages in some small proportion
> as the prices of necessaries increased . . . Their wages have been
> raised within these three weeks, pretty generally, one shilling a
> week; had it been done some time past, they would not have
> been discontented, for a want of loyalty [to Nelson the worst of
> crimes] is not amongst their faults; and many of their superiors,
> in many instances, might have imitated their conduct with
> advantage.

He appends a most carefully worked out budget for an agri-
cultural labourer's family, showing "not quite two pence a day
a head for food," and "to drink nothing but water."

And Mrs Nelson? It must be remembered that the change
from the President's house at Nevis, where she was the great
lady of the island, with scores of servants at her beck and call,
courted by the younger men among the colonists, and by visiting naval officers — the change from this to the quiet little
parsonage house in Norfolk, where her husband was just a
half-pay captain, among many others in the county also
waiting for jobs, was a step not up but down in the social
world. We know that Nelson's Walpole relations were in-

clined to forget her existence. She was not invited to the funeral of Lord Orford, and, though there were apologies when the mistake was discovered, still she must have felt the slight. She and Nelson had no children. There was Josiah, of whom they were both very fond; but it requires little knowledge of human nature to guess that Nelson was disappointed, and that the very existence of Josiah made him feel it more. He was restless and worried. He had got it into his head that everybody, even Lord Hood, was against him, and, on the whole, making all allowance for his natural kindliness of disposition and his thoughtfulness for those around him, he cannot have been an easy man to live with at this time.

Yet every letter he wrote to Fanny after he was given a ship — and there are dozens of them — seems to show that they got through this difficult period remarkably well. There is no hint of any kind of disagreement, and for that a large share of the credit must go to her. In trying circumstances and with some cause for discontent she played the part of an uncomplaining, obedient, understanding wife. It is a point that should be remembered in her favour.

Then at last things began to move. War was in the air. The French Revolution, at first merely an internal fire which seemed likely to burn itself out amid blood and ashes, had now been got under control by the Committee of Public Safety and the revolutionary tribunals, and had become a danger to the peace of the world. The new rulers of France were seeking a safety-valve and found it in an aggressive foreign policy, with the avowed object of imposing their theories upon the rest of the world. Nelson, in Norfolk, had, as we have seen, taken due note of the formation of clubs and societies of a more or less revolutionary character. He was not more panicky about it than others — rather less so. The whole world was alarmed, and it was only a question of time before a revolution designed to restore peace and prosperity to man should plunge him (as revolutions do) into all the miseries of war.

War was declared on February 11, 1793. Long before that

the Admiralty had remembered Nelson. Ships were being commissioned rapidly, and, no doubt, Prince William Henry (now Duke of Clarence) and probably Lord Hood would hasten to put forward his name — if, indeed, any reminder were needed. On January 7 the First Lord sent for him and, after apologizing for not being able to give him a 74-gun ship, offered him a sixty-four, if he would take it till there should be a seventy-four available. On January 30 he was appointed to the *Agamemnon*.. Nelson was elated. All his discontents vanished at a touch. Here at last was work to be done. Already the French in Brest had fired on the English brig *Childers,* and Nelson himself saw the round-shot which had been brought to the Admiralty. He was now a man of thirty-four. Six of the best years of his life had been wasted. What matter! He prepared eagerly to go down to his new command. "After clouds comes sunshine," he wrote.

CHAPTER VII

THE MEETING WITH EMMA

THE PERIOD from February 1793 to October 1805 has been well described as "Nelson's page in history." * During that period there were spectacular actions fought on land, oceans of money poured out to support the rival armies, ceremonial meetings between kings and diplomatists, all of which take up a good deal more space in the history books than the achievements of the British fleet. But it was during these years that the British established their ascendancy at sea, which, as we can now see, was one of the decisive factors in the war. British ships destroyed the enemy's commerce, they bottled up his fleets in harbour, and they made it quite clear that, whatever might happen to his opponents on land, he could never invade the most obstinate and active of all the countries opposed to him — Great Britain. And in this great achievement the name of Nelson figures prominently. His service up to date had been useful, no doubt, and had won the recognitions of men like Lord Hood and the Duke of Clarence. But it had not made history. It was no more distinguished than that of many other naval officers of his age. From the time of his taking command of the *Agamemnon* he is always in the limelight. He is making history at last.

Moreover, when he stepped on board his new ship, he was taking over the longest command he ever held. With the exception of the *Victory*, on whose decks he died, no vessel is so intimately associated with Nelson's name as the *Agamemnon*. As usual he was favourably impressed. "I have the

* Mahan, *Life of Nelson*, Chapter III (London, 1899).

pleasure of telling you," he writes to Mrs Nelson, "that my ship is without exception the finest 64 in the service." He is "well appointed in officers," and has "no doubt but we shall acquit ourselves well should the French give us a meeting . . . to me it is perfectly indifferent to what quarter of the world we go; with a good ship and ship's company we can come to no harm."

As a matter of fact, the *Agamemnon* turned out to be one of the best sailers in the fleet. But the manning of her had not been so easy as these letters might suggest. Nelson went about it carefully. He put out his bills all over Norfolk and Suffolk before any were allowed to be issued in London; so that most of the ship's company came from those parts where his name was known, and the men would share a sort of local patriotism. Young Josiah was among the midshipmen. It did not really matter where Nelson got his crew from; they always followed him with the same devotion. But the *Agamemnon's* may be regarded as picked men, and it is worthy of notice that Nelson during the next few years several times refused promotion to higher commands because he would not leave this ship, which was certainly nearer his heart than any other he ever sailed in. And if he conferred immortality on the *Agamemnon,* it was also the *Agamemnon* that made him. It took him for the first time to the Mediterranean, where some of his greatest exploits were to be performed and the foundations of his fame securely laid.

The ship was ordered to join Admiral Lord Hood's fleet, which sailed for Gibraltar in the early part of June. The health of the crew was excellent. "We are all well," writes Nelson, "indeed, nobody can be ill with my ship's company, they are so fine a set." We can understand that there was a general reluctance to "report sick" on any ship commanded by Nelson. The great secret of his success was that he always assumed everybody to be as efficient and loyal and enthusiastic as himself. In the Bay of Biscay the *Agamemnon* and five other ships were sent into Cadiz to water, in order that the whole fleet might not be watering together at Gibraltar, which would mean loss of time. At Cadiz Nelson made his first close acquaintance with the Spanish Navy (Spain was then still neutral), and his comments have a refreshing candour. "The Dons make fine ships," he says, "they cannot, however, make men."

He liked the Dons well enough personally — until they took him to see a bull-fight. It is amusing — and astonishing — to see the typically modern English view of bull-fighting expressed by this eighteenth-century sailor. The resemblance is so remarkable that his letter to his wife on the subject is worth quoting in full. It is dated June 23, just after leaving Cadiz:

A bull feast was exhibited, for which the Spaniards are famous; and from their dexterity in attacking and killing of these animals, the ladies choose their husbands. We English had certainly to regret the want of humanity in the Dons and Donnas. The amphitheatre will hold 16,000 people: about 12,000 were present. Ten bulls were selected, and one brought out at a time. Three cavaliers on horseback and fourteen with flags were the combatants. We had what is called a fine feast, for five horses were killed, and two men very much hurt; had they been killed it would have been quite complete. We felt for the bulls and horses, and I own it would not have displeased me to have had some of the Dons tossed by the enraged animal. How women can even sit it out, much more applaud such sights, is astonishing. It even turned us sick, and we could hardly go through it: the dead, mangled horses with the entrails torn out, and the bulls covered with blood, were too much. We have seen one bull feast, and have agreed that nothing shall tempt us to see another.

Yet in England foxes, stags, and badgers were hunted and cruelly killed without any of the risks to the sportsmen which the Spanish toreador had to face. Bear-baiting and bull-baiting and running were going strong, and were not suppressed in England until 1835, nearly half a century after Nelson wrote the above. Nelson, in fact, was expressing the typical, sentimental modern English point of view. He hoped that the bulls would succeed in tossing the toreadors; and modern visitors to Spanish bull-fights may often be heard expressing the same pious wish. It sounds simply wicked; but in fact it is neither wicked nor even merely muddle-headed, being based upon the profound English conviction that a bull is nearer to a human being than a foreigner. Bosh!

And so, on to Gibraltar. Off Cape St Vincent he paid Lord Hood a visit, and found him "very civil." "I daresay we shall be good friends again." From Gibraltar the fleet was ordered to Toulon, and in the Gulf of Lyons Nelson writes: "Lord Hood is tolerably good friends with me." Finally, on December 1 of the same year, we note the usual hero-worship of an efficient chief: "Lord Hood," he writes to Locker, "is certainly the best officer I ever saw." As a matter of fact, on a careful reading of the whole of the evidence, the conclusion is forced upon one that all his talk about Hood having become his enemy was pure imagination, born of a long period of unemployment and nervous strain.

In the middle of July the fleet arrived off Toulon, and proceeded to blockade the place. Nelson had been writing a remarkable series of letters to the Duke of Clarence, giving an almost daily journal of events, from which it appeared that the blockade was very strictly maintained, while every effort was made to induce "these red hot gentlemen" as Nelson called the French fleet (for they were reported to be preparing red-hot cannon-balls) to come out and fight. At the end of August, however, peace was arranged on the terms that Toulon should turn Royalist and hoist the fleur-de-lis. The British fleet then entered the harbour, and marines were landed and preparations made to defend the town against the expected Republican attack. The rest of that tragic history need not be recorded here, since Nelson had no hand in it. It is enough to say that the Republican army advanced against the town in December and was immediately successful. A young artillery officer named Buonaparte distinguished himself in the attack. The defenders, outnumbered and divided among themselves, put up a feeble resistance. Hood burned much of the shipping in the harbour, and took on board some fifteen thousand refugees before putting out to sea. But at least another six thousand, men, women, and children, were mercilessly slaughtered by the Republicans as they stood, crowded helplessly together, on the quays.

Nelson, as we have said, was not there. He was making his first visit to Italy and, incidentally, to Naples. As the *Agamemnon* was the best sailer in the fleet she was sent away by Lord Hood on August 25 with letters to the Courts of Naples and Turin. Nelson set off joyfully. It was the first of his many independent commands in the Mediterranean. He could not guess what Fate had in store for him. He had probably no more than barely heard of Sir William Hamilton, English Ambassador at Naples, and his charming wife.

The business at Turin was soon transacted, and they proceeded southward making for the famous bay, which a man is advised to see and then die. On September 11 he wrote to his wife, Fanny: "We are now in sight of Mount Vesuvius, which shows a fine light to us in Naples Bay, where we are lying-to for the night, and hope to anchor early to-morrow." Nothing in that to alarm her. The first thought in her mind as she read the letter was probably of her midshipman son, Josiah, and how pleased he would be to see these famous places. As for Nelson, he cast anchor next morning and went ashore to deliver his papers at the Neapolitan Court. Before he sets foot on the quay we may glance briefly at the small group of people with whose affairs he was presently to be so closely connected — the King and Queen, the British Ambassador and his wife.

The King of Naples was as nearly mad as makes no difference. It is true that he showed a certain shrewdness in regard to the foreign policy of his little kingdom, which was at that time in rather a delicate situation, threatened by French armies from the north and by the British fleet from the south; but though there are some who maintain that he was not such a fool as he looked, his personal behaviour was, to put it mildly, eccentric. The British officer Bunbury has left us an unforgettable picture of the King at a somewhat later date than this, when the French had driven him out of Naples, and the Straits of Messina had become, so to speak, a no man's land between the French on the one side and the British and Neapolitans on the other. Bunbury saw the King standing on one of the batteries in the town of Messina, watching an engagement between some of his gunboats and a number of Sicilian boats in the French service which were trying to creep along the Calabrian coast with supplies for Reggio. Bunbury writes:

> I chanced to be standing beside his Majesty: he was watching the skirmish on the opposite coast with childish eagerness; at every shot he laughed aloud, threw one of his long bony limbs in strange gesticulations, and poured forth volleys of buffoonery in the Lazzaron dialect. It never seemed to occur to him that the people in the boats on both sides were his subjects, and that the shots might strike off their heads or legs. No, it was a sight he had never witnessed before, and he was himself in perfect safety.

Of his good-natured, rather theatrical, but not unintelligent Queen even less need be said. She was a friend of Lady Hamilton and a friend of the British. How far those two friendships depended upon each other it is difficult now to decide, though it is clear that Nelson, in commending Lady Hamilton to the British Government in his will, greatly exaggerated the strength of her influence and the importance of her services.

It has been said by a biographer of George Washington * that we shall never see the figure of the great American clearly until we drag him forth from the impenetrable shade of the cherry-tree. In the same way it may be said of Nelson that — at any rate, as far as the casual modern reader is concerned — he urgently needs to be rescued from behind the petticoats of Lady Hamilton. So many books have been written about Lady Hamilton within the last fifteen or twenty years, and so many studies of Nelson solely in his relation to her, that the occasional reader who prefers to take his or her

---

* Mr Philip Guedalla.

history in the biographical form and in the modern manner might be excused for supposing that Nelson's passion for Lady Hamilton was the central fact of his life. Nothing could be more absurd, of course: it gets him more out of proportion than if we think of him as a naval commander and nothing else. But this modern pre-occupation with Lady Hamilton is not merely a reaction against the prudery of the Victorians and the unfairness of their attacks upon her memory; it is based upon the fact that we understand her type better than any intervening generation has understood it. The female adventurer may not be so common now nor so influential as she was in the eighteenth century, but at any rate we no longer deny her existence, as the nineteenth century did — indeed, we are, perhaps, unduly interested in her.

Emma Hamilton was the daughter of a humble workman in the parish of Great Neston, Cheshire, and was born probably in the year 1761. She was christened Amy, but for some reason adopted the name Emma. She came to London as a nurse-maid, and after an adventurous career as shop-girl, barmaid, and the mother of at least one illegitimate child, she went, in 1780, to live under the protection of Sir Harry Fetherstonhaugh of Up Park in Sussex. It was a noisy, dissolute household, and one day, after a row, Fetherstonhaugh turned her out with barely enough money to get home to her mother. Nor did he ever afterwards so much as answer her letters. She then went to live with Charles Greville, that gentlemanly, cold-hearted, ambitious young man, taking her mother with her to act as cook and housekeeper — a typical eighteenth-century arrangement. She was really in love with Greville (ready to be in love with anyone, probably, poor child!) but he treated her stingily. Though an earl's son, he had but £500 a year of his own, out of which he allowed Emma only £20 for dress and pocket-money. But he introduced her to Romney, who adored her — perhaps more than was good for him — and to Reynolds and Lawrence and Hopner, whose portraits of her are now well known. Romney used to declare that she was the inspiration of everything that was best

G

in his art, and he painted her so often that about this time, 1783 (when Nelson was taking his broken heart to the West Indies to be cured), she must have sat to him incessantly, like a regular model. Romney was then a man of fifty, and it is generally thought that his unbalanced admiration for the beautiful girl hastened his nervous breakdown.

At any rate, Emma Harte, as she then was, became an acknowledged beauty and a general favourite. No doubt Greville, in his own way, was proud of her. But his money difficulties continued, and he was not slow to see the financial possibilities in this wonderful mistress whom he had bought so cheap. So he decided to sell her. It happened that in the summer of 1784 his maternal uncle, Sir William Hamilton, British Ambassador at Naples, happened to be home on leave. He saw Emma, and was captivated. Sir William is described as a man "of spare figure and of great muscular power and energy"; he was a keen sportsman, a bit of a musician, a member of the Society of Antiquaries and of a society of dilettanti, who made important gifts to the British Museum, and was "the best dancer at the Neapolitan Court." But he was now a man of fifty-four, and there was always something curiously fatherly about his attitude towards Emma. To the modern mind his behaviour is almost as difficult to defend as Greville's; yet we feel instinctively that he was a decent kind of man, whereas Greville was not.

To put it briefly, Greville offered to hand Emma over in return for a consideration in his uncle's will. Thus it was arranged. But Emma was genuinely in love with Greville; so she had to be inveigled out to Naples under the pretence of being taught music and the Italian method of singing. Her wretched old mother, who had now changed her name to Cadogan and probably knew quite well what was happening, accompanied her. Why prolong the miserable story? Emma soon discovered the trap. She appealed again and again to Greville — foolish, illiterate, tearful, moving appeals — "Greville, my dear Greville, write some comfort to me!" Not he! At last she gave way; and it was the best thing she could do,

SIR WILLIAM HAMILTON
From the painting by Sir Joshua Reynolds in the National Portrait Gallery.

for she was undoubtedly happier in the end with this easy-going old libertine than with a cold cad like Greville. Hamilton could refuse her nothing. In May 1791, when they were again in England, he married her in Marylebone Church.

In Naples she had been a social success from the start. Returning now as the Ambassador's wife, she was received at Court and became Queen Carolina's closest friend — to the great advantage of the English, and to the disgust of the pro-French party, who did not hesitate to spread the most disgraceful scandals about this friendship. Distinguished English visitors called on her and were enchanted. Sir William Hamilton, at their first meeting, had declared that her beauty was "even superior to the classical"; and it is about this time that we hear so much of her famous "attitudes," a series of poses in classical drapery, now familiar to every one in Friedrich Rehberg's engravings. "You never saw anything so charming as Lady Hamilton's attitudes" wrote the Countess of Malmesbury from Naples in 1792, "the most graceful statues or pictures do not give you an idea of them." Emma's pretty Greek nose was, no doubt, a great asset, but it is obvious, as Lady Malmesbury seems to suggest, that no statues and pictures could ever recapture and hand on to us the most devastating of her charms — her natural grace and vivacity in every movement. She must have been the perfect model; her "attitudes," we feel convinced, were entirely her own. But the play of ever changing emotions upon that extraordinarily vivid little face of hers has caught the painters unaware, so that their ideas of her — and even the same painter's ideas of her — will differ so widely that it is almost impossible to believe that some other model has not been substituted. All show the big eyes, the bright colouring, and the wavy hair. Beyond that there is no agreement — except that all are charming.

It is recorded by Harrison, who must have got it from Emma herself, that "on Sir William Hamilton's returning home after having first beheld Captain Nelson [no doubt on that same first morning of his arrival in the Bay, when his papers were presented at Court], he told his lady that he was about to introduce a little man to her acquaintance who could not boast of being very handsome." He is alleged to have added, however, that this Captain Nelson, judging from his conversation, would become "the greatest man that ever England produced." It is at this point that we remember that Harrison's book was not written till after Trafalgar. A more convincing and homely detail is Hamilton's order to his wife, "let him be put in the room prepared for Prince Augustus."

So he went to stay with the Hamiltons, and it may be, as Harrison says, that he was "charmed with the characteristic sweetness of disposition which she so fascinatingly displayed for the promotion of his ease and comfort." There is nothing, however, to suggest love at first sight. On the other hand, she did, clearly, produce an impression. Three days after his arrival he wrote (again to Fanny):

> Lady Hamilton has been wonderfully kind and good to Josiah. She is a young woman of amiable manners, and who does honour to the station to which she is raised.

So kind to Josiah. A psychologist might discuss that statement at much length. Was it only Nelson's excuse to himself for the interest he felt in this new and fascinating acquaintance? Or was Lady Hamilton really so very, so markedly, kind to Josiah? If so, we can only feel the very gravest suspicions about her motives.

In the meantime there were more serious matters to attend to. The purport of Nelson's letters to the King was to request the help of Naples, both naval and military, in the defence of Toulon against the impending Republican attack. It was great news in Naples that Toulon had hoisted the Royalist flag. Even the King became quite enthusiastic, and not only received Nelson with cordiality on several occasions, but honoured him with a visit on board the *Agamemnon*. He told Nelson that the English were "the saviours of Italy and his dominion in particular." In four days from the arrival of his ship in harbour Nelson had extracted a promise of

six thousand men, with transports and convoy, and naval assistance as well. Moreover, the arrangements for their dispatch
went forward with unexampled promptitude: his very presence seemed to make those sleepy quays come to life.   But
he saw no more of his charming hostess and admiring host,
for on the fourth day there was a rumour of a French frigate
on the coast, and the *Agamemnon* instantly put out to sea
in pursuit, carrying with her the King's letters to Lord Hood
at Toulon.

It had been a brief visit, and the hurried departure turned
out to have been unnecessary, for no French frigate material-
ized, and an attempt to intercept another one at Leghorn
failed.   Discipline in the French fleet was suffering from the
effects of the Revolution, and Nelson discovered that one reason why the ship at Leghorn had not sailed was that the crew
had suddenly deposed their captain and made him sergeant of
marines instead; while the lieutenant of marines had become
captain, and the sergeant was promoted to fill the lieutenant's
place. "What a state!" he exclaims contemptuously. On October 5 he was back at Toulon, reporting the success of his
mission, and delighted with his kind reception by Hood,
whom "all the foreigners at Toulon absolutely worship." At
Toulon he remained for a few days "only as a spectator," he
says. But we know of one activity of his, for in a characteristic rapid, newsy letter to his wife he describes how he was
member of a court-martial on Vice-Admiral Hotham's flagship in the harbour, and how, throughout the proceedings, a
French Royalist 74-gun ship, the *Princess Royal,* three frigates,
and several mortar-boats kept firing over their heads at a Republican battery on shore. It is interesting to hear of shooting
at this high angle. The mortars, of course, would be firing
shell. On October 6, after the Neapolitan troops had arrived,
he got a friendly letter from Sir William Hamilton, in the
course of which he said: "Lady Hamilton and myself will always be happy to see you." Nelson was now sent to join
Captain Linzee's squadron off Sardinia.

On his way to this rendezvous he had an encounter which

must have shown him that the French, whatever he might think of their discipline, were still able to shoot. He sighted five enemy ships, and, by clapping on all sail, succeeded in bringing the rearmost, a frigate, to action. But the frigate was a better sailer than the *Agamemnon* and, moreover, was ably handled. She kept yawing and firing broadsides, to which the line-of-battle ship could reply only with her three foremost guns. The result was that the *Agamemnon* was badly cut about, her main topmast shot to pieces, and her main-mast, mizzen-mast, and foreyard all seriously damaged, so that when the other frigates returned to their consort's assistance, there was little disposition on either side to renew the engagement.

We get a lively account of this "scrap" with the frigates from young Midshipman Hoste, son of the Rev. Dixon Hoste, of Godwick, Norfolk, an old family friend of the Nelsons. Nelson, of course, was young Hoste's hero, and he concludes his narrative with the proud boast that, "Captain Nelson is acknowledged to be one of the first characters in the service, and is universally beloved by officers and men." More interesting to Nelson's biographer is the Captain's strong affection for this boy. He writes frequently to Mr Hoste about him, assuring the father that his son is "an exceeding good boy, and will shine in our service." He offers good advice: "Do not, I beg, spoil him by giving him too much money — I love him, therefore I shall say no more on that subject." And a few months later, after a boat attack off the coast of Corsica, he writes: "You cannot, my dear Sir, receive more pleasure in reading this letter than I have in writing it, to say that your son is everything which his dearest friends can wish him to be; and is a strong proof that the greatest gallantry may lie under the most gentle behaviour."

It is interesting to speculate as to the effect upon Nelson's character if he had been so fortunate as to have had a son. Josiah did not fill the gap. He was no doubt "a good boy," as Nelson often assures his mother. But it is clear to anyone who has read these references that Josiah must have been rather a colourless, unlovable youth; and there is evidence that he had a nasty temper. It is interesting again to speculate as to what might (or might not) have happened if Josiah had been a real bond between Nelson and Fanny. "Josiah is very well," writes Nelson a little later, "I have not seen him these ten days, but have written to invite him and Hoste to dinner: that lad is a charming good boy." "That lad" is, of course, Hoste.

Linzee, following his orders, proceeded to Tunis, the *Agamemnon* with him, to negotiate with the Bey for the surrender of a French convoy then in harbour there. The Bey bargained interminably, in the manner of the East, and the negotiations fell through. Nelson was indignant. "The English seldom get much by negotiation except the being laughed at," he writes to his uncle. In his opinion Linzee should first have seized the convoy, and then have offered the Bey £50,000 for it — that is, act first and argue afterwards. Probably he was right. Anyhow he was thankful when Hood ordered him away from Linzee, and gave him a command of his own — a squadron of frigates to cruise off Corsica and Italy and blockade the port of Genoa. This command he rightly considered "a very high compliment," there being five older captains in the fleet. In pursuance of his instructions he visited Leghorn, and there, in December, witnessed the arrival of several shiploads of refugees from Toulon. This was the first news he had of the fall of that place and the massacre of the inhabitants, and he hastened to report it to the Admiralty.

Nelson did not remain long on the Italian coast. All eyes were now turned to Corsica, where the inhabitants, led by that picturesque patriot Paoli, were still putting up a gallant fight against the French. As long ago as 1745 Corsica had offered to place herself under British protection, and it was to England that the patriotic party looked for help. Nelson was always strongly in favour of a forward policy in regard to Corsica — as in regard to most places; and indeed it was obvious that if the French could be turned out of the fortified positions they still held in the island and British garrisons substituted, the fleet would have a valuable base, and all subsequent operations in the Mediterranean, both naval and military, would be greatly facilitated. On the other hand, the French fleet in Toulon (for it was clear by now that only a small number of their warships had been destroyed when Hood evacuated the place) would be severely handicapped by being refused the Corsican harbours, while their coastal trade with Italy would be constantly threatened. It was a happy day for Nelson when, at the end of January 1794, Lord Hood having definitely decided to reduce the island, joined him off Calvi with a fleet of transports, conveying about eighteen hundred troops. This was the beginning of the Corsican adventure.

CHAPTER VIII

HARD KNOCKS

THE CONQUEST of Corsica really resolved itself into the taking of just three towns in which the French had garrisons — Bastia, on the north-east coast, San Fiorenzo on the north, and Calvi on the west. On January 28, 1794, Nelson, with the *Agamemnon* and his attendant frigates, was already off the coast and had even got in touch with Paoli, the Nationalist leader. The officer sent ashore for that purpose was Lieutenant Andrews, brother of the parson's daughter of Saint-Omer. But on the 28th it blew great guns, and the squadron was scattered; and by the time they were got together again there was Lord Hood, already arrived from Toulon in the Bay of San Fiorenzo, with transports carrying Lieutenant-General Dundas and his eighteen hundred men. A further twelve hundred soldiers were to serve as marines in the fleet, since many landing parties would be required. In the early days of February the little army was disembarked, and on the 13th the town of San Fiorenzo surrendered without a fight, as Nelson had prophesied it would in a letter to Hood.

The army then advanced to Bastia. Nelson was already cruising off that port with his two frigates, and through his glasses he could plainly see the English redcoats on the surrounding hills. He was greatly stirred. "A noble sight"; "the grandest thing I ever saw." But he adds that if he had only five hundred soldiers, with his "invincible" seamen from the *Agamemnon,* he would have stormed the town without more ado. "Armies go so slow that seamen think they never mean to get forward." We can imagine, then, his shame and disgust when, a few days later, he saw the troops retire, and heard that Dundas had fallen back upon San Fiorenzo, after flatly refusing to attempt an attack on Bastia.

Hood was no less disgusted than Nelson, and there broke out one of those unfortunate quarrels between the army and the fleet which were too often a feature of any combined operations attempted by the British during the eighteenth and nineteenth centuries. Nelson usually got on very well with the military, but the lethargy of Dundas nearly drove him mad. Hood had returned to San Fiorenzo to appeal to the general, and Nelson wrote to him there that the town might yet be taken if they had only a thousand soldiers to help the ships. Two military officers, Duncan of the artillery and De Butts, an engineer, reported in the same sense. But Dundas sat tight, and when he was recalled to England his successor, D'Aubant, proved equally determined not to move.

Hood, that wonderful old man — "upwards of seventy, he possesses the mind of forty," says Nelson — determined to take matters into his own hands. The twelve hundred soldiers entered on the ships' books as marines had been landed with Dundas. Hood demanded them back (D'Aubant could not refuse) and forthwith sailed to Bastia. At the same time Paoli's Corsican forces closed in on the town. Nelson was to land the heavy guns (the *Agamemnon's* 24-pounders) and plant the batteries. He writes in high glee to Sir William Hamilton, concluding with his "most respectful compliments" to her ladyship.

It was on April 4 that Nelson landed with his men, a little to the north of Bastia, and began the laborious task of dragging the guns up the cliffs to their selected positions. He probably never dreamed that he was to remain on shore with short intervals for the next four months, and experience by far the hardest fighting of his life up to date. He was to become so expert in the planting of batteries and siege operations in general, that, as he humorously wrote to his wife when it was all over, "I feel almost qualified to pass my examination as a besieging general." And he was to be

wounded and lose an eye — the first of a long series of such
sacrifices in the service of his country.

It was "very hard service for my poor seamen, dragging
guns up such heights as are scarcely credible." But they got
them there in the end, and at once commenced an artillery
duel with the forts protecting the town, at a range of seven
or eight hundred yards. Nelson was beginning to enjoy himself. "We are in high health and spirits besieging Bastia," he
says. "We are few but of the right sort . . . I am very busy,
yet own l am in all my glory." As for his seamen, "they mind
bullets no more than peas." With the assistance of the Corsi-
cans a strict blockade was maintained by land, and Nelson saw
to it that not a boat slipped through from the sea. Nelson's
one fear was that "these soldiers will advance when Bastia is
about to surrender, and deprive us of part of our glory." But
D'Aubant made no move until it was too late. On May 19
the garrison, seeing the hopelessness of their position, sent in
a flag of truce; and on the very same day the British general
advanced from San Fiorenzo! The French, to the number of
four thousand five hundred men, marched out and laid down
their arms on the 24th. It was a great achievement, though
Nelson, when he writes exultantly about five thousand men
surrendering to one thousand, forgets the presence of the
Corsican nationalists and also of the British fleet. He writes
to Josiah's mother: "Josiah has been with me at the head of
the British grenadiers, taking possession of the forts and
posts."

When Hood's dispatches were published Nelson's name, of
course, appeared, but not so prominently as he had hoped.
At first he made no complaint, but later he seems to have
come to the conclusion (perhaps with the help of some mis-
chief-making friend) that he was slighted. He wrote to his
uncle, William Suckling:

> The whole operation of the siege was carried on through Lord
> Hood's letters to me. I was the mover of it — I was the cause of
> its success. Sir Gilbert Elliot [the new Viceroy of Corsica, who

had come out with Hood] will be my evidence, if any is required. I am not a little vexed, but shall not quarrel. We shall be successful here [Calvi] and a stranger and a landsman will probably do me that credit which a friend and brother officer has not given me.

The complaint is ill founded. Hood could hardly announce in an official report that it was Nelson who had pushed him to the decision of attacking the place, even if he would have admitted it; and in mentioning the officers concerned he was bound to state that Colonel Villettes was in command of the soldiers who composed the greater part of the attacking force, and that even the command of the seamen was shared between Nelson and Captain Hunt. In private he fully realized Nelson's large share in the victory, and the two men continued to be excellent friends.

The next objective was Calvi. The French fleet had ventured out from Toulon, and Hood went in pursuit of them — unsuccessfully, as it turned out. But the *Agamemnon* was sent on to Calvi to make preparations for the siege. Nelson found that there had been another change in the command on shore, the new G.O.C. being General Stuart, an officer of great ability, whose early retirement, owing to disagreements with his superiors, is today recognized to have been a serious loss to his country. Stuart's conduct of the operations was in almost startling contrast to that of D'Aubant. "Every time I write *delay*," he said to Nelson, "I suffer more than I can describe." Nelson was keeping a journal of the siege, and he notes that Stuart "is not sparing of himself on any occasion: he every night sleeps with us in the advance battery." They were kindred spirits, and should have formed a powerful combination. Unfortunately the usual misunderstandings arose, for which Nelson and Hood were inclined to blame Colonel (afterwards General Sir John) Moore. There were delays on the part of the military engineers, and there was a shortage of ammunition. When Nelson said that neither shot nor powder could be spared from the ships, Stuart suggested that the ships should be "laid against the walls."

Whereupon, says Nelson, "I took the liberty of observing that the business of laying wood before walls was much altered of late." It was a fatiguing siege; both soldiers and sailors were "harassed to death."

On July 11, when Nelson was in the advance battery, a shot struck the parapet close beside him — dashing stones and gravel in his face, so that his head was badly bruised, and his right eye injured. He made light of his hurt, only staying away from duty one day and writing reassuringly to Hood and Mrs Nelson. But his eye got steadily worse, and must have given him great pain. On July 16 he could "distinguish light from dark, but no object." Soon it had to be admitted that the sight was gone. Otherwise his health was better than might have been expected. He boasted afterwards that he was "almost the only person in army or navy at the siege of Calvi who was not completely knocked up." "I am the reed amongst the oaks," he wrote to the Duke of Clarence, "all the prevailing disorders have attacked me, but I have not strength for them to fasten upon: I bow before the storm, whilst the sturdy oak is laid low." Among others "poor little Hoste" was "extremely ill" (he afterwards recovered and served, with Josiah, as Nelson's *aide-de-camp* in Hotham's engagement with the French fleet); and Mrs Moutray's son, "a very fine young man for whom I have a great regard," unfortunately died of fever. Nelson himself composed an inscription for the tomb signed "H.N." and wrote to Fanny: "What a shock it will be to his poor mother . . . he was Second Lieutenant of the *Victory,* and at this moment, had he survived, would have been a captain."

In the meantime Nelson was "always on the batteries," and from there, no doubt, watched the French march out in surrender on August 10. In the harbour was captured the French frigate *Melpomene,* with which Nelson had fought the action of October 22, 1793. That was the end of the Corsican adventure. He may well have felt that it had been an acid test of his powers of physical endurance. Never again need he seriously worry about his health.

Nelson had been too busy — perhaps he was always too busy — to have room for more than one woman in his heart. During this Corsican rough-and-tumble his thoughts often turned to Fanny in Norfolk. A whole series of letters addressed to her at this time breathe a deep and genuine affection. He seems seldom to have gone into action without first sitting down and writing to her. For instance:

> I need not, I am certain, say that all my joy is placed in you: you are present to my imagination be where I will. I am convinced you feel interested in every action of my life; and my exultation in victory is two-fold, knowing that you partake of it. Only recollect that a brave man dies but once, a coward all his life long.

"A glorious death," he says, "is to be envied," but, should any "accident" happen to him, he reminds Fanny of the financial provision he has made for her. He even finds time to write, as it would seem almost in the heat of battle, "except with you I would not be anywhere but where I am." Perhaps, without knowing it, he was as much in love with England as with Fanny. After praising the beauty of the Italian cities he adds: "However I trust we shall soon quit these magnificent scenes and retire to England where all that I admire is placed"; and in a later letter he even talks about looking out for "some little cottage," when he gets back. It is the typical dream of the Englishman in exile. Of Emma he probably thought not at all.

Hood had decided to pay a visit to England, whether to confer with the Admiralty or on private business is not known. The command was to be left temporarily in the hands of Vice-Admiral Hotham. As it happened Hood quarrelled with the authorities in London and never returned. Nelson would almost seem to have had some presentiment of this, for he was miserable when he heard that his friend was to go — "the greatest sea-officer I ever knew." He could have gone with him had he wished, for Hood was anxious to take him and had offered him the command of a seventy-four; but he would not leave the *Agamemnon* — could not "bring myself to part with the ship's company with whom I have gone through such a series of hard service as has never before, I believe, fallen to the lot of any one ship." True, he longed for home, but, as he wrote to Fanny, "we must not repine: at all events I shall cheat the winter." Hood left on October 11, 1794. The *Agamemnon* was ordered first to Leghorn and then to Genoa, to secure the neutrality of the Republic; but Nelson went there in a gloomy frame of mind, having half his men sick, and he was not sorry when the time came to rejoin the fleet. In a letter written about now he tells Fanny frankly about his eye*: "The pupil is nearly the size of the blue part, I don't know the name"; he can still just distinguish darkness from light. He also, for the first time, discloses the fact that this was not the only wound he received in Corsica; at Bastia, it appears, he got "a sharp cut in the back." However, he is now about the fittest man on the ship, though somewhat out of temper.

Now if only the French fleet could have been enticed out of Toulon and destroyed, there would have been no difficulty at all about securing the neutrality of Genoa. Instead of occasional visits from a single line-of-battle ship, the *Agamemnon,* the whole British fleet, released from its duty of watching Toulon, could have been employed on the Italian coast, with the best possible moral effect. The coastal trade with France must immediately have ceased; and, since this was the principal means by which the French were supplying their armies in Italy, it is even a question whether the invasion of that country would not have been abandoned, and General Buonaparte forced to seek his laurels elsewhere. Hood was always looking for an opportunity of eliminating this inconvenient French fleet; but they never gave it to him, and he was now vainly pleading with the Admiralty in London to send out more ships so that the British naval forces might be strong

---

* He was wonderfully considerate of her feelings. On a rumour that the *Agamemnon* had been captured, he wrote immediately: "Never believe anything you may see in the papers about us."

enough to perform both duties — Toulon and the Italian coast — at once.

Then the opportunity came — to Hotham, alas, not to Hood! Fickle fortune never played England a scurvier trick. Hotham's idea of watching Toulon was to remain in harbour at Corsica or Leghorn. He was at the latter place on March 8, 1795, with his whole fleet, including the *Agamemnon,* when he heard that the French, numbering fifteen sail (the same strength as his), were at sea, and set out to intercept them. On the morning of the 12th the enemy were in sight, and there followed the first of those two scrambling, unsatisfactory engagements with which Hotham's career in the Mediterranean closed. The wind was light and fitful, and the two fleets drawn out in long scattered lines. The *Agamemnon* was in front — that is to say, in front of the ships of the line, for there was one frigate a little ahead of her. She was a good sailer, of course, though old and crazy; but it is a fact, explain it how you will, that, whatever ship Nelson happened to be in, this is the position where you always find him when the enemy comes in sight.

This was his first fleet action. Even now that astonishing fact makes us gasp. It was his first fleet action; but he dominated it — and his second one too, as we shall see in a moment, and every other afterwards. The excitement of the moment must have been almost enough to kill him — to tear his flimsy little body apart. As he stared eagerly after the French ships, now so close that he could see their stern windows — and a familiar sight it was to be to him in future years! — steeling himself to the necessary self-restraint, now that his great chance had come, now that he was in his element, where he knew himself supreme — suddenly he saw something which must have made him shout for joy. One of the ships in the French rear carried away her topmasts. Instantly she fell astern. She was one of the biggest of them, too — the *Ça Ira,* as it turned out, of eighty-four guns. The *Agamemnon* had every stitch of canvas set. If he can only get up to her, and oppose his sixty-four guns to those eighty-four!

But first the *Inconstant* frigate (Captain Fremantle), being somewhat ahead of the *Agamemnon,* made a gallant attempt to cut the big Frenchman off; but when she came under the guns of that powerful broadside, she was badly mauled and compelled to draw off. Nelson saw this. Looking round, he noted that there was no British ship of the line within several miles of him, whereas two French ships, the *Sans Culotte* (120) and the *Jean Bart* (74), were close enough to come at any moment to the assistance of the *Ça Ira.* He adapted his tactics accordingly. He was drawing closer every minute now, but he was careful to keep astern of the *Ça Ira,* so that she could not bring her broadside to bear. He has said that it was his intention not to fire a shot until his bowsprit actually touched her stern. But the French ship was using her chasers all this time, and shooting so well that the masts and rigging of the *Agamemnon* began to suffer. Should she be crippled now she would be at the mercy of the French. If anything was to be done, it must be done at once. At a hundred yards range the *Agamemnon* yawed, and fired a broadside into the *Ça Ira's* stern, raking her destructively. Then, having fallen behind by this manœuvre, she put her helm over and pursued again, until she was close enough to repeat the dose. This went on for two hours. Over a hundred men were killed on the *Ça Ira* and — an important point — all her rigging so cut to pieces by the British shot that it was found impossible to get new topmasts up during the night. Nelson had only seven men wounded. In the afternoon Hotham, in his flag-ship, the *Britannia,* signalled Nelson to rejoin the fleet. He did so, and set his men to work repairing the damage aloft. The *Ça Ira* was taken in tow by a French frigate.

Next morning the two fleets were still close together, sailing in line ahead; but a fresh breeze had sprung up from the north-west, and this gave the English the weather gage. They took advantage of it to interpose their line between the

H

crippled *Ça Ira,* now towed by a line-of-battle ship, the *Censeur,* and the rest of the French fleet. The *Captain* and the *Bedford* were detached and fought the *Ça Ira* and the *Censeur* until all four ships were crippled. The French fleet, returning on the opposite tack, engaged about half the English line, so that four of the English ships, the *Illustrious, Courageux, Princess Royal,* and *Agamemnon,* were fighting on both sides, directing their starboard broadsides against the *Ça Ira* and the *Censeur,* and their port broadsides against the French fleet. The French Admiral could have brought on a general action had he wished; instead he turned away into the wind, leaving his two ships to their fate. They were soon dismasted and forced to strike, and the *Agamemnon,* happening, very suitably, to be the nearest British ship, Nelson sent Lieutenant Andrews to board them and make them prizes. Andrews seems to have stood well with him. "As gallant an officer," he says, "as ever stepped a quarter deck."

He himself was in a fever to be after the retreating Frenchmen. It happened that the Admiral's ship, the *Britannia,* was next astern of him in line. She was one of the slowest sailers in the fleet, and no one but Hotham would have kept his flag on her; but moving one's quarters was a nuisance, and anyway he probably had an instinctive preference for sluggish sailers. Thus we find that his share in these actions was confined to lumbering along behind, flying signals of recall to his more advanced ships, like a lame hen anxious about her chickens. Captain Nelson went on board the *Britannia.* He met Hotham on the quarterdeck. His solitary blue eye was blazing as he urged upon the Admiral the desirability of leaving the two shattered prizes with the *Captain* and the *Bedford* and pursuing the French fleet. Hotham waved a soothing hand. He was "much cooler than myself," says Nelson. "We must be contented," he said. "We have done very well." Nelson, in desperation, had himself rowed over to the *Princess Royal,* next ahead of him, where he interviewed Rear-Admiral Goodall, second-in-command, who quite agreed with his proposal, and sent an urgent note to Hotham. But nothing was done. The truth is that Hotham had no desire for a pitched battle. His one idea was to get through this last command he was ever likely to hold with as little loss as possible and retire on a comfortable pension — which is what eventually he did. Nelson liked him, but despised him. "Hotham," he said, "must get a new head; no man's heart is better, but that will not do without the other." "Had I commanded our fleet on the 14th," he adds, "either the whole French fleet would have graced my triumph, or I should have been in a confounded scrape."

This victory, though not a great one, aroused much enthusiasm in those Mediterranean countries where popular opinion was on the English side. Nelson found himself, deservedly, the hero of the hour. "French verses" were written about him, though where, or by whom, he does not say. "I am so covered with laurels, that you would hardly find my sallow face" — a good touch. He is "the dear Nelson, the amiable Nelson, the fiery Nelson," and these expressions, "however nonsensical are better than censure," and are we not all of us "open to flattery?" Yes, but none more open than Nelson, as we are beginning to see. "All hands," he writes to the Duke of Clarence, "agree in giving me those praises which cannot but be comfortable to me to the last moment of my life."

In the meantime he is "absolutely in the horrors," partly at Hotham's inactivity, which continues for another four months, and partly because he is dreading promotion to flag rank as a reward of his duel with the *Ça Ira,* since this would mean a return to England and loss of money and opportunities of distinction. What he wants is a colonelcy in the marines — a sinecure rank often given to naval officers, and more or less justified in his case by his recent services ashore. He is worried about money, in fact, as many lesser men have been before and since, and his thoughts turn once more to that country cottage. "I hope to save my pay," he writes to Fanny, "which, with a little addition, will buy us a very small cottage where I shall be as happy as in a house as large as Holkham." He also applied to the War Office for pay during his time ashore in Corsica, and was promptly refused. But he got the colonelcy, and that must have eased his mind.

Four months of lethargy. Hotham is "perfectly satisfied that each month passed without any losses on our side." But on July 7 the *Agamemnon* and a few frigates, on their way to Genoa, sighted the French fleet, which chased them to San Fiorenzo in Corsica, where Hotham lay. He got under way and pursued the French, and another rearguard action followed. The *Alcide,* a French seventy-four, had an explosion on board. She was carrying a large case of "combustibles" consisting of some kind of liquid fire, which had been sent to the fleet by the Directory in Paris, but which the sailors would not use. She fell behind and was captured. At dusk the leading English ships, the *Agamemnon* and the *Cumberland,* were just getting into close action when Hotham called them off. The French wriggled into the Gulf of Frejus, where they anchored after dark, and Hotham would not follow them. The losses were slight on either side. That was the end of Nelson's first two fleet actions. The French, more frightened than hurt, did not venture out again, and Hotham sent Nelson once more to the Italian coast to watch over the neutrality of Genoa.

The next year in Nelson's life is one of comparatively little interest to his biographer, so far as public events are concerned. He found the situation extremely delicate, the French and Austrian armies facing each other, the Genoese anxiously waiting to see which way the cat would jump, his own force just strong enough to be a mild nuisance to the French and a worry to the Genoese, but not to cut off the French supplies by sea. His main business was with the Austrian general, De Vins, and at first, of course, he took him for a great man, "an officer of great abilities," and even went out of his way to write to the First Lord of the Admiralty that De Vins was "well disposed to act with vigour on every proper occasion." De Vins, on his side, admired Nelson, and sang his praises to Mr Drake, the British Minister at Genoa, who duly passed on the testimony to Hotham. Nelson soon discovered his mistake. "Very hard at work in pushing the Austrian general forward" is his own eloquent description of his life at this time. In fact, he bounced off De Vins like an india-rubber ball, exhausting himself in the process. He wrote to his wife: "I am not, Fanny, quite so pleased as I expected with this army, which is slow beyond all description; and begin to think that the Emperor is anxious to touch another four millions of English money." He gives an interesting account of the French Republican army at this time, as described to him by some of his officers who had been prisoners in their hands. "Few of the French soldiers are more than twenty-three or twenty-four years old; a great many do not exceed fourteen years, all without clothes; and my officers add they are sure my barge's crew would have beat a hundred of them." Poor Fanny gets a good many political disquisitions about this time; but most of his letters are addressed to Mr Elliot, the Viceroy of Corsica (afterwards Lord Minto, Viceroy of India), who had become his close friend.

We have already had examples of Nelson's physical courage, his perfectly genuine and instinctive delight in danger, his gallant swagger — which Mr Shaw would try to persuade us is the mark of the supreme coward. This kind of courage is perhaps the most attractive, but not the most uncommon, of virtues. It is less generally recognized that Nelson had also, in the highest degree, a rarer kind of courage — political courage. He would always take responsibility; he went to meet a difficult decision with the same enthusiasm with which he boarded an enemy ship; and he did so just as cheerfully when his whole future career depended upon the decision as when his life might depend upon the direction of a roundshot in action. For instance, when he reached Genoa on July 17, Mr Drake urged upon him the desirability of trying to stop not only French trade, but even neutral trade with the districts occupied by the French armies. It was a grave step to take, and it was no use consulting Hotham. Nelson slept on it. Next day he told Drake that if he would tell him officially "it is for the benefit of H.M.'s service," he (Nelson) would take the responsibility. So it was arranged. And immediately there is a note of exultation in his letters. He knew that he was acting "not only without the orders of my commander-in-chief, but in some measure contrary to them." But "if we are to finish the war with France, we must not stop at trifles," and, "political courage in an officer abroad is as highly necessary as military courage." There was no doubt that he delighted in these dangerous decisions, and may have been secretly glad that he was under an unenterprising chief, who allowed him to do as he liked. Hotham, for his part, was grateful to Nelson — since his decisions always turned out to be the right ones — and highly commended him to the Admiralty.

Then came the disastrous battle of Loano, and complete dis-illusionment as regards the efficiency of the Austrian Army. The French drove the Austrians before them like sheep. There was some complaint that the British had been unable to prevent French gunboats from creeping along the coast and bombarding the left wing of the Austrian Army. Nelson re-plied indignantly and at great length, pointing out that he had remained at Genoa during the battle at the particular request of the Genoese, who feared a Jacobin rising, and that anyhow the break in the Austrian line had occurred not on the coast, but twelve miles inland. It is characteristic of him that he could never bear criticism, and would always rush in with a defence of his conduct before it had been seriously im-pugned. On this occasion he wrote letters all over the place, as well as making a formal defence to his Admiral. Mahan quotes in this connexion the remark of his friend Captain Ball, when Nelson some years later showed him a long memorandum explaining the failure to intercept the French fleet on its way to Egypt. "I was particularly struck," wrote Ball to Nelson, "with the clear and accurate style, as well as with the candour of your statement in the letter, but I should recommend a friend never to begin a defence of his conduct before he is accused of error." That was a lesson Nelson could never learn.

General Beaulieu succeeded De Vins, but did no better, except that he had the honour of being beaten by Buonaparte himself, in a series of engagements, each of which took place farther into Italy and farther from the French frontier — while Nelson looked on in helpless rage. In the meantime an important event had taken place. Hotham had gone home on the plea of ill health, and Sir John Jervis was in command of the British Mediterranean Fleet. The personality of this fierce, stooping little man, this relentless disciplinarian and indomitable fighter, would stand out conspicuously in the popular traditions of the Navy if he had not happened to live at the same time as Nelson. His arrival had an almost humorously galvanic effect upon the fleet. He found the British ships comfortably at anchor in San Fiorenzo Bay. Within twenty-four hours they were out of it and, almost before they knew what had happened, were tossing outside Toulon harbour, there to remain indefinitely until the French surrendered or came out to fight.

Nelson came from Genoa to report himself to his new chief. There was an instantaneous liking between the two men. Nelson's well-known theatricality, of which we hear so much, seems never to have jarred upon the nerves of a single one of his naval chiefs, however different from him in temperament — nor, it may be added, upon any other great leader of men with whom he was brought in contact, Wellington only excepted. Jervis at once began to treat Nelson, as the latter says himself, "more as an associate than a subordinate officer." He sent him straight back to Genoa, with no written orders, and verbal instructions so vague as to give him practically an independent command. There is another interest in this occasion. It affords one of the few examples in the record of Nelson's career of a feeling of jealousy against him among his brother captains. Writing to his wife on January 17, 1796, he mentions an incident which occurred before he left the fleet:

The fleet was not a little surprised at my leaving them so soon, and I fancy there was some degree of envy attached to the surprise, for one captain told me, "You did just as you pleased in Lord Hood's time, the same in Admiral Hotham's, and now again with Sir John Jervis; it makes no difference to you who is commander-in-chief." I returned a pretty strong answer to this speech.

Yet it seems a mild enough remark, compared with many others that must have been made in the Navy since in similar circumstances. Soon afterwards the Admiral authorized Nelson to hoist a distinguishing pennant as a commodore.

CHAPTER IX

"WESTMINSTER ABBEY OR VICTORY!"

"Had all my actions been gazetted," wrote Nelson to his wife in August 1796, "not one fortnight would have passed during the whole war without a letter from me." "One day or other," he added — and this was not the only time he made the boast — "I will have a long gazette to myself: I feel that such an opportunity will be given me." It was to be given to him sooner than he thought.

He was sick to death of the Italian coast and the excuses and delays of England's so-called allies. "I have nothing to write about but myself," he apologises to his father, "for no-one else attempts to do anything." He had other troubles of a more private character. His old servant, Frank Lepée, took to drink, and Nelson, who "never would keep a drunkard another hour," had to get rid of him. Even his health began to suffer, and he went so far as to write to Jervis about the possibility of a few weeks' leave, but added characteristically, "I do not much like what I have written." It was the old trouble in his chest; it felt "as if a girth were buckled taut over my breast, and my endeavour, in the night, is to get it loose." In fact it sounds very much like common-or-garden indigestion. But every time he saw Jervis he cheered up. Here was some one who would listen to what he had to say, and would, no doubt, have agreed with his own claim that not one of his plans had failed, "nor of the opinions given has one been in the event wrong."

The fact is that he was eating his heart out. He was like an actor waiting impatiently in the wings for his cue to appear upon the world's stage in the part for which he was designed by nature and of his own deliberate choice — that of a national hero. That moment was now at hand. Already, as young Hoste had said, he was recognized in the fleet as one of its "first characters"; but he could not delude himself into believing that he cut any such figure in the popular estimation at home. Few of his countrymen had so much as heard of him. But on Valentine's Day, 1797 — only six months from the date we have now reached — he was to win that place in the hearts of the English people which he never lost, and never will lose.

The preliminaries to the battle of Cape St Vincent may be briefly recorded. On June 11, 1796, Commodore Nelson left the *Agamemnon* and hoisted his pennant in the *Captain* (74). A month later, on instructions from Jervis, he seized the port of Ferrajo in the Island of Elba. But it was becoming daily more apparent that Spain was about to enter the war on the French side, thereby upsetting the balance of naval power in the Mediterranean. At the same time England's Italian allies were falling away — and with the French armies at their very gates it was difficult to blame them. In these circumstances there was no longer any object in maintaining outposts such as Corsica and Elba. In October 1796, therefore, Jervis sent Nelson to superintend the evacuation of Corsica. He hated the task, and bitterly lamented its necessity, but carried it out with his usual expedition. Next he was dispatched to Elba for a similar purpose, but on his way fell in with an adventure which deserves to be recorded at somewhat greater length.

For the purpose of this mission Nelson, since speed was important, had transferred his pennant to the *Minerve* frigate, and had with him in company another frigate, the *Blanche*. On December 20, in cloudy weather and with a fresh gale, they sighted two Spanish frigates and (war having just been declared) engaged them. The *Minerve's* opponent, the *Santa Sabina,* after three hours' fighting, struck her colours, and her captain, Don Jacobo Stuart (a descendant of the Duke of Berwick), came on board and surrendered his sword. A little later another frigate was seen approaching, and was at first mistaken for the *Blanche;* but she hailed the *Santa Sabina* in Spanish, and finding her in the hands of the English, fired a broadside into her. Then three other Spaniards appeared in the failing light, two of them line-of-battle ships. There was nothing to do but make off; but the wind had dropped, and there were only light and baffling airs. At one time it seemed certain that the *Minerve* would be overtaken and shot to bits; but the officers in charge of the Spanish prize, Lieutenants Hardy and Culverhouse, very sportingly took this occasion to hoist English colours over the Spanish at the main, and this was more than the leading battleship could stand. She turned aside to capture them, and the *Minerve* escaped. The *Blanche* also got clear.

Returning from Elba (where the officer in command of the troops absolutely refused to be taken off in the absence of orders from his own commander!), Nelson arrived at Gibraltar. He was unnecessarily ashamed of the loss of his prize, the *Santa Sabina,* and concluded his report to Jervis with the words: "This is, Sir, an unpleasant tale." To us it may seen a fine one, but to Nelson all tales were unpleasant which did not end in British victories. However, there were three Spanish ships in Gibraltar Bay, and Nelson promptly addressed himself to the local authorities, with a view to recovering his missing lieutenants, who, as he correctly guessed, were on board one of these. His letter to Don Miguel Gaston, Captain General of the Department of Carthagene, is so courteous and so elegant, so characteristic both of the writer and of his times, that I cannot resist giving it in full:

His Brittanic Majesty's ship
the *Minerve,* at sea
December 24th, 1796

SIR,

The fortune of war put *La Sabina* into my possession, after she had been most gallantly defended: the fickle dame returned her to you with some of my officers and men in her. I have endeavoured to make the captivity of Don Jacobo Stuart, her brave commander, as light as possible; and I trust to the generosity of your nation for its being reciprocal for the British officers and men.

I consent, Sir, that Don Jacobo may be exchanged, and with full liberty to serve his King, when Lieutenants Culverhouse and Hardy are delivered into the garrison of Gibraltar, with such others as may be agreed on by the cartel established between Gibraltar and St Roche, for the exchange of prisoners.

I have also a domestic taken in *La Sabina,* his name is Israel Coulson. Your Excellency will, I am sure, order him to be immediately restored to me, for which I will consider myself to be obliged to you.

I also trust that those men, now prisoners of war with you, will be sent to Gibraltar. It becomes great nations to act with generosity to each other, and to soften the horrors of war. I have the honour to be, with the most perfect esteem,

Your most obedient servant,
HORATIO NELSON

The exchange was duly effected, and the two lieutenants restored to liberty; but before releasing Don Jacobo, Nelson wrote to his commanding officer, the Spanish Admiral, Don Juan Marino:

I cannot allow Don Jacobo to return to you without expressing my admiration of his gallant conduct. To you, who have seen the state of his ship, it is needless to mention the impossibility of her longer defence. I have lost many brave men: but, in our masts, I was most fortunate; or, probably, I should have had the honour of your acquaintance. But it pleased God to order it otherwise, for which I am thankful.

That must surely be one of the most chivalrous letters ever written in such circumstances. The truth is that Nelson liked the Dons — as much as he disliked the Frenchmen. The Dons were gentlemen. It is a prejudice not uncommon among Englishmen even today.

The *Minerve* sailed from Gibraltar on February 11, 1797, seeking the British fleet, which was cruising off Cape St Vincent. Two of the Spanish ships immediately followed, and nearly succeeded in capturing her in the Straits. For a man had fallen overboard, and the jolly-boat had been lowered, under the command of Lieutenant Hardy, to try to pick him up. The man was lost, and the current carried the jolly-boat far astern towards the approaching Spaniards. Nelson did not hesitate for a moment. "By God, I'll not lose Hardy! Back the mizzen topsail!" The Spaniards, seeing this manœuvre, could only suppose that the *Minerve* had sighted the British fleet approaching from the West. They accordingly put about and sailed back towards Gibraltar, leaving the *Minerve* to pick up the jolly-boat and proceed at her leisure. The *Minerve* rejoined the fleet on February 13, the day before the battle of St Vincent, and Nelson at once returned to his own ship the *Captain*. He was in the nick of time. As he says in one of his letters, "Wherever there is anything to be done, there Providence is sure to direct my steps."

The position of the rival forces, British and Spanish, on February 14 was as follows. The Spanish had twenty-seven sail of the line. Jervis had expected to be joined by Mann from Gibraltar, but Mann, though he had received Jervis's order, had disobeyed it and taken his squadron back to England two months before this. As a set-off to this defection the English Admiral had received certain reinforcements from home; but he had also lost two ships during the recent stormy weather, and two others were in Lisbon for repair; so that he had now with him just fifteen sail of the line — that is to say, about the same strength as before the Spanish declaration of war. It was most important to bring England's new enemies to action immediately, and deal them such a blow as would teach them to keep to their harbours. Never once did it occur to Jervis, or anyone under his command, to hesitate about taking a fleet of fifteen in pursuit of twenty-seven.

At dawn on St Valentine's Day, as the English fleet sailed southwards, in close order, groups of strange ships could be seen standing across their van on the larboard tack. These were the Spaniards. They had become scattered during the night, and there was a gap of something like eight miles between their two divisions. Jervis was striding up and down the quarterdeck of his flagship, the *Victory,* grumbling fiercely to himself. He was heard to growl something about a victory being essential to England. And then he would pause, and strive to measure with his eyes the long stretches of water separating the Spanish ships. Could he risk it? Fifteen against twenty-seven? But would he ever get such a chance again? Without further hesitation he set his course for that eight-mile gap. The English were in line ahead, and, for once, Nelson was at the rear (third from it, as a matter of fact). But, as we shall see presently, he soon turned the rear into what, for all practical purposes, was the van.

It was too late for the Spaniards to reclose their ranks. Their lee division, to the left (or larboard) of the English attack, was cut off. Only two of the windward division succeeded in getting across to it ahead of the attacking van, thus bringing its strength up to nine ships of the line. As the leading English entered the gap they engaged this division with their larboard broadsides. The remainder of the Spanish windward division, seeing themselves too late, turned up north, with the idea of getting round the English rear, and so joining their friends, or making off westwards to the Spanish ports. Now if the English line had been a little longer — only five or six ships — this manœuvre would have been impossible; but, as it was, it seemed likely that the Spaniards or, at any rate, their leading ships of this division, could refuse action if they liked, and get clean away. Meantime they were exchanging distant shots with the English line as they passed on opposite tacks.

This was the position when Jervis made the signal to tack in succession and fall among the Spanish windward division (the smaller leeward division had so little liked the English larboard broadsides that it took no further part in the fight). The leading English ship, the *Culloden* — commanded by Captain Troubridge, whom we remember on the *Seahorse* with Nelson in 1773 — immediately tacked and pursued the rearmost Spaniards. But it was obvious by now that if the English

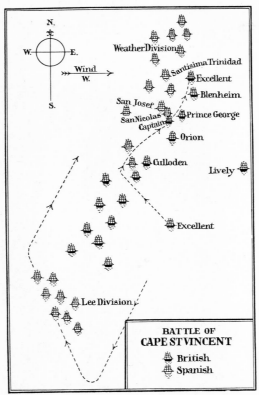

N.

W. E.

Wind
W.

S.

Weather Division

Santísima Trinidad
Excellent
Blenheim
San Josef
San Nicolas
Captain
Prince George
Orion
Culloden
Lively
Excellent

Lee Division

BATTLE OF
CAPE ST VINCENT
British
Spanish

ships had waited to tack "in succession," at the point at which the *Culloden* tacked, the result would have been no more than a rearguard action, since the Spanish showed so small stomach for the fight, and nothing much might have been achieved.

The captain of the third ship from the rear in the British fleet saw this. Without waiting for orders he left the line and threw himself across the path of the leading Spaniards — the *Santissima Trinidad* of a hundred and twenty-six guns, the Spanish admiral, and the largest vessel afloat; the *San Nicolas* (80), the *San Josef* (112), the *Salvador del Mundo* (112), and another first-rate and a seventy-four, whose names Nelson could not read through the smoke. It was magnificent, but was it war? Evidently Jervis thought so, for he signalled the *Excellent,* the last ship in the line, to support Nelson. Jervis was a great man. The *Culloden,* pursuing the Spaniards, came up and, in Nelson's words, "most nobly supported" him. For nearly an hour, as it seemed to Nelson (I am quoting from his own notes), the *Culloden* and the *Captain* maintained this "apparently but not really unequal contest." The *Blenheim* relieved the pressure for a moment by passing between the *Captain* and her immediate opponents and pouring a broadside into the Dons. The *Captain* by this time was almost helpless, her wheel shot away and her foremast gone. She was engaged in close action with the *San Nicolas,* and was hard pressed.

In the meantime the *Excellent,* commanded by Collingwood, Nelson's friend, upon receiving Jervis's signal, had fallen in with others of the leading Spanish ships, and had compelled one of them to strike (and it is a question whether a second had not done so), when Collingwood, seeing the condition of his old messmate, left his prizes without taking possession of them — an act of extraordinary magnanimity in those days — and ranging up within ten feet of the *San Nicolas,* gave her such a broadside as practically settled her business. She luffed up, and fell on board the three-decker *San Josef,* while Collingwood passed on in pursuit of the Spanish flagship, the *Santissima Trinidad.* The *Captain,* being in no condition to pursue anyone, Nelson ordered Captain Miller to put her helm astarboard, so that he might grapple with the two Spanish giants, the *San Nicolas* and (beyond her) the *San Josef*. It is important to remember how these three ships hung together: first the little *Captain,* then the *San Nicolas* in the middle, then the towering *San Josef,* by far the biggest of the three.

He called for boarders. It was a call he never made in vain. Captain Berry, late lieutenant of the *Captain,* but now only a passenger waiting for promotion to another ship, climbed out along the spritsailyard, and jumped into the enemy's mizzen chains. Others followed him. (Captain Miller, commanding the *Captain,* would have been among them, but Nelson ordered him to remain.) Meantime, on the next deck below, a soldier of the 69th Regiment, (many of whom had been serving as marines in the fleet ever since the Corsica affair) reached across the intervening space and, with his musket, smashed the upper quarter-gallery window of the *San Nicolas.* He jumped in and Nelson followed him. They found the cabin doors closed, and the Spanish officers firing at them with their pistols through the windows. But this soldier — or some other coming in behind, for it cannot have been little Nelson — hurled himself against the door and burst it open.

They drove the Spaniards onto the quarterdeck, where, in Nelson's words, "I found Captain Berry in possession of the poop, and the Spanish ensign hauling down." There was still the fo'c'sle. Across the middle, or waist, of the ship ran narrow gangways at each side, and these were the only direct means of communication between quarterdeck and fo'c'sle. Nelson started across the larboard gangway, with Lieutenant Pierson of the 69th Regiment and some others of "my people." On the way he met three Spanish officers, who delivered up their swords. The *San Nicolas* was taken. But at this moment from the "admiral's stern gallery" (that is, behind the quarterdeck) of the *San Josef* a destructive volley of musketry and pistols was fired into the *San Nicolas,* killing seven Englishmen and wounding many more; for the *San Josef,*

NELSON BOARDING THE "SAN NICOLAS" AT THE BATTLE OF ST VINCENT, FEBRUARY 14, 1797

From the picture by Sir William Allan in the Painted Hall, Greenwich.

By permission of the Lords of the Admiralty

being a three-decker, overlooked the other ship, and the range was only a few yards.

The soldiers of the 69th replied to this fire; and Nelson, calling again for boarders, managed to scramble into the main chains of the *San Josef,* assisted by Captain Berry, and to get upon her decks. As he found his feet he is said to have shouted his war cry — "Westminster Abbey or a glorious victory!" Then a Spanish officer put his head over the quarterdeck rail and said that they surrendered. It was "welcome intelligence." Nelson mounted to the quarterdeck, and there the Spanish captain, with a bow, presented his sword, explaining that the Admiral was unable to be present, since he was in the cockpit dying of his wounds. Nelson thanked him, and stood there waiting while the other Spanish officers were summoned. And there "on the quarterdeck of a Spanish first-rate did I receive the swords of vanquished Spaniards; which, as I received, I gave to William Fearney, one of my bargemen, who put them with the greatest sangfroid under his arm."

It was a great moment. Nelson says that as he took the Spanish officers' swords he was surrounded by Captain Berry, Lieutenant Pierson, John Sykes (his coxswain, who afterwards saved his life), John Thompson, Francis Cook, and others, "all old *Agamemnons.*" As Jervis's flagship, the *Victory,* passed the *Captain* and her two prizes, still locked together, the crew lined the bulwarks and gave them three hearty cheers. Two other Spaniards of their windward division had surrendered; but the *Santissima Trinidad,* though apparently willing to strike her colours, had not been taken possession of, because the *Excellent's* rigging was so much cut about that she could not pursue, and she succeeded in wriggling away as evening fell. It remains to record the extraordinary behaviour of the Spanish lee division. They had at last worked round the English rear to windward, and there was nothing to prevent them from renewing the engagement with Jervis's sorely battered fleet. The choice lay with them. The *Culloden* and the *Excellent* were in hardly better state than the *Captain,* and Jervis had only twelve ships with which

I

to oppose twenty Spaniards. These twelve formed a line between the prizes and the enemy. The Spanish Admiral took a good look at them (he is said to have called a conference of his captains to discuss what to do), and then made sail and stood away to Cadiz. It is hardly surprising to hear that this Spanish admiral was afterwards court-martialled and dismissed the service.

Covered with bruises from his boarding exploits, fainting with fatigue, intoxicated with the sense of victory, Nelson went on board the *Victory,* and Jervis — who knew a victory when he saw one — received the little hero with a great bear's hug of an embrace that must have hurt him damnably. He told him that he could never sufficiently thank him, and "used every kind expression which could not fail to make me happy." We get a sudden vivid glimpse of Nelson at this great moment of his life from his having happened to describe the scene to his brother-in-law, Bolton, after returning to England. He stood there upon the Admiral's quarterdeck, his face blackened with powder, his clothes hanging in shreds, and half his hat shot away. Yet he would not have changed places with any man living.

Back in his own cabin in the small hours, Nelson sat down and wrote to Collingwood:

My dearest friend, — "A friend in need is a friend indeed," was never more truly verified than by your most noble and gallant conduct yesterday in sparing the *Captain* from further loss; and I beg, both as a public officer and a friend, you will accept my most sincere thanks. I have not failed, by letter to the Admiral, to represent the eminent service of the *Excellent*.

To which "Coll" answered cheerfully that "it added very much to the satisfaction which I felt in thumping the Spaniards that I released you a little."

It had been a great day for England. So swift and dramatic a reply to the Spanish declaration of war had never been expected by her enemies. They were dazed. They huddled into Cadiz; and Jervis, after rapidly refitting, followed them,

THE EARL OF ST VINCENT
From an engraving by H. Robinson after the painting by John Hoppner in
St James's Palace.

with his much smaller fleet, and coolly blockaded them there. "It absolutely appears a dream," wrote Nelson to his wife, describing this rush of events. Yet he knew in his heart that even now there was something lacking. St Vincent had not been a perfect work of art — not the smooth, solemn symphony that he would play out to the very last crashing chord when he found the enemy in Aboukir Bay. Why had no more enemy ships been captured? Why had the *Santissima Trinidad* been allowed to escape? Her masts were gone, and she was said to have had five hundred casualties. Collingwood could not quite reach her, but if there had been a few more Collingwoods among the English captains whose ships were still seaworthy, the big Spaniard must surely have been laid by the heels. And the *Soberano,* a Spanish seventy-four, was almost equally a wreck. These two ships "belonged to us by conquest"; they "only wanted some good fellows to get alongside them, and they were ours."

To his brother he wrote that he would not accept any praise which did not include Collingwood and Troubridge. "We are the only three ships who made great exertions on that glorious day; the others did their duty." And he tells an anecdote that was going about the fleet to the effect that when the *Captain* turned out of the line, and the *Culloden* tacked (according to orders), Calder, the Captain of the Fleet approached Sir John Jervis and, pointing out that these two ships had separated from the rest of the fleet, asked "Shall we recall them?" "I will not have them recalled," was the answer, "I put my faith in those ships." There was another saying in the fleet that pleased Nelson — "Nelson's patent bridge for boarding first-rates," alluding, of course, to the manner in which he had crossed the decks of the *San Nicolas* to get at the big *San Josef.* It was this incident in the battle which appealed most strongly to the imagination of the common sailors, and also to the people at home. At the same time, though he liked the flattery, no one knew better than Nelson that both these ships were on the point of surrendering when he boarded them. It was like him to get there first,

was not his greatest moment on St Valentine's Day.
occurred when he took the rapid, heroic decision of
throwing himself alone across the enemy's path, and so turned
what might have been a minor success into a resounding
triumph.

However, it had been a great day, and this was no time
for grumbling. At home in England they went wild with joy
at the news. It was a weight off the nation's mind. We had
soon taken the measure of the Spaniards! Jervis's dispatches
were extraordinarily brief and unilluminating. He mentioned
the services of the *Captain* in the baldest terms. In a private
letter to the Admiralty, however, he praised Nelson highly,
but again without giving many details. This has been
attributed to the jealousy of Calder, the Captain of the Fleet.
From what we know of Jervis's character it seems unlikely
that he was influenced by anyone. He preferred to be brief;
and, anyhow, he would not wish to emphasise that Nelson
had acted without orders. Probably the first full and authori-
tative account of the battle to reach England was taken by Sir
Gilbert Elliot, the late Viceroy of Corsica, who was on his
way back to England on the *Lively* frigate, and had induced
Jervis to let him delay the frigate's voyage, so that he might
watch the battle from her decks. It must have been an inspiring sight, and we may be sure that, in describing it to the
Lords of the Admiralty and others, he did not fail to do justice to the part played by his friend Nelson. To Nelson he
wrote, with the picture of the battle still bright in his mind,
"the glorious group of your ship and her two prizes fast in
your grip was never surpassed, and I dare say never will."
With Elliot on board the *Lively* was Colonel Drinkwater, a
member of the Viceroy's staff, to whom we owe the best and,
indeed, the only adequate account of this famous engagement.
It is a fortunate thing that he was there to supplement Jervis's
curt phrases.

Honours were now showered upon the victors. Sir John
Jervis became Earl St Vincent. Nelson might have been
made a baronet — there seems to be no doubt about that —

but, anticipating something of the sort, he had written to Elliot two days after the battle, expressing his preference for the K.B. on the ground that "to take hereditary honours without a fortune to support the dignity, is to lower that honour it would be my pride to support in proper splendour." In fact he was still a poor man. Thus it was arranged; and, notification of his promotion to flag rank arriving by a happy coincidence about the same time, he now became Rear-Admiral Sir Horatio Nelson, K.B. He was not made Rear-Admiral for his services at St Vincent, but in the ordinary course of advancement. The Spanish Admiral's sword, which William Fearney had tucked under his arm on the quarter-deck of the *San Josef,* was presented by Nelson to the city of Norwich, and Norwich responded by conferring on him its freedom. He also received the freedom of the city of London. His father wrote from Bath that "the name and services of Nelson have sounded throughout this city," so that the old man was "obliged to retire from the public eye so that he might weep tears of joy in secret."

Nelson was transferred to the *Irresistible,* but soon returned to the *Captain,* and hoisted his flag there as Rear-Admiral of the Blue. A fortnight later he was sent to Elba to fetch away the garrison whose commander had before refused to move. He found them already embarked on another ship and returned with them to Gibraltar. The *Captain* was now sent to England for repair, and Nelson moved his flag to the *Theseus,* which had just arrived from home, and joined the fleet off Cadiz, where the blockade continued.

CHAPTER X

HE LOSES AN ARM

ONE NIGHT — probably about June 10 or 11 — a piece of paper was dropped on the quarterdeck of his Majesty's ship *Theseus*. It lay there for some time unnoticed in the darkness. Eventually some one found it, and it was carried down to the Rear-Admiral's cabin — which would open out on to the upper gun-deck, the captain's cabin being on the quarterdeck above. Read by the light of a lantern, swinging from the roof, the paper was found to have written upon it the following message:

> Success attend Admiral Nelson! God bless Captain Miller! We thank them for the officers they have placed over us. We are happy and comfortable, and will shed every drop of blood in our veins to support them, and the name of the *Theseus* shall be immortalised as high as the *Captain's*. — SHIP'S COMPANY.

Nothing much in itself — Nelson was accustomed to such adulation; but at this particular moment it was an extraordinary message to receive, so extraordinary that he immediately passed it on to Jervis.

The *Theseus* lay tossing outside the harbour of Cadiz. She was part of the advance squadron kept there by Lord St Vincent, under the command of Rear-Admiral Nelson, so close inland that they could see every manœuvre in the forts, and even watch, through their glasses, the Spanish ladies walking on the foreshore, and doubtless taunting the officers of their own navy (as Nelson often heard they did) for not going out to fight. The ship was cleared for action. Nelson tells us that all her bulkheads were down. Any reader who

has followed me through Chapter II of this volume will
appreciate what that means. The cabins had simply disappeared. The midshipmen and pursers found themselves
camping out in the open on the orlop deck; all those comfortable little messes, which might be more properly described
as wigwams, had become no more than a right to a certain
corner of the deck; and even the Admiral's hammock might
be seen swinging between its beams by any sailor who took
the trouble to peep under the quarterdeck, for the bulkheads
which divided his dining-room and sleeping apartments had
all been removed. There was precious little comfort in a ship
cleared for action in those days; and in this advance squadron
outside Cadiz, they were cleared for action all the time.
Jervis had been reinforced from England, so that in number
he was now almost equal to the Spaniards, but the latter did
not know this, and nothing but their own pusillanimity prevented them from coming out.

But the *Theseus* only three or four weeks before had been in
England and had been engaged in the mutiny of the Nore.
There is no dispute that her crew had been wholeheartedly on
the side of the mutineers. It is an astonishing fact — but perhaps not really so astonishing to those who know him — that
at the period of his greatest victories the British sailor was
most thoroughly "fed up." The worst mutiny in the whole of
England's naval history occurred during the period of her
greatest naval triumphs. There is no need to go into the
miserable history of the mutiny of the Nore. Nelson was not
concerned in it. After the usual fumblings and hesitations the
authorities at home suddenly took strong action, and Parker,
the ringleader, was hanged. But the spirit of rebellion had
spread through the fleet. Four men of the *St George,* one of
the line-of-battle ships under Jervis's command, were arrested,
and it was found that elaborate plans had been made for a
corresponding mutiny in the Mediterranean command. One
of the prisoners confessed to the clergyman who attended him
after his condemnation that he had fellow-conspirators on the
Britannia, Captain, Diadem, and *Egmont,* where plans for

the rising had been carefully prepared. It is astounding to think that among the men who followed Nelson across the blood-stained decks of the *San Nicolas* and the *San Josef* on Valentine's Day were some who had signed their names to an agreement to raise a mutiny in the fleet.

The four mutineers of the *St George* were condemned on a Saturday evening, too late — as Jervis remarked — to hang them that night. But he had it done next morning, Sunday or no Sunday. Vice-Admiral Thompson, who was in the fleet, took the liberty of writing to the Admiral, publicly protesting against this profanation of the Sabbath. Jervis instantly demanded and secured his recall. The criminals, he reported to the Admiralty, had asked for five days in which to prepare themselves for death; but "in that time they would have hatched five hundred treasons." On the Sabbath morning their corpses dangled from the yard-arm. Nelson has sometimes been accused of winning popularity by pandering to the mob. He now wrote to Jervis's Captain of the fleet: "I am sorry that you should have to differ with Vice-Admiral Thompson, but had it been Christmas day instead of Sunday, I would have executed them." He added that no one could tell "what might have been hatched by a Sunday's grog."

It was in these circumstances that the ship's company of the *Theseus*, supposed to be one of the worst ships in the fleet, dropped their scrap of paper on Nelson's quarterdeck. He was always served loyally, but never more so than by these men from the Nore. There was something about him that even Hood and Jervis lacked: something that made the common sailor — a criminal from the county gaol, an escaped debtor, or an embittered victim of the press-gang — follow him blindly into the cannon's mouth. Every crew that he commanded was, in his own fair words, a "band of brothers." His discipline was a model to the fleet, but he loved his "poor brave fellows"; and they knew it, and loved him.

Shortly after this, going on board the *Swiftsure*, which was in his squadron, he found two men there in irons. They were apparently mad, but Jervis suspected them of what we should nowadays call "swinging the lead" in order to get their discharge from the service. Nelson could not bear the sight. Returning from his visit to the *Swiftsure,* he wrote to the Commander-in-Chief: "The sight of the two men in irons on board her has affected me more than I can express." "I hope," he continued, "for the poor men's sake that they are imposing on me, but depend on it that God Almighty has afflicted them with the most dreadful of all diseases; they do not sham, indeed you will find I am not mistaken." He offered to pay £50 out of his own pocket in order to place the younger of the two "in some proper place for his recovery." He was obviously in an agony of mind lest Jervis should take some stern action against them in the exceptional circumstances of the moment. But Jervis could not resist him, and the men were sent home.

He gave his men plenty of opportunities about this time of showing their affection. There were some vigorous skirmishes with the Spanish mortar-gunboats and launches. In particular the night of July 3, 1797, was made, as Nelson puts it, "a warm night at Cadiz." The *Thunderer* bomb was run in under the walls, and a number of shells dropped into the town, whereupon the Spanish gunboats came out like a swarm of angry wasps, and Nelson, in his turn, ordered his boats out to attack them. He himself went in command of his barge, having with him Captain Miller, who had been transferred from the *Captain,* and Fremantle, formerly of the *Inconstant.* In the course of a confused conflict the barge was laid aboard by an armed launch, carrying twenty-six men. Nelson had only his crew of ten men with the three officers. It was always difficult to protect Nelson on these occasions. As he jumped for the other boat a Spaniard aimed a blow at him, which Sykes, the coxswain, interposing, received upon his head (and was in hospital for weeks afterwards in consequence). Fremantle also was slightly wounded. But the end of it was that eighteen Spaniards were knocked out and their launch captured. Nelson pauses, in his report to Jervis, to record that the Spanish commander, though beaten, put up such a resistance "as did honour to a brave officer."

His relations with the Spaniards were, indeed, almost humorously cordial. As he remarked in a letter which he sent to the Spanish Admiral when returning some prisoners, "the distresses occasioned by the known laws of war are miserable enough without adding to them." In the same spirit he had previously written to this Admiral, requesting him to inform "the ladies at Cadiz" (how charming they had looked through his glasses!) that the following day, being King George's birthday, the blockading English fleet would be firing salutes, and he particularly desired that this should be explained to them, "that they might not be alarmed at the firing." But business was business all the same, and when he ran the *Thunderer* bomb in under the walls and proceeded to shell the town, there is no evidence, as Harrison remarks, that he sent any polite intimation to the ladies of this real danger.

We have seen that Nelson, though no one in history was ever less introspective, was childishly proud of certain qualities of his which he had deliberately cultivated — all those, in fact, which went to complete his portrait of himself as a national hero. Recording this and other skirmishes with Spanish gunboats in his *Sketch of My Life,* he solemnly states that "it was during this period that perhaps my personal courage was more conspicuous than at any other period of my life." But even then he forgets to tell us what he did himself, and talks only about John Sykes and Captain Fremantle. He thinks it important to his biographer to know how brave he, the great Nelson, was, but he has not the kind of conceit that enables him to retail any personal act of bravery.

If the Admiral's brief dispatches after the battle of St Vincent had done rather less than justice to Nelson's personal share in that victory, his report of the comparatively unimportant boat skirmish off Cadiz more than made up for the deficiency. He gave a glowing account of "Rear-Admiral Nelson's actions which," as he said, "spoke for themselves,"

so that "any praise from my pen would take from their merit."
In the meantime he and Nelson were busy concocting a new
plan for the vexation of the Spaniards. For a long time —
ever since St Vincent in fact — they had been wondering what
was happening to the rich treasure-ships from Manila and the
West Indies, which were due in Cadiz about this time. What
would they do when they found the British fleet between them
and Spain, and their own fleet beaten and bottled up in
harbour? To Lord St Vincent and Nelson, discussing this
matter by letter, or over a bottle of port in the cabin of the
flagship, it seemed likely that the treasure-ships would put
into Santa Cruz, the harbour of Teneriffe. Troubridge was
consulted, and agreed. Nelson got a report on the defences of
Santa Cruz and passed it on to the Commander-in-Chief.

Obviously this was a case for a combined military and naval
operation, and Nelson's first idea was that General de Burgh,
now returning from Elba under naval escort, should be induced to allow the former garrison under his command to
be diverted to Teneriffe. Need it be said that he refused?
The more enterprising O'Hara, commanding the troops at
Gibraltar, was next approached; but neither would he have
anything to do with it, though he agreed to lend artillery.
Not even the prospect of certain loot would move the soldiers.
Definite information now came to hand that a Manila
treasure-ship had put into Santa Cruz. St Vincent could bear
it no longer. He determined to attack, and, not unnaturally,
he selected the most active of his subordinates for this dangerous duty. When Nelson heard that he was to command
the expedition his spirits went up with a bound. His letters
are full of jocularities about what he will do to Santa Cruz.
He was taking Troubridge with him, and declared that
"under 'General Troubridge' ashore and myself afloat, I am
confident of success. Whenever I see it [Santa Cruz] ten
hours shall decide its fate."

He made elaborate plans. He had been allowed to choose
his own ships, and took with him the *Theseus* (Captain
Miller, formerly of the *Captain*), *Culloden* (Captain Trou-

bridge), *Zealous* (Captain Samuel Hood), *Leander* (Captain Thompson), *Seahorse* (Captain Fremantle), *Emerald* (Captain Waller), *Terpsichore* (Captain R. Bowen). It will be noticed that most of the captains are old friends. Nelson sent forward the frigates *Seahorse, Terpsichore,* and *Emerald,* carrying on board the landing party of one thousand men, commanded by Troubridge and including two hundred and fifty marines under Captain Oldfield. They were attended by all the boats of the squadron, and had with them scaling-ladders for use on shore. Special instructions were issued about warm clothing for the men.

The town of Santa Cruz lies surrounded by heights, which, to the south-west, are practically inaccessible and tower over the little white town so that one half of it is thrown into deep shadow. On the other side (that is, to the right of the English as they approached), and at some little distance from the town, lies the fort, also surrounded by cliffs.

The intention was for the boats to dash ashore in the darkness just before dawn, landing on the low beach between the town and the fort. They were then to seize the fort and turn its guns upon the town, which must have surrendered. But the luck was against Nelson from the start. At midnight the frigates were within three miles of their objective; but a strong current against them, and a wind off shore, so kept them back that when the sun rose over the hills behind Santa Cruz they were still, with every stitch of canvas set, one mile from their landing place — and were so discovered to the startled inhabitants. Instantly the place came to life like a disturbed hive of bees. Behind the frigates the big line-of-battle ships now appeared in the offing, and Troubridge, who had been eagerly scanning the shore through his glasses, jumped into a boat, and with Oldfield and Bowen was rowed back to the *Theseus* to consult with Nelson. They thought that if they could seize the heights above the fort, it might be stormed from thence; so Nelson brought his big ships in, with the intention of battering the walls of the place from the sea, and so creating a diversion while the heights were attacked. But, in the first place, it was found that the line-of-battle ships could not get within three miles of the walls on account of the currents; and, in the second, that the heights were now covered with men prepared to dispute their possession. It must be added here that there might have been a better chance of carrying the heights if Troubridge had led his landing party on shore at once instead of going back to consult the Admiral. He showed, for once in his life, an unfortunate lack of initiative which Nelson — one would have thought — would have found it particularly hard to forgive. He does remark somewhere that if he himself had been with the frigates the attack must have succeeded; but he never blamed Troubridge, and continued to place great confidence in him.

Nelson now changed his plan. A De Burgh or an O'Hara would have given up the expedition at once, and in this case the soldiers would have been right. But there was a confident pugnacious spirit in the Navy in those days which simply refused to admit defeat, and if Nelson was the outstanding example of this spirit, it is only fair to point out, now that we are recording his first serious failure, that in his determination to go on with the attack he appears to have had the cordial support of every officer in his squadron. The idea now was to make a night attack upon the town itself. The men who had been landed in the neighbourhood of the fort were re-embarked on July 22; but throughout the whole of the next day the ships continued to demonstrate against the fort, firing shots at long range, so as to give the impression that this was still the objective. Nelson spent the day drawing up his plan of attack — a lengthy and wonderfully explicit document. The boats were to advance against the town in six separate divisions, some towing, some pulling, so arranged that when they landed the boats from each ship would find themselves together. They were to make for the mole in the centre of the harbour. As soon as fire was opened upon them, they were to cast off the tow ropes and pull in separately. Nelson himself would be in the centre and have Fremantle and Bowen with him. The *Fox* cutter, commanded by Lieutenant Gibson and carrying a hundred and eighty men, was to follow the boats in. The attack was timed for eleven o'clock on the night of the 24th.

On that fatal evening, not long before what we should now call zero hour, Nelson and some of his oldest friends in the squadron — Troubridge, Miller, Fremantle — met for supper on board Fremantle's ship, the *Seahorse*. Nelson had been busy in his cabin, going through his papers, and burning private letters, with the assistance of his stepson, Josiah. "I never expected to return," he told Jervis afterwards. He even suggested to Josiah that he should stay behind, on the ground that if both of them were killed, there would be nobody to look after Lady Nelson. But the lad had been detailed for the attacking party, and insisted vehemently that he would go.

The Captain of the *Seahorse* had just recently been married, while on service in the Mediterranean, and, in the easygoing manner of those days, he had his wife on board. This was a great attraction. The blushing bride presided at the supper-table, and no doubt her presence contributed vastly to the success of the meal; but the nervous strain of these social duties at a moment when her husband was about to engage in a life-and-death struggle must have been enough to agitate even one of her much cooler sisters of today. However they had their supper, these hardy sunburned men, and no doubt enjoyed it, and drank to the King, "God bless him!" and to the success of the expedition; and so went quietly over the side at about five minutes to eleven, and were rowed out to their respective stations in the irregular line of boats already floating there in the darkness; until, at a given signal, the whole mass moved forward silently and disappeared in the direction of the town. Little Mrs Fremantle had three hours to wait.

All the boats, as already stated, had orders to get alongside the mole. What would have happened if these instructions could have been carried out it is difficult to say, for the Spaniards, as afterwards appeared, had cannon trained upon this spot, and a strong force of soldiers at the landward end of the mole. As a matter of fact, however, most of the boats missed the mole, and found themselves going ashore among the breakers, either to the south-east (right) or south-west (left) of it. According to Nelson's memorandum of the affair, every boat that attempted to land to the left of the mole was wrecked, but from Troubridge's report to Nelson, dated July 25, it would appear that this was a slight exaggeration. Troubridge was in command on the right. No one would have suspected him of journalistic gifts, but his account of the landing on that side is extraordinarily vivid. He says that many of the boats, seeing the big breakers ahead of them, put back and returned to their ships. Of those that landed most were capsized, and all the small arms ammunition carried by the marines was soaked. Not a single scaling-ladder was brought ashore. Indeed, the invaders were not so much landed as thrown ashore by the waves. Troubridge, however, with Waller of the *Emerald,* who had landed near him, collected what men he could find and advanced through the streets of the town to the principal square, which had been appointed by Nelson as a rendezvous.

We can see them in the square of this Spanish town, a few red-coated marines and a larger party of seamen, armed with cutlasses, small arms, and pikes, expecting every moment to be attacked. Nearly all their muskets were useless. They waited there about an hour, hearing heavy firing close at hand — no doubt at the mole — and Troubridge, hoping to bluff the Spaniards into surrender, "sent a sergeant with two gentlemen of the town to summons the citadel." But, "I fear the sergeant was shot on his way, as I heard nothing of him afterwards." To attempt the citadel without scaling-ladders would, of course, have been absurd. Hearing that Captains Hood and Miller had landed to the left of the mole, Troubridge marched to join them, and by daybreak he found himself once more in the centre of the town at the head of about three hundred and fifty men, and with a certain amount of dry ammunition,

which had been obtained from the Spanish prisoners. Not a
man had joined them from the mole, where Nelson was! As
delay was dangerous he got his little force in motion "to try
what could be done with the citadel without ladders"; but
"found the whole of the streets commanded by field pieces,
and upwards of eight thousand Spaniards and one hundred
French under arms approaching by every avenue." Even if
we assume these numbers to have been exaggerated, the position was hopeless, for they had not a boat that was not stove
in, they had no provisions and no time to look for them, and
no orders from their Commander-in-Chief, who was presumably dead.

In these circumstances Troubridge acted with commendable
initiative. He sent a flag of truce to the Spanish governor,
declaring that he should immediately set fire to the town and
retire fighting, unless his terms were agreed to, which were
these — that the invaders should be taken off and returned
to their own ships with all the honours of war, the British
squadron undertaking not to molest Santa Cruz any further,
and that prisoners should be given up on both sides. Of
course it was bluff, and must have been recognized as such;
but the Spanish governor did not choose to call it. He
agreed to the terms. He did more: he put all the wounded
English prisoners in hospital, where they were given the very
best provisions available, and he made it known that, so far
from wishing to hurry his departing guests, the English ships
"were at liberty to send on shore and purchase whatever refreshments they were in want off, during the time they might
lie off the island." "Noble and generous conduct," as Nelson
said.

But what had happened at the mole? This was the first
great failure of Nelson's career, and his biographers have been
accustomed to dismiss it briefly. But if it was a failure, it was
a heroic one, worthy to be classed with Zeebrugge. Nelson
says that they were not discovered till they were "within half
gun-shot of the landing place." Then, as the first round shot
whistled over their heads, he gave the order for the boats to

cast off from each other, which they immediately did, and the whole flotilla, with a loud cheer, pushed for the shore. What happened to the right and left of him he could not see, but his own boat, with those of Fremantle and Bowen and four or five others, being in the centre of the line, came direct to the mole. There was a concentrated fire of thirty or forty pieces of cannon, some of them situated on the mole itself; but the boats pushed in right under the muzzles of the guns, and the sailors and marines springing ashore dashed at the defenders and drove them off. Every gun was spiked. But it was impossible to advance another step. "Such a heavy fire of musketry and grape-shot was kept up from the citadel and houses at the head of the mole," says Nelson, "that we could not advance, and we were all nearly killed or wounded." Bowen was killed. Fremantle was down. There was not a leader left.

Nelson, as he was stepping out of the boat, was shot through the right arm. The elbow was completely shattered. His arm was "nearly shot off" says Harrison. He fell back, into the arms of his stepson, Josiah Nisbet. "I am shot through the arm," he exclaimed, "I am a dead man." But when the sword, which he so greatly valued, given by his uncle, Maurice Suckling, slipped from his nerveless right hand into the bottom of the boat, he reached down quickly with his left and picked it up . . . This was Josiah's great moment. At no other point in his history can the biographer of Nelson make anything out of this uninteresting relative. But now Josiah, finding the slight figure of his stepfather and benefactor fainting in his arms, acted with a coolness and promptitude which — as Nelson ever afterwards acknowledged * — undoubtedly saved his life. The blood was flowing freely, and, seeing that the sight of it increased Nelson's faintness, Josiah covered it up with his hat; then, taking a silk handkerchief from his neck, he tied it tightly round the arm above

---

* "The boy is under obligations to me; but he repaid me by bringing me from the mole of Santa Cruz."

K

the wound. A man named Lovell, one of the crew of Nelson's barge, tore his shirt into shreds and made a sling. Josiah then seized an oar and called upon the boat's crew to assist him to get under the guns of the batteries that were still firing at them, so that the shot might pass over their heads. What remained of the other boats' crews pushed off at the same time.

Nelson lay at the bottom of the boat. Presently he asked to be lifted up, so that he might see what was going on around him. It was still dark, but in the scene of destruction in that fatal harbour — boats floating bottom uppermost, or pulling desperately to safety, the lost scaling-ladders bobbing about on the waves — he must have recognized all the signs of defeat. And at that moment, as he still looked round him, there was "a general shriek from the crew of the *Fox*": the cutter had been hit between wind and water, and she went down in a moment, with her whole crew, of whom Lieutenant Gibson and ninety-seven men were drowned. The Admiral's barge turned aside to help in the work of rescue; and much of Josiah's good work was quickly undone, for Nelson insisted upon sitting up and using his left arm to pull the struggling men out of the water. They took in so many that the boat was full, and then they pulled away towards the English ships — none too soon. And not a man in that wet, beaten, unhappy company but was sick at heart to see Nelson lying there among them, white and suffering.

At last they reached the foremost ship; but, even as they were about to take him up, Nelson recognized it and refused to go on board. It was the *Seahorse*. "I had rather suffer death," he exclaimed (and it is evident that he thought himself dying) "than alarm Mrs Fremantle by her seeing me in this state, and when I can give her no tiding whatever of her husband." (Fremantle was brought off later, also wounded in the right arm, and so badly that he was unable to serve again for a whole year, and missed Aboukir.) He made them row on to the *Theseus.*. When some one suggested a chair from the yard-arm he cried out impatiently that the boat must return immediately to the scene of action, and that a rope over the side would do, and this he seized with his sound left arm and so was dragged up, and on to the deck. Arrived there, he said: "Let me alone: I have yet my legs left and one arm. Tell the surgeon to make haste and get his instruments. I know I must lose my right arm, so the sooner it is off the better."

It is plain that, after the first shock of being hit, Nelson behaved with the kind of histrionic heroism which was natural to him. The gestures and sayings quoted above come from Harrison, or Clarke and MacArthur, and may have been a little embroidered. But the latter have included an account of Nelson's return to his ship, written by his young friend, Midshipman Hoste, who was one of the officers who had been left on board instead of going with the landing party. Hoste says:

> At two o'clock in the morning Admiral Nelson returned on board, being dreadfully wounded in the right arm with a grape-shot. I leave you, Sir, to judge of my situation when I beheld our boat approach with him who I may say has been a second father to me, his right arm dangling by his side, whilst with his left he jumped up the ship's side, and displayed a spirit that astonished everyone. He underwent the amputation with the same firmness and courage that have always marked his character.

Nelson's one memory of that operation seems to have been, in his own words, "the coldness of the knife" as it made the first circular cut through the integuments and muscles. He remembered it all his life. Years later on the *Victory,* the ship's surgeon, Magrath (afterwards Sir George Magrath, Medical Inspector of Hospitals and Fleets), having heard him on the subject, made a rule of always keeping hot water in the cockpit to dip the knife and instruments in. They cut very high, quite near to the shoulder, so that we must assume either that the injury was not confined to the elbow, or that they were afraid of gangrene. Anyhow, instead of severing a few broken threads, they cut right through his upper arm.

What was worse, though he did not know it at the time, they applied the ligature so clumsily to the humeral artery that the wound would not heal for months.

In the meantime Nelson continued his amazing display of stoicism. The Spanish Governor, hearing of his hurt, sent him two large flasks of the best Canary wine; and he replied with some English beer and cheese — a sort of last shot before leaving the place. Less than three days after his arm had been sawn off at the shoulder — with unsterilized instruments, without anæsthetics or antiseptics, while in the dim light of a hurricane lamp he writhed upon a table which the midshipmen had probably been using an hour or two before for their supper — less than three days later he was sitting up in his cabin, perfectly cool and collected, slowly scribbling one of the first letters he had ever written with his left hand. It was a brief note to Lord St Vincent — but how long it took to write! It mentioned the death of "poor Bowen," and asked that, in the series of promotions that was bound to ensue, Josiah Nisbet might get a move up.* And there is a laborious and rather formal epistle to Fanny, written a week or two later, while the expedition was on its way back to Cadiz from Teneriffe:

My dearest Fanny, — I am so confident of your affection that I feel the pleasure you will receive will be equal whether my letter is wrote by my right hand or by my left. It was the chance of war, and I have great reason to be thankful; and I know that it will add much to your pleasure in finding that Josiah, under God's Providence, was principally instrumental in saving my life. As to my health, it was never better [this less than three weeks after the amputation!]. I am much more recovered than anyone could have expected [as indeed he was]. I beg neither you nor my Father will think much of this mishap.

Every one was kind to him. His Commander-in-Chief met him with nothing but commiserations for his injury and praise for his conduct. He was sent straight home to England on the *Seahorse,* where Mrs Fremantle no doubt divided her

* St Vincent immediately made Josiah a Master and Commander.

attentions between him and her husband. He reached Spithead on September 1, 1797, and proceeded at once to Bath, where he found his father "not in the smallest degree altered" and his wife, and where many other friends and relations came to see him. Lord Spencer, the First Lord of the Admiralty, wrote to congratulate him upon his "glorious though unsuccessful attack," and to express the hope that he (Lord Spencer) might soon have the pleasure of making the personal acquaintance of "one whom I have so long been in the habit of admiring." To an equally cordial letter from the Duke of Clarence Nelson replied that, though he had lost an arm, "not a scrap of that ardour with which I have hitherto served our King has been shot away." At the same time, however, he was writing miserably to St Vincent that "a left-handed Admiral" would never be considered any use, and therefore "the sooner I get to a very humble cottage the better, and make room for a better man." There is no doubt that his mental sufferings were terrible: he feared that he might be regarded as a cripple, and that his career was at an end. At the same time he very properly put in an application to the Admiralty for wound pension, pointing out that he had been in four fleet actions, three actions with frigates, six engagements against batteries, ten cutting-out expeditions in boats, that he had served four months ashore in Corsica, and had lost his right eye and arm, and been "severely wounded and bruised in his body." The pension was promptly granted, at the rate of £712 a year, with the usual deductions.

But it was his physical suffering that was the real crux of the situation. He was pronounced a cure, but the pain in the stump of his arm continued to torment him day and night. A week after his arrival at Bath, while his wound still required a daily dressing, his wife wrote to Mr William Suckling that it was only by means of opium that he ever got any sleep. In October they moved to London, and took lodgings in the house of a Mr Jones in Bond Street; but Nelson was still in constant pain. He was cheered up by the kindness of the King, who received him twice, and he wrote to St Vincent:

"the moment I am cured I shall offer myself for service." But it was obvious that he was very far from cured.

It was in this same month of October that the celebrated incident related by Clarke and MacArthur is alleged to have occurred. The news of Admiral Duncan's victory at Camperdown reached London; and the patriotic mob, as it cheered and shouted its way down Bond Street, was disgusted to find one single house without any kind of illumination. Approaching this dark, silent dwelling, they "knocked repeatedly and violently at the door." A servant answered the summons, and was asked who his master was who had put no lights in his windows for the victory. He replied that his master had taken a dose of laudanum and gone to bed, in the hope of getting a little sleep, and that his name was Rear-Admiral Nelson. The mafeking mob fell back ashamed. The story is at any rate *ben trovato*. We know, as a fact, that Nelson was deeply stirred by the news of Duncan's victory. He first heard of it from Colonel Drinkwater — whom we have met before at St Vincent. Drinkwater had called to inquire about Nelson's health, and he gives the following account of what happened:

> I told him there was a rumour that the British fleet had been engaged with that of Holland. He started up in his peculiar, energetic manner, notwithstanding Lady Nelson's attempts to quiet him, and stretching out his unwounded arm—"Drinkwater," said he, "I would give this other arm to be with Duncan at this moment."

Nelson at first supposed that he had caught a cold in the wound which prevented it from healing; but the truth is that the ligature had been put on in such a way as to include a nerve; and apparently none of the distinguished surgeons who attended him almost daily in London had discovered this. The agony he suffered must have been almost unendurable. Then one morning, towards the end of November, he waked up to find that he had slept right through the night and was entirely free from pain. On sending for his surgeon, the ligature came away almost at a touch, and from then on his wound healed rapidly. He was back at Bath on January 29, and evidently in excellent spirits, for he writes to a friend in his old jocular manner, describing how he shared with some others a box at the opera.

> Some of the handsomest ladies in Bath are partakers in the box, and was I a bachelor I would not answer for being tempted; but as I am possessed of everything that is valuable in a wife, I have no occasion to think beyond a pretty face.

He had discovered, too, that the Admiralty were not only willing but anxious to find a ship for the popular hero of St Valentine's Day. Before the end of December he was promised the *Foudroyant,* a new 80-gun ship, to be launched in January. In making up his list of officers he thought of the gallant coxswain Sykes. It appeared that he was now gunner of the *Andromache;* but his former Captain, Miller, wrote to Nelson that if Sykes had had longer service he (Miller) would have "endeavoured to prevail on Lord St Vincent to make him a lieutenant; his manners and conduct are so entirely above his station that Nature certainly intended him for a gentleman." Nelson also got a short letter from Sykes — the last, it is feared, before the gallant fellow was killed. After all, the *Foudroyant* was not ready in time. Nelson was therefore ordered to hoist his flag on the *Vanguard* which he did on March 29, and on the 10th of the following month sailed from St Helens to join Lord St Vincent. Berry, formerly of the *Agamemnon,* was his flag captain.

It is said * that "a gloomy foreboding hung on the spirits of his affectionate wife" when Nelson bade her farewell. It may have been so; though, in view of the biographer's later knowledge of certain events which took place at Naples before the couple met again, it is a statement that we must regard with suspicion. What we do know is that, before he sailed, Nelson had realized one small ambition — he had bought that "coun-

---

* Clarke and MacArthur.

try cottage" of which he so often spoke. It was near Ipswich, a house rather than a cottage, and was called Roundwood. As things turned out, he was never to live there. In the meantime he left England before his wife could be settled in; but she wrote out to him a month later, praising the place, and telling him how much his father liked it, so that the old gentleman even talked of staying there with her, although there was "little or no accommodation" (evidently she did not want him), and then hurriedly adding, so as not to hurt Nelson, "the house is quite large enough." It is clear that the old friendly, quite unloverlike relations between Fanny and her husband had been, if anything, strengthened by his painful illness, through which she had doubtless nursed him with conscientious care.

CHAPTER XI

THE BATTLE OF THE NILE

So HE started on the long chase that was to end in Aboukir Bay. From the very beginning, somehow, this voyage had the air of a pursuit. He was at Lisbon within a fortnight of leaving St Helens, and there he found Josiah, aged seventeen, already in command of a hospital-ship, the *Dolphin*. He was delighted, and wrote to tell the boy's mother; nor did he forget to let Lord St Vincent know how well Josiah was handling his first ship, adding that "he also improves in manners and conversation." On the last day of the month he joined the fleet off Cadiz (where the Spaniards were still blockaded) and was able to look round him and take stock of the situation. It is significant that in his first letter, written upon arrival there, he is able to assure his wife confidently that "England will not be invaded this Summer."

Yet there were those who thought she might be. The naval position was extraordinarily puzzling, and there were almost as many opinions as to what would happen next as there were sailors in the fleet. The French at Toulon had their fleet intact (thanks to Hotham), and it was known that for months past they had been assembling there a great flotilla of transports, and that troops were arriving from all parts of France. In a few weeks time this formidable armament would be ready to move. And, thanks to the secrecy of the French staff work, no one could do more than guess at its destination! Some thought Sicily, some Corfu, others suggested Portugal, or even Ireland. None mentioned Egypt. It was a situation calculated to test even the iron nerve of Lord St Vincent, for, until reinforcements came out from England, he was not

ng enough to keep both the Spanish and the French in
their harbours, and in the meantime he could not tell when
or where this French menace would develop. He wanted
some one he could send to Toulon to find out for him, and he
longed hungrily for the sight of that battered little figure
which he had last seen groaning in a cot on the *Seahorse* so
many months before. "The arrival of Admiral Nelson," he
wrote to Lord Spencer, "has given me new life." He sent him
off to Toulon immediately in the *Vanguard*, with the *Orion*
and *Alexander*, ships of the line, the frigates *Flora, Emerald*,
and *Terpsichore*, and the sloop *Bonne Citoyenne*.

Nelson started off eagerly on his new quest, and on May
4 was at Gibraltar, where he was rather disgusted at the social
junketings he found going on there — dances given by the
garrison, and so forth. "I have no turn for such things when
we had better be alongside the Spaniard." He hurried on,
and on the 17th, off Cape Sicie, reported to St Vincent that he
had taken a French corvette and learned that Buonaparte was
already at Toulon, and that troops were constantly arriving.
Twelve thousand men, including some cavalry, had embarked,
and many times that number were to follow.

Almost from the first Nelson suspected that the real objective of the French was Egypt. Many incidents in his career
suggest that he had an uncanny intuition in these matters;
but on this occasion the idea had been given to him by the
English Consul-General at Leghorn, a Mr Udney, who, as
early as April 20, had written to him personally on the subject,
and, after mentioning the various suggestions that had been
made, concluded with these prophetic words:

I for my part, reflecting on the plan the late Empress of
Russia attempted to put in execution, of getting possession of
Egypt, am convinced that Buonaparte will hereafter, with more
reason in his unbounded enterprises, pursue the same scheme of
seizing and fortifying Alexandria, Cairo, and Suez. If France
intends uniting with Tippoo Sahib against our possessions in
India, the danger of losing half an army in crossing the desert
from Egypt would be no obstacle.

REAR-ADMIRAL SIR HORATIO NELSON IN 1798
From the painting by L. F. Abbott in the National Portrait Gallery.

144

In the meantime the British Admiralty, rather late in the day, was sending out naval reinforcements to Cadiz under Sir Roger Curtis, so that Lord St Vincent might be able to spare for Toulon a squadron strong enough to tackle the French Armada, if and when it emerged.   They did not bind St Vincent in any way, but they went so far as to drop a pretty broad hint as to who should command the Toulon squadron.   "If you determine to send a detachment into the Mediterranean," wrote Lord Spencer, "I think it almost unnecessary to suggest to you the propriety of putting it under the command of Sir H. Nelson, whose acquaintance with that part of the world, as well as his activity and disposition, seem to qualify him in a peculiar manner for that service." *

Such advice was indeed "unnecessary."   St Vincent would never have dreamed of choosing anyone else.   He waited impatiently for the promised reinforcements, and on the day of their arrival gave a fine example of what may fairly be called the "Jervis touch."   The high state of discipline and efficiency in every fleet under his command, and the change which this marked from the easy-going methods of his predecessors, has already been alluded to.   He now without delay detailed ten of his best ships — *Culloden, Goliath, Minotaur, Défense, Bellerophon, Majestic, Audacious, Zealous, Swiftsure,* under the command of Captain Troubridge, to join Nelson off Toulon, and kept them ready to sail at a moment's notice. And Captain Berry has recorded that "as soon as Sir Roger Curtis with the squadron under his command from England was visible from the masthead of the Admiral's ship, Captain Troubridge with his squadron put to sea, and was actually out of sight on his course to the Straits of Gibraltar, before the former cast anchor at the British station off Cadiz Bay." If there would be nothing very remarkable in such promptitude nowadays, we have to thank for it, very largely, the new

---

* It afterwards appeared that both the Duke of Clarence and Lord Minto (Sir G. Elliot) had put up this suggestion to Lord Spencer, who, however, had already thought of it himself.

spirit infused into the Navy by that fine old warrior Lord St Vincent. This was on May 24.

Meantime, on May 19, disaster had overtaken the little squadron off Toulon. One of those sudden Mediterranean gales, as unaccountable then as they are now, but a much greater danger and nuisance, sprang up from the north-west. During the night of the 20th it blew harder and harder until, in the small hours of the morning, the *Vanguard* was dismasted, her main topmast, mizzen topmast, and foremast going over the side, and her bowsprit being sprung in three places. It was just possible to wear the ship with a remnant of the spritsail, and, with the assistance of the *Orion* and *Alexander,* the *Vanguard* was at last got safely into the anchorage of San Pietro at the southern end of Sardinia at noon on the 23rd. But all the frigates had parted company in the storm, and, supposing that the *Vanguard* would have to go into dock at Gibraltar, had returned there themselves. "I thought Hope would have known me better," wrote Nelson, referring to the senior captain of the frigates who had taken the others off. Moreover, the Sardinian authorities found the three line-of-battle ships uncomfortable guests, and would not help them, and it was only by tremendous exertions on the part of every one concerned that jury masts were rigged on the *Vanguard* so that she was able to put to sea again in four days' time. Reporting to St Vincent, Nelson praises Captains Saumarez, Ball, and Berry, as they no doubt deserved; but he characteristically adds the name of the ship's carpenter, James Morrison, and begs "most earnestly" that "your Lordship will have the goodness to recommend Mr Morrison to the particular notice of the Board of Admiralty."

Nelson always looked upon this unexpected accident as a direct interposition of Providence. "Figure to yourself," he wrote to his wife, "a vain man on Sunday evening at sunset, walking in his cabin with a squadron about him, who looked up to their chief to lead them to glory, and in whom this chief places the firmest reliance, that the proudest ships, in equal numbers, belonging to France, would have bowed their flags, and with a very rich prize lying by him — figure to yourself this proud, conceited man when the sun rose on Monday morning, his ship dismasted, his fleet dispersed, and himself in such distress that the meanest frigate out of France would have been a very unwelcome guest."

But the long arm of coincidence was at work even more strangely than he thought. That same north-wester which had scattered his squadron before it like so many paper ships blew much more moderately in the north, so that to the French in Toulon it seemed no more than a brisk and favourable breeze — in fact just what they had been waiting for. Seizing the opportunity, the Armada slipped out to sea and was away, no one knew where, long before the British ships staggered back to their station. Thus Nelson and Napoleon missed each other for the first time. And from Nelson's point of view it must be confessed that, though it was doubtless most annoying to lose the enemy like this, after taking so much trouble to keep in touch with them, he could consider himself fortunate, with his tiny squadron, not to have met the powerful French fleet as they emerged. And if he had seen them, and followed them at a safe distance, hanging upon their skirts, he might have missed Troubridge and the reinforcements now on their way to him.

As it was, while he sailed from point to point along the coast, seeking vainly for news, tearing his hair with impatience, he was joined by the *Mutine* brig, commanded by his friend Captain Hardy, who brought him what he calls the "flattering account" of his having been appointed to command the new fleet in pursuit of Buonaparte. Two days later he was joined by "dear Troubridge," and the great pursuit began. "The French have a long start," he wrote to St Vincent. "You may be assured I shall fight them the moment I can reach their fleet, be they at anchor or under sail." It seems already a hundred years since Hotham's days!

Southward; first to Naples — hardly a pause on the way. No time to go ashore; no time to see Lady Hamilton, if ever he thought of her. But he sends Troubridge in on the *Mu-*

tine brig, and Hardy anchors in that glorious harbour at five o'clock in the morning. Sir William Hamilton is in bed, but he gets up in a hurry, and hastens to make arrangements for Troubridge to see the authorities and endeavour to obtain that authorization which Nelson is demanding for the British ships to be provisioned in Neapolitan ports. Nelson wants an explicit order from the King; all he gets is a letter from the Minister, General Acton (an Italian of British descent). It is now that Lady Hamilton is supposed to have obtained, through her friend the Queen, some secret order or "talisman" (as Harrison puts it) which gave Nelson all he required. Although he himself later confirmed this story, it is clear from his own correspondence at the time that no such document existed.

As soon as Hamilton discovered who was in command of the British fleet he wrote privately to Nelson in the most affectionate terms, wishing him every success and adding, "Emma's most kind love attends you, who, you may be sure, joins with me heart and soul in wishing you to crown your glory by the destruction of this boasted armament." Nelson had not set eyes on Lady Hamilton since his visit five years ago; the one or two letters they had exchanged had been couched in most formal terms; and, in fact, it is impossible not to wonder whether she was aware of the manner in which Sir William now introduced her name — or whether she herself had suggested it. She must have heard of his fame by now, and how he was already a popular hero in England. In the meantime there was nothing further to do but to stare at the distant ships through glasses. "It is very tantalising," wrote Sir William, "to see, as we do, your ships at a distance and to have no communication with you." At the same time he was able to convey certain assurances from the King on the subject of victualling, and Nelson, who was all this time thinking of nothing but the French fleet and of what might be passing in the minds of General Buonaparte and the Admiral, De Brueys, felt that he had stayed long enough. He must push on to Sicily, where some one might be able to tell

him where the French had gone. He wrote one typical letter
to St Vincent, just before sailing. "My lord: I have only to
assure you I will bring the French fleet to action the moment
I can lay my hands on them. Till then, Adieu."

He was entirely without frigates — "the eyes of the fleet."
"My distress for frigates is extreme." If he died, he said, the
word "frigates" would be found written on his heart. Passing through the Straits of Messina, he was still without news,
though the Sicilians stood up in their fishing-boats to cheer
the English ships and would have given any information they
had. The vast majority of the population was strongly on the
English side, though their Government at Naples, living under
the continual threat of French invasion from the north, was
afraid to give open support. Off Cape Passero, the southern
extremity of Sicily, Nelson got his first news of the French.
They had seized Malta, which surrendered without firing a
shot, and had sailed on into the unknown. That was only
six days ago. He was close on their heels. The wind was
from the west when the French had sailed from Malta, and it
seemed clearer than ever that their destination must be Alexandria. Nelson had thought so all along, and he now, with
his customary decision, staked everything upon that opinion.
He set sail for Egypt.

One of his captains — Berry, of the *Vanguard* — has given
us a little glimpse of life on board the fleet at this critical moment. Every ship, of course, was cleared for action, and every
man felt keyed up to meet the approaching crisis. The captains — sometimes all of them, sometimes only the four sen-
iors — would frequently be rowed across to the flagship for
consultation with the Admiral. He used those few days, between Malta and Alexandria (and every other free day he
could get), to work out in advance and explain to his captains
the tactics to be adopted in whatever situation they might
come upon the French. "There was no possible position in
which they could be found," says Berry, "that he did not take
into his calculation." When we catch ourselves thinking of
Nelson merely as a heroic figure, more a spell-binder than

a tactician, it is well to remember that no commander on land or sea has ever prepared his tactical schemes more carefully.

All this time, of course, he was expecting to catch the French at sea, when he would have to deal not only with a slightly superior fleet, but with a crowd of transports carrying forty or fifty thousand men, an army big enough to conquer England. He therefore divided his force into three sub-squadrons, two of them to attack the hostile fleet, while the third, consisting of the *Culloden, Theseus, Alexander,* and *Swiftsure,* was to make hay among the helpless transports. Even if the French fleet had put up a successful resistance, it seems certain that Troubridge in the *Culloden,* and his three consorts, would have made terrible havoc of the troop-ships. "Boney," the bogyman of the English nursery, would probably have been drowned, and that to every Englishman of the period would have seemed an unmixed blessing — even from the wretched Boney's point of view, for, as Southey said:

> It would have spared him his defeat at Acre—his only disgrace; for to have been defeated by Nelson upon the seas would not have been disgraceful; it would have spared him all his after enormities . . . a romantic obscurity would have hung over the expedition to Egypt, and he would have escaped the perpetration of those crimes which have encarnadined his soul with a deeper dye than that of the purple for which he committed them — those acts of perfidy, mid-night murder, usurpation and remorseless tyranny, which have consigned his name to universal execration, now and forever.

But they did not sight the French fleet. The information obtained in Sicily was false; the French had left Malta not on the 15th, but on the 19th, and Nelson had actually overtaken and passed them on a foggy night, without knowing of their presence. The French were bearing east, in order to sight the southern coast of Crete before turning south for Alexandria. Nelson took the direct route, south-east; and consequently he arrived before them. On June 28 the Pharos of Alexandria came in sight — that most celebrated of lighthouses, once one of the seven wonders of the world, where

Cæsar and Cleopatra had dallied, now falling into decay under Turkish rule — springing suddenly out of the sea as any high building does on that flat coast, and on either side of it the two harbours, the new and the old, crowded with shipping; for Alexandria was then, as today, one of the leading ports of the Mediterranean. But among all that shipping there was not a French tricolour to be seen, as the English officers, crowding to the bulwarks, stared at it eagerly through their glasses. The only warship present was a Turkish line-of-battle ship, which was disembarking men and guns, possibly with some vague idea of resisting the anticipated French invasion, for Egypt was still nominally under Turkish rule. Nelson sent messages ashore to the English consul, only to find that he had left Alexandria three months before. The one thing certain was that the French had not arrived.

If Nelson had stuck to his theory of an Egyptian objective, and if he could have possessed his soul in patience, and just waited there for the French to arrive, we know now what must have happened. The history of the world would have been altered. But he could not stand it. He was mortified by his failure to intercept the enemy, and was beginning to think that perhaps he had been wrong after all, and that — as nearly everybody else had thought — Corfu and the Adriatic was their destination. It was at this moment that he seized his pen and dashed off his long apologia to Lord St Vincent, to which reference has already been made. "I am before your Lordship's judgment," he declares theatrically; and he shows the state of his nerves by wildly accusing the Government of Naples and Sicily of having deliberately concealed the whereabouts of the French fleet. As his friend Captain Ball very rightly remarked, it was a mistake to defend himself before he was accused. At the same time it is clear, from some of St Vincent's letters to him about this time, that there did exist an anti-Nelson faction in the Navy, headed by Admiral Sir William Parker and Sir John Orde, a faction "fraught with all manner of ill will to you," who were never tired of complaining that so young an officer had been sent

L

upon this vital mission, and would be sure to proclaim his failure now. His old friend Admiral Goodall, who had served with him under Hotham, wrote from London, "knowing my attachment to you, how often had I been questioned: 'What is your favourite hero about? The French fleet has passed under his nose!'"

Angry and disappointed, Nelson could not wait. He plunged for the Syrian coast, searched it northwards, then turned aside to Crete, which the French had just left (though he never knew it), and so back to Sicily, where this wild goose chase had begun. His nerves were wearing thin. When the Governor of Syracuse not unnaturally hesitated to supply him openly with provisions, he burst out to Hamilton, "Our treatment is scandalous for a great nation to put up with, and the King's flag is insulted at every friendly port we look at." There was still no news of the French, and he added bitterly: "It is an old saying, the Devil's children have the Devil's luck: I cannot find, or to this moment learn, beyond vague conjecture, where the French fleet are gone to." "But if they are above water," he again assures St Vincent, "I will find them out, and if possible bring them to battle." On July 25 he left Syracuse again, and on the 28th was in the Gulf of Coron, in the Peloponnese. Here, for the first time, he got definite news. The French fleet had been sighted, nearly a month ago, steering south-east from Crete. So it was Egypt after all! The luck had been dead against him, but now at last he knew where he stood. The transports would have been emptied of their soldiers by now, but there was still De Brueys and his fleet to be reckoned with. Crowding on all sail, he steered for Alexandria.

On August 1 the Pharos was in sight again. The harbours seemed fuller than before, and there was a new air of animation. As the English fleet appeared in the offing, every vessel flying the white ensign (for this was Lord St Vincent's order, though Nelson, as it happened, was a Rear-Admiral of the Blue), the officers once more turned their glasses on those crowded harbours, and "soon," says Captain Berry, in his excellent narrative of the battle of the Nile, "soon we had the satisfaction of seeing the French flags flying on board some of the ships." The *Alexander* and *Swiftsure* were sent in to reconnoitre the ports, while the main body of the squadron kept in the offing. As De Brueys was plainly not in harbour, Nelson stood along the coast to the eastwards, when almost immediately (that is, about a quarter to three in the afternoon) the *Zealous* (Captain Hood), at the eastern end of the line, signalled that she could see the French fleet at anchor in Aboukir Bay. Nelson at once recalled the *Alexander* and *Swiftsure* and made the signal to prepare for battle. They had smooth water and fair weather. He had hardly eaten or slept for many days; but now to the general surprise he ordered dinner to be prepared, and, while the ship was being got ready for action, he sat with his senior officers in the great cabin and dined at his ease. A weight seemed to be lifted from his mind. Then, as the officers rose to go to their battle stations, he said: "Before this time tomorrow I shall have gained a peerage or Westminster Abbey." It was the old war-cry of Cape St Vincent.*

The wind was at NNW. and blew what seamen call a top-gallant breeze. As the fleet steered SE. by E. for Aboukir their line was very much scattered. Captain Miller of the *Theseus,* in his narrative (really a letter to his wife), tells us that "the *Zealous* and *Goliath* were the most advanced ships next the Admiral, and a posse of us near him." Next came the *Majestic,* with the *Leander* and the *Culloden* several miles astern, the latter towing a French brig loaded with wine,† which had recently been captured. Still farther away — probably eight or nine miles — and closer inland, were the

---

* According to Parsons (*Nelsonian Reminiscences,* London, 1843) Nelson in later life fell into quite a habit of using this or some similar expression as he went into action. "Now for a monument in Westminster Abbey," he would exclaim as the first broadside was shot.

† Nelson was a great believer in wine as part of the men's dietary in hot climates. During the land fighting in Corsica in 1794 he used to say that the reason why the seamen were so much healthier than the troops was that plenty of wine was allowed to them.

Swiftsure and *Alexander,* returning from their reconnaissance.

Then Aboukir Bay opened out; and now not only the leading English, but Nelson also from his flagship, could see the French fleet as they lay at anchor, thirteen line-of-battle ships, stretching in a long, slightly convex line from one arm of the bay to the other. In the curve of the line, inshore, were a few frigates. The afternoon was now wearing on. In this brilliant, jewel-like little bay, on an August evening, everything is blue and gold; the desert sands run down to the water's edge without a trace of vegetation, either there or on the small island which now bears Nelson's name; there is no hint of any warmer colour to relieve the eye, until sunset comes, and the wonderful green afterglow, for which Egypt is famous, bathes the whole scene in its gentle light. And now, as the leading English ships, the *Goliath* and the *Zealous,* turned into the bay, the sun behind them was already falling quickly in a big red ball towards the long horizon.

So the curtain went up on the completest and most devastating of all Nelson's victories — the neatest and most perfect of his works of art. It is customary to pause here and consider the rival strengths of the two fleets, as to which there has been some controversy. The French had thirteen sail of the line, nine seventy-fours, three eightys, and one, the *Orient,* De Brueys's flagship, of a hundred and twenty guns. They had also four frigates, two of forty and two of thirty-six guns. The English had fourteen sail of the line, all of them seventy-fours except the little *Leander;* but the *Culloden* never came into action, and of frigates, as we know, Nelson had none. In the number of men engaged the French were greatly superior, even without their frigates, as also in weight of metal (for a French seventy-four carried heavier guns than an English seventy-four, and a French hundred and twenty was in mere weight of metal equal to any two ships under Nelson's command). But the French discipline was bad, and their crews half trained. For the first they had to thank their Revolution; for the second John Jervis, who, ever since his arrival in the Mediterranean, had forbidden them the use of the sea. What effect this lack of sea experience may have had upon an action which was fought while riding at anchor, it is impossible to estimate exactly, but we may note that, with characteristic slovenliness, they had failed to clear their ships for action on the larboard side, never expecting any of the English to get inshore of them; and also that, when the attacking fleet came in sight, most of their working parties who were on shore preferred to remain there, and did so, in spite of the Admiral's signals.

As to tactics, Nelson and his captains had worked it all out in advance. The simple principle of British naval tactics in those days (and it was precisely the same principle that Napoleon used on land) was to defeat a numerically superior enemy by bringing an overwhelming force to bear upon one part of his line. The method of cutting the enemy's line in half and overwhelming the windward section before the leeward section could get round to help them had been practised by Jervis and Nelson at Cape St Vincent, and with great success; and it was to be used again, even more effectively. But a fleet at anchor was a different proposition, especially when it was drawn up in such a way that there was no room to pass between any two ships in the line, and the wings were so near the shore that it was impossible to pass round and envelop either of them. This is precisely the arrangement that De Brueys thought he had made. He must have realized, if he thought the matter out, that, where a French ship had room to swing at anchor, according to the direction of the wind, there must also at the windward end of his line, be just room for an English ship to slip round without going ashore. But he never dreamed that any hostile fleet would attempt such a feat of seamanship. Moreover the western and, at this moment, the windward, end of his line, was further protected by the shoals round Nelson Island. Yet he beheld each English ship, as she entered the bay, steer unhesitatingly, and without waiting for the Admiral, for that narrow passage at the end of his line, sounding as she went. "No further signal was necessary," says Captain Berry. "The Admiral's designs were as fully known to his whole squadron as was his determination to conquer or to perish in the attempt."

Still De Brueys was undisturbed. Each English ship, he perceived, as she approached that passage must be raked fore and aft by the broadside of the leading Frenchman, and the French gunnery, whatever may be thought of their seamanship, was extremely good. The thing was impossible. They could never get round. He had his greatest strength, the *Orient* (120), the *Tonnant* (80), and the *Franklin* (80) in the centre of the line, but he did nothing to alter his dispositions. The leading English ships approached in the following order: *Goliath, Zealous, Vanguard, Theseus.* But the Admiral hove to for a moment to speak to the *Mutine,* and, says Captain Miller, "I took this opportunity to pass the Admiral to leeward, and endeavoured to obtain the honour of leading the fleet into battle, as the *Culloden,* the only ship ahead of us in the regular line, was still considerably distant; but Captain Berry hailed as we passed, and gave me the Admiral's order to become his second a-head, in consequence of which I hove to close ahead of him, and the *Orion* and the *Audacious* passed us."

The action began exactly at sunset. At 6.31 the *Goliath* came under the fire of the first two ships in the French line, the *Guerrier* (74) and the *Conquérant* (74). Without firing a shot in reply Captain Foley brought his ship, "in a very gallant and masterly manner,"* towards the enemy's line, gradually closing with their van until he was across the bows of the first ship, the *Guerrier,* which he raked with his larboard broadside, and, passing round inside the enemy line, took station abreast of the second ship, the *Conquérant,* and engaged her at close quarters. The *Zealous,* following, also raked the *Guerrier,* bringing down her foremast, and, anchoring just inshore of her, proceeded to complete the ruin which the *Goliath* had begun. The third English ship, the *Orion,*

---

* Captain Miller's narrative.

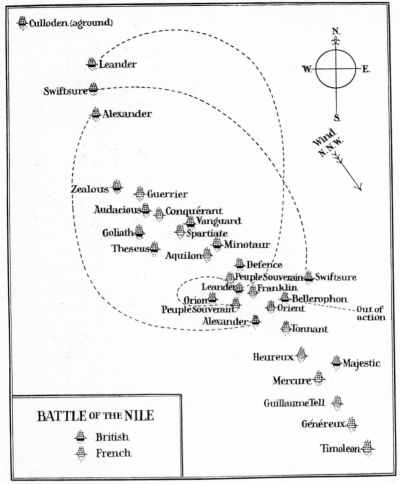

Culloden (aground)

Leander

Swiftsure

Alexander

N.
W. — E.
S.

Wind
N.N.W.

Zealous
Guerrier
Audacious   Conquérant
            Vanguard
Goliath   Spartiate
Theseus   Minotaur
    Aquilon
        Defence
    PeupleSouverain   Swiftsure
    Leander   Franklin
    Orion   Bellerophon
PeupleSouverain   Orient
    Alexander   Out of
            action
        Tonnant

        Heureux   Majestic

        Mercure

        GuillaumeTell

        Généreux

        Timoleon

BATTLE OF THE NILE

British
French

156

took a wider sweep, to avoid the others, and Captain Miller thinks she must have touched the ground, before she eventually reached a position opposite the fifth and sixth ships of the French line, the *Peuple Souverain* and the *Franklin*. On the way she poured a broadside into the *Serieuse* frigate, which lay in her way inside the French line, and the frigate drifted on to a shoal, a helpless wreck with all its masts gone. The *Audacious*, passing between the *Guerrier* and the *Conquérant*, came to close against the bows of the latter, which was already engaged in a desperate duel with the *Goliath*, while Miller, in the *Theseus*, running down upon the *Guerrier*, in the wake of the *Zealous* and *Goliath*,

> observed their shot sweep just over us, and knowing well that at such a moment Frenchmen would not have coolness enough to change their elevation, I closed them suddenly, and running under the arch of their shot, reserved my fire, every gun being loaded with two and some with three roundshot, until I had the *Guerrier's* masts in a line and her jib-boom about six feet clear of our rigging; we then opened with such effect that a second breath could not be drawn before her main and mizzen masts were also gone.

Then, passing between the *Zealous* and the *Guerrier*, and inside the *Goliath*, the *Theseus* took station opposite the *Spartiate*, the third in the French line. But "we had not been many minutes in action with the *Spartiate*, when we observed one of our ships (and soon after knew her to be the *Vanguard*) place herself so directly opposite to us on the outside of her, that I desisted firing on her, that I might not do mischief to our friends." The *Theseus*, therefore, directed her larboard broadside half at the *Conquérant*, astern, and half at the *Aquilon*, the fourth ship in the French line.

Nelson had seen five of his ships get in between the enemy and the shore. His tactics were obvious — to lead the rest down the outside and thus envelop the French van. The *Guerrier* and *Conquérant* being already practically out of action, he anchored beside the *Spartiate*, and exchanged broadside for broadside with her. The *Minotaur*, following him down, engaged the *Aquilon;* and the *Défense* anchored opposite the *Peuple Souverain.* The *Bellerophon* let go her anchor either opposite the *Franklin* (already engaged with the *Orion*) or on the starboard bow of the *Orient;* but the anchor dragged, and the *Bellerophon,* having still some way on her, came under the full force of the three-decker's broadside, which blew two of her masts out of her, wounding the captain and killing many of her crew, so that she drifted along the French line in an almost helpless condition and was not seen again until morning.

It was now almost dark, and the faint glow in the sky was obscured by the thick pall of smoke which hung over Aboukir Bay. Yet the remaining English ships, as they arrived on the scene, managed to pick out a suitable station with a certainty which does credit to the enterprise and courage of their captains. The *Majestic,* following the *Bellerophon,* missed the *Orient* and the *Tonnant,* and fell aboard the *Heureux,* the ninth French ship, and was for some held by her jib-boom, while the *Tonnant* and the *Heureux* fired into her, doing great execution. At last she got clear, and getting across the bows of the *Mercure,* the tenth French ship, she took a terrible revenge, with a raking broadside. Of the remaining English ships the *Swiftsure* and the *Alexander,* by some happy instinct, made direct for the dangerous French flagship, the *Alexander* passing inshore and engaging the *Orient* on the larboard side, while the *Swiftsure* anchored on her starboard bow, the position which the unfortunate *Bellerophon* had attempted to occupy.

Nelson had signalled to Troubridge to cast adrift his wine-cellar of a prize and follow with all speed into action, and Troubridge had done so, and crowded on all sail; but in trying to cut off a corner, as he passed the shoals round Nelson Island (and it must be remembered that there was no pilot on board the English fleet) he ran aground, and nothing that he could do would get the *Culloden* off until long after the battle was over. It nearly broke his heart. The *Leander,* waiting to offer him assistance, was somewhat delayed, but she eventually took position between the *Aquilon* and the *Peuple Souverain*. The latter, already severely battered by the *Défense* and the *Orion*, drifted helplessly away inland, while the *Leander* continued to pump broadsides into the next French ship, the *Franklin*, and, since she was athwart their line, any shot that missed the *Franklin* hit the *Orient* just beyond. The *Leander* was the last of the British ships to enter the battle, and the skill with which Captain Thompson took position was one of the decisive events of the day.

Darkness had fallen, and only that long line of stabbing lights across the bay, and the thunder of the guns, indicated to the watcher on shore the progress of the historic battle. The flashes seemed to be moving now from west to east. The first five ships in the French line had been overwhelmed. The *Guerrier* and the *Conquérant* surrendered early; but the *Spartiate* put up a gallant fight, holding out longer than the *Aquilon*, which was behind her in the line. Between the *Spartiate* and the *Vanguard* it was a battle to the death. No one else interfered. About nine o'clock the *Spartiate* was silenced, her main and mizzen masts having gone by the board, and Captain Berry sent an officer on board to take possession of her, and collect the French captain's sword, which was delivered to Nelson in his cabin. He had been wounded again. About 8 P.M., shortly before the *Spartiate* struck her colours, he was standing on the quarterdeck, looking at a map, when some missile from the French ship, probably a langridge shot, cut across his head, so that a flap of skin from his forehead fell across his eyes, blinding him. He staggered, and Captain Berry caught him in his arms. The flag captain afterwards told Lady Berry that Nelson exclaimed: "I am killed: remember me to my wife."

As usual, he thought he was dying. Yet, when they carried him down to the cockpit, he refused to allow the surgeon, Jefferson, to attend to him first. "No, I will take my turn with my brave followers." When Jefferson found time to probe the wound, he assured Nelson that there was no danger. But the pain was intense, so much so that he still seemed to have thought himself seriously hurt, for he summoned the chaplain, to whom he gave a last message to Lady Nelson, and it is further asserted by some biographers that he sent for Captain Louis of the *Minotaur* to thank him for the support which his ship had been giving to the *Vanguard,* while engaging the *Aquilon* at the same time*— as though this were his last chance of thanking anyone. When his wound was sewn up and dressed they put him in the "bread room" (a storeroom in the after part of the orlop deck) and urged him to keep still. Instead he sent for his secretary, Campbell, and forthwith began to dictate his dispatches to the Admiralty! The unfortunate Campbell, sitting there in the stifling heat of the dark, evil-smelling little storeroom, beholding his Captain apparently desperately injured, and listening to the infernal din up above and the shrieks of the wounded in the cockpit beside them, found his hand shaking so much that he was unable to write. Nelson thereupon seized the pen and himself began writing with his left hand. A strange scene!

The writing was interrupted by the arrival of Captain Berry, who came to announce that the French flagship was apparently in flames. Nelson immediately rose and, with Berry's assistance, ascended to the deck. He looked round him. What had happened to the French ships? In the darkness it was possible to distinguish the *Aquilon,* and the dismasted *Peuple Souverain.* Beyond them was a group of English and French ships, and in the midst of them a blaze of light, where the *Orient,* the French flagship, was on fire. So bright were the flames that it was easy to observe the ensigns and fix the positions of the opposing fleets. This was the climax of the battle. The crew of the *Orient,* under fire from the *Alexander, Swiftsure,* and *Leander,* were unable to control the flames, which soon spread over the whole ship. At ten o'clock the *Orient* blew up, with a "tremendous ex-

---

* Three months later there was an attempted mutiny on the *Minotaur;* but Nelson, usually quite ruthless in these matters, consented to overlook it on a petition from the loyal majority of the ship's company backed by their captain, explaining that he was only induced to do so by his remembrance of the *Minotaur's* support at the battle of the Nile.

plosion," and there ensued, says Captain Berry, an "awful pause and deathlike silence for about three minutes," when the wreck of the masts and yards, which had been carried to a vast height, fell down into the water and upon the decks of the surrounding ships.

Captain Miller on the *Theseus* was horrified to hear his ship's company raise a cheer, and endeavoured to stop them, for, as he says, the spectacle of the *Orient's* destruction was "such as formerly would have drawn tears down the victor's cheeks"; but, on reflection, this patriotic Briton found his pity "stifled as it rose by the remembrance of the numerous and horrid atrocities their unprincipled and bloodthirsty nation had and were committing." On the deck of the *Orient,* where every Frenchman had done his duty to the end, the son of the Captain, little Casabianca, remained at his post long enough to supply the subject for a sentimental English poem by Mrs Hemans. The Admiral, De Brueys, was cut nearly in half by a roundshot, shortly before the explosion occurred.

Nelson, who was still on deck, gave orders that the only boat on the *Vanguard* which had not been shot to pieces should be sent out to pick up the drowning Frenchmen. He was then, though with difficulty, persuaded to go to bed. But he continued restless, and presently got up again and signed a number of orders, such as Hardy's commission to take Berry's place on the *Vanguard,* while Berry went home with the dispatches. Then he lay down again, still in great pain.

There was a pause in the fighting. Not a shot was fired for the space of about ten minutes, and during that time it was seen that the line-of-battle ships of the French rear, many of whom had hardly been engaged, had fallen still farther away to the eastwards, so that there was a big gap in their line, which was occupied by the *Alexander,* the *Majestic,* and the *Swiftsure,* who were presently joined (on a signal from the Admiral) by the *Theseus* and the *Zealous,* who all bore down in the small hours of the morning to make an end of the French resistance. Only two out of the five line-of-battle ships at this end of the French line had been seriously engaged; yet they had made no attempt by towing, or any other means, to come to the assistance of their hard-pressed centre and van. Now, after an exchange of shots at long range, the *Guillaume Tell* and the *Généreux* stood out of the bay and escaped, accompanied by two frigates. The *Zealous* gallantly attempted to intercept them, but was recalled by a signal from the Admiral, as she could not be supported. The *Heureux* and the *Mercure* struck their flags, and the *Timoleon* went ashore and was set on fire by her crew and abandoned.

It was now broad daylight on August 2, and the battered English ships, with their canvas in shreds and many of their masts shot away, lay scattered about the bay, their crews so exhausted that they had fallen on the decks beside the guns, and were sleeping there like dead men. Of the seventeen units of the French fleet nine were prizes, four had been blown up or sunk, and four had escaped with their tails between their legs. The French fleet had ceased to exist. And the French army, with Buonaparte at its head — though it might march hither and thither across the deserts, slaughtering the Mamelukes in the shadow of the pyramids, following the trail of the children of Israel across Sinai to Jerusalem and Acre, and back again to Cairo — was as effectually put out of action, from the point of view of European politics, as if Nelson had caught and sunk every one of its transports in the Mediterranean Sea.

CHAPTER XII

FANFARE OF TRUMPETS

THE LAST shot had scarcely been fired, and the hulls of the four escaping Frenchmen were still clearly visible from the bay, when Nelson issued the following general order:

> Almighty God having blessed His Majesty's arms with victory, the Admiral intends returning public thanksgiving for the same at two o'clock this day, and he recommends every ship doing the same as soon as convenient.

Having regard to the exhausted condition of the crews, and the urgent necessity of repairing their masts and yards unless they wanted them tumbling about their ears, we may guess that this was not a particularly popular church parade.

But Nelson could not rest. He was in a condition of feverish, nervous reaction, issuing orders to his captains, arranging about sending the French wounded ashore, obtaining fresh provisions for his own wounded, and writing out his dispatches to Lord St Vincent at least three days before there was a chance of any of his battered ships being in a condition to carry them to Gibraltar. Troubridge, having at last got his unlucky ship off the shoals, was able to relieve him of much of the work. Troubridge liked this sort of thing, for he was a great "hustler." "Dear Troubridge," wrote Nelson not long afterwards, in praising their common favourite to Lord St Vincent — "Dear Troubridge, the active business and the scolding he is obliged to be continually at, does him good." But still Nelson could not or would not rest, but continued to scribble letters in his cabin or pace hurriedly up and down the quarterdeck, looking alarmingly ill, as though he might collapse at any moment.

Captain Berry, with the dispatches, left by the *Leander* on August 6. Twelve days later, off the coast of Crete, they had the misfortune to encounter the French seventy-four the *Généreux,* just escaped from Aboukir. The ships were unevenly matched, for the *Leander* carried only fifty guns, and those of a light calibre, with a crew of three hundred and twenty men against the seven hundred on board the heavily armed *Généreux.* The English line-of-battle ship, in fact, was hardly bigger than a frigate. Moreover, she had been considerably knocked about in the battle, whereas the *Généreux,* thanks to her prudent retirement, was still as fresh as paint. We can imagine the glee with which the Frenchmen seized this opportunity of getting a little of their own back. After a vigorous engagement, the *Leander* was forced to strike; Captain Thompson was severely wounded, Captain Berry too, and his dispatches were taken from him. They contained a full account of the victory, and cannot have made very pleasant reading for Berry's captors. He and the other English officers were brutally treated, and even robbed of their clothes; but eventually Berry was exchanged, and reached England in the following December.

The shouts and antics of joy of the little groups of mounted Mamelukes and Egyptian peasants, who, on the morning of August 2, attracted by the sound of firing, had assembled on the shores of Aboukir Bay, and there beheld the ruin that had been made of the fleet of their invader — these shouts and antics were but a prelude to a wave of hysterical enthusiasm which swept through those Mediterranean lands which had long been cowering under the menace of Buonaparte's irresistible armies. Nelson had tied him down to Egypt, and there might he stay; Nelson had left Captain Hood to blockade the Egyptian ports, so that his army might starve; Nelson had captured all his dispatches; Nelson had written a long letter to the Governor of Bombay, telling him what had happened, and warning him to be on the look-out lest Buonaparte should attempt to get in touch with Tippoo Sahib via the Red Sea. Nelson had lifted a nightmare from their minds — and done it with such dash and gallantry, with such a sunny disregard for the old rules about never attacking a fleet anchored in harbour, and with such a dramatic and ruthless completeness as could not be equalled in the whole history of naval warfare — so that their hearts warmed towards him. It was Captain Capel, now in command of the *Mutine* (Hardy having been transferred to the *Vanguard,* in Berry's place) who brought the good news to Naples. Nelson had very wisely had a copy made of the document sent with Berry, and Capel was to take this overland, through Italy and Germany, and deliver it direct to the Admiralty in London. Our old friend Midshipman Hoste, now a lieutenant, was also on board, and was to take command when Capel landed.

Thus it happened that Naples was the first to hear the news. Naples promptly went mad with joy. The Hamiltons led the way, even the dignified Sir William quite shaken out of his usual calm. As for his wife, she fainted on hearing of the victory. Faints are out of fashion nowadays, but this seems to have been a genuine one, for she fell so heavily that when Nelson reached Naples a month later she was still suffering from bruises! Later she paraded the streets with a bandeau on her head, inscribed with the words: "Nelson and Victory." Hoste has left us a short account of the scene as he and Capel passed through the streets. Shouts of "Viva Nelson!" resounded on every side. "You can have no idea of the rejoicings," he says, "bonfires and illuminations all over the town."

Presently the two young officers met Lady Hamilton (they had been formally presented to her earlier in the day), and she would not be satisfied till she had them into the carriage with her and so continued her drive, the mob crowding round them cheering, Emma very much in her element, the two English officers rather stiff and shy, and Hoste, that "charming good boy," undoubtedly covered with blushes. In the evening she and Sir William took them to the opera, where was more enthusiasm, and a noticeable absence of French cockades (though it was here that the supporters of France had been wont to congregate). The Neapolitan Jacobins seem to have belonged to the middle or upper classes: the *lazzaroni* were as loyal, and as ecstatic at the news of victory, as the Queen herself. Of the latter Lady Hamilton wrote to Nelson:

> How shall I describe the transports of the Queen! 'Tis not possible, she cried, kissed her husband, her children, walked frantic about the room, cried, kissed and embraced every person near her, exclaiming O brave Nelson! O God bless and protect our brave deliverer! O Nelson, Nelson! What do we not owe you! O Victor! Saviour of Italy! O that my swollen heart could now tell him personally what we owe to him.

Nelson quotes all this in a letter to Fanny; but even he, with all his appetite for flattery, adds drily that he hopes these transports will have subsided before he himself reaches Naples.

Meanwhile Capel had got to London, and on the day after he arrived, October 3, the city voted two hundred guineas and a sword of honour to Nelson. Special prayers of thanksgiving were read in every church in the country on the following Sunday; and when the Houses of Parliament met on November 20, there was a handsome reference to the victory in the King's Speech, votes of thanks were passed, and Nelson was voted a pension of £2000 a year, and was raised to the peerage with the title Baron Nelson of the Nile. Jervis, it will be remembered, had been given an earldom for St Vincent, a far less crushing victory; but it was explained that it was impossible to go higher than a barony for Nelson, because he was not the senior Admiral in the Mediterranean — a poor excuse. A gold medal was struck for him and for every one of his captains; the Sultan of Turkey sent him a diamond aigrette (the famous *chelengk* valued at £18,000), together with a purse of two thousand sequins to be distributed among the British wounded; the Tsar presented him with his portrait set in diamonds; the King of Naples sent a sword of honour, the King of Sardinia a diamond-encrusted box, the Turkey Company a piece of plate, and the East India Company

£10,000. There were congratulations from Hood, St Vincent, the Duke of Clarence.

But what he probably valued most of all was a letter from Lord Howe, for whom he had always felt so much admiration. He had probably never spoken to the veteran since that visit to the Admiralty in 1784, when he was just back from St Omer, and was trying to get another ship. Howe now wrote, trusting that he would "forgive the additional trouble of my compliments on this singular occasion, not less remarkable for the skill than the cool judgment testified under the considerable disadvantages in the superior force and situation of the enemy, which you had to surmount." Nelson in reply, after suitably acknowledging the honour of such a flattering letter from "the first and greatest sea officer the world has ever produced," went on to pay this correspondent the very real compliment of giving him a brief outline of his tactics. There are many points of interest in these few sentences. He wrote:

I had the happiness to command a band of brothers; therefore, night was to my advantage. Each knew his duty, and I was sure each would feel for a French ship. By attacking the enemy's van and centre, the wind blowing directly along their line, I was enabled to throw what force I pleased on a few ships. This plan my friends readily conceived by the signals (for which we are principally, if not entirely, indebted to your Lordship) and we always kept a superior force to the enemy. At twenty-eight minutes past six, the sun in the horizon, the firing commenced. At five minutes past ten, when *L'Orient* blew up, having burnt seventy minutes, the six van ships surrendered. I then pressed further towards the rear; and had it pleased God that I had not been wounded and stone blind, there cannot be a doubt but that every ship would have been in our possession. But here let it not be supposed that any officer was to blame. No: on my honour I am satisfied each did his very best. I have never before, my Lord, detailed the action to anyone; but I should have thought it wrong to have kept it from one who is our great master in naval tactics and bravery.*

---

* As a matter of fact, the greatest naval tactician, in Nelson's opinion, was not Howe, but Hood, to whom he owed — so far as he owed anything to anyone — the ideas behind his own masterly tactics. Howe he thought pre-eminent in "the management of a fleet"— which is not the same thing.

M

One curious gift remains to be recorded. After the battle the *Swiftsure* had picked up the mainmast of the *Orient* which was floating in the bay; and Halliwell, her captain, with a strange twist of humour, had a coffin made out of it and presented it to Nelson, so that "when you have finished your military career in this world you may be buried in one of your trophies." Nelson was thoroughly pleased, and for a long time kept the coffin propped up beside his dining-room table.

All this meant a heavy burden of correspondence for Nelson, who, it must be remembered, had only learned to write with his left hand twelve months before. And, as usual, he was going out of his way to help people — writing to the Admiralty, for instance, begging for a cadetship for the son of an officer of marines who was killed in the battle. He should really have been in bed. Every letter he wrote was a terrible nervous strain. "My brain is so shook with the wounds in my head," he wrote to the Governor of Bombay, "that I am sensible I am not always so clear as could be wished." "My head is ready to split," he complained to Jervis, adding that he was continually vomiting. On top of this came a recurrence of his old enemy malaria. On the day that Hoste and Capel left him "I was taken with a fever which has very near done my business; for eighteen hours my life was thought to be past hope; I am now up, but very weak both in body and mind, from my cough and this fever." There was nothing unusual in an attack of fever at that time of year in a semi-tropical climate; but Nelson was in no condition to resist it. He even thought of throwing up the sponge and going home, but happily changed his mind. His wound had healed, leaving an ugly scar across his forehead; so he brushed his hair forward (as some of the portraits show) to hide it. But nothing could hide his emaciated appearance and the signs of the cruel strain he had undergone.

He had got his frigates now — they had been trailing after him while he trailed after the French, like a game of "follow-my-leader." And the most damaged of the English ships, the

Vanguard, the *Culloden,* and the *Alexander,* had been so far repaired that they could put to sea for a week or two (that is, long enough to reach a friendly port) if the weather held. He thought of Naples. It was the nearest large port with the necessary facilities for refitting. He did not want to go there. Certainly, he had no sentimental thought about it. Indeed he wrote: "I detest this voyage to Naples; nothing but absolute necessity could force me to the measure." He left Hood with the *Zealous, Goliath, Swiftsure,* and a good supply of frigates to blockade the Egyptian coast. Buonaparte's army, he said, was "in a scrape" for lack of food, and he proposed to keep it so. He sent Saumarez with a small squadron and six of his prizes to join Lord St Vincent. Three prizes, the *Guerrier,* the *Heureux,* and the *Mercure,* he burned, as not being worth the time and cost of refitting, and then wrote to the Admiralty, demanding their value in prize money for the fleet. The Admiralty agreed, though the First Lord did venture to point out that "the case is one for which there has never yet been any precedent." And having settled all that, he set sail for Naples.

At Naples they had been warned of his coming. The town was *en fête.* A sort of pageant of boats had been arranged. The Hamiltons were to go in one decorated barge, the King in another, and the Queen in another (though for some reason or other she failed to arrive), and all the loyal population of Naples was to follow them in a long flotilla. The boats pulled out across the bay, and, as they did so, they saw the leading ships of the fleet of Aboukir rounding the promontory in the sunlight. The scene that followed is best described in Nelson's own words. Writing to his wife, he tells her how he saw the boats approaching, with their flags and banners flying, portraits of himself held aloft, and heard the cheers of the people coming clear across the water. He admitted that he found it "terribly affecting." The Hamilton's barge came alongside, and "up flew her Ladyship, and exclaiming: 'O God is it possible?' she fell into my arm more dead than alive."

Again, there seems to be no reason to doubt the genuineness

of the faint; for Nelson's appearance had altered shockingly since she had first seen him, and had perhaps begun to think of him as her hero. One arm and one eye had gone, the hair brushed over his forehead scarcely concealed his latest scar; and he was thin and haggard and obviously on the verge of a collapse. A cooler woman than Lady Hamilton might have fainted; and it must be remembered that this was a highly emotional scene. "However," says Nelson, "tears soon set matters to rights." Some one escorted the beautiful, tearful lady to the cabin, where refreshments had been prepared.

Meantime, the King's barge had also come alongside. Stepping on deck, Ferdinand advanced to Nelson, and, seizing him by his only remaining hand, greeted him, in that loud, harsh voice of his, as "my deliverer and preserver!" From the boats all round rose cries of "Nostro liberatore!" as their occupants strove to be first up the gangway. "My greeting from the lower classes," says Nelson, "was truly affecting." The King insisted upon seeing all over the ship, and then departed, scattering congratulations. Down in the cabin, where refreshments were being taken, there was a pretty scene, which has been preserved for posterity by a Miss Knight, who was among the English visitors. A little bird was seen to hop across the table, and land familiarly on Nelson's shoulder. Questioned about it, he said that the bird had joined the ship the day before the battle of the Nile, and he added that it was a curious coincidence but this was not the first time it had happened; before several of his engagements a small bird had suddenly appeared and taken up its quarters in his cabin. Lady Knight, Miss Knight's mother, ventured to ask the Admiral whether August 1, the date of Aboukir, was not the happiest day in his life. "No, Madam," he answered firmly, "the happiest was that on which I married Lady Nelson."

There followed a mad round of gaiety ashore. He was received by the King and Queen, and there were bonfires and illuminations in his honour every night. His birthday coming round, Sir William Hamilton entertained him at a ball and supper which was estimated to have cost two thousand ducats. The plate, specially made for the occasion, bore the initials "H.N.", and from one of Nelson's letters it would appear that even the buttons worn by the guests were similarly inscribed. He was so popular with the common people that he found it impossible to walk or even drive in the streets. All this must have been terribly tiring to a man in his state of health, however soothing to his pride. But the Hamiltons were looking after him. Sir William had weeks ago written to Nelson — indeed as soon as he heard of his latest injury — "a pleasant apartment is ready for you in my house, and Emma is looking out for the softest pillows to repose the few wearied limbs you have left." And there, when he had no public engagements, he reclined at his ease, looking out over the Bay of Naples, and tended by one of the most beautiful women of her time, under whose spell he was insensibly falling. "I hope some day to have the pleasure of introducing you to Lady Hamilton," he wrote to Fanny. "She is one of the very best women in this world; she is an honour to her sex."

What precisely was the relationship between these two people at that moment can never now be explained. In its more obvious aspects it is clear enough. Somewhere about this time — though one or two biographers put it much later — Nelson must have become Emma's lover. That he did not do so without a mental struggle may be taken for granted; and the elaborate pretence of a purely Platonic friendship which he kept up (whenever he could remember it) during the rest of his life no doubt represents the measure of his reluctance to make a cuckold of his friend and hurt the feelings of a wife for whom he felt real affection and respect. Sir William, though in his old age he did petulantly complain that Nelson monopolized Emma, always adopted this comfortable theory. Even Nelson kept fiercely assuring himself that his love for Emma did no harm to anyone. He was always so frank about his admiration for her — as though there

were no more than that in it. For instance, he writes from
Naples to old Lord St Vincent, now well on his way to the
seventies:

> I am writing opposite Lady Hamilton, therefore you will not
> be surprised at the glorious jumble of this letter. Were your
> Lordship in my place, I much doubt if you could write so well;
> our hearts and our hands must be all in a flutter. Naples is a
> dangerous place and we must keep clear of it.

No one who has not been through the strain of months
and months of active service, without sight or touch of woman,
been wounded and broken in battle, suffered the awful reaction that follows victory, and at last come back to a triumph
— "the softest pillows," and a face bending over you that the
greatest artists in the world were dreaming of — no one who
has not been through such an experience has the right to
blame him. Here in Naples, on the fringe of that sea so often
swept by sudden and violent storms, these two also were swept
by a great and violent emotion that bound them together for
the rest of their lives. Later on things would settle back, as
the sea does after a tempest, and the waves and winds subside.
But who can doubt that at first, when they discovered their
mutual love, they lived in an enchanted land, where they two
seemed the only living creatures, and all the rest mere
shadows? The love of Nelson and Emma Hamilton, by one
of the ironies of history, was left to be recorded by Victorian
biographers who either could not understand it, or would not
permit themselves to speak the truth. To them it was always
a "guilty" love. But to this generation, whose experience of
life has been so much more like the experience of Nelson's
generation, it is plain that the love of these two people was a
great and beautiful thing, dignifying them both by its depth
and strength.

About this time, Nelson's letters to Fanny almost ceased.
Poor Fanny, poor shadow! No doubt she worried about it.
Her friends at Roundwood would ask her for details of
Nelson's latest victory, knowing how regularly he had always

LADY HAMILTON AT THE SPINNING-WHEEL
Romney
Photo W. F. Mansell

written to her, and she would have to confess that she had not heard. But nor had the relations at Burnham Thorpe; and it is fair to add that Nelson, in one of the few letters his brother received from him at this time, complained that he had not heard from Burnham Thorpe for weeks and only once from Roundwood. The posts were very irregular. Though Lady Nelson felt uneasy, there is no evidence that she ever suspected the truth. In December, some weeks after Nelson had left Naples, she got a letter from Lady Hamilton — a typical, indiscreet, hurried scrawl. "Lord Nelson's wound is quite well," wrote Emma, "he was not well when first he arrived, but by nursing and asses' milk he went from Naples quite recovered." Then, with a woman's instinct she proceeds to praise Josiah, saying how much he is improved (that seems to be the highest praise he ever gets from anyone) and adding, "although we quarrel sometimes he loves me, and does as I would have him." She concludes with a characteristic reference to the British Government's action in rewarding Nelson with a mere barony — "hang them, I say!" There was always a touch of Drury Lane about Emma.

On the other hand, there was rather less than her usual honesty here, for Harrison, who presumably got it from her, asserts that Josiah became disgracefully drunk at Nelson's birthday party, and had to be led away by Troubridge and another officer. The estrangement between Nelson and Josiah dates from this time. How far it was due to this alleged drunken scene, which rests only on the authority of Lady Hamilton, and how far to the boy's dawning suspicion as to the kind of relations that existed between his stepfather and the beautiful lady who was always so nice to him, it is impossible to say. But Nelson ever after expressed himself as "disappointed" in Josiah. It must be admitted that, quite apart from any personal difficulties between the two, Josiah was not a man of mark.

The fleet remained at Naples until October 15. In a letter to Lord Spencer Nelson admits that "three weeks is a long time to refit a fleet after a battle," but draws attention to the battered condition of the ships, and the heavy swell in the Bay of Naples, which made it difficult to work aloft. The ill-natured may think of another reason. However, on October 15, he set sail in the *Vanguard,* with the *Minotaur, Audacious, Goliath,* and *Mutine* brig in company. The business in hand was the recapture of Malta, which Buonaparte had snapped up on his way out East. Nelson put Captain Ball of the *Alexander* in charge of the squadron which was to blockade the island, and himself returned to Naples, from whence he sent Lord Spencer a very frank account of the political situation. He had come to the conclusion that the Neapolitans were "a nation of poets and fiddlers, whores and scoundrels." He no longer trusted them an inch. But he was invited to attend the councils of state (a curious proceeding when Naples was still supposed to be neutral), and there he soon found that he could do what he liked with them. His plain, nervous speech and his dynamic personality were altogether too much for the Neapolitan King and his odd collection of ministers — old Acton, the tall, scraggy Scottish-Italian, "Cardinal" Ruffo, the leader of irregulars, and Caracciolo, the smooth-tongued Admiral. He wrote to St Vincent: "I have scolded; anger is necessary; his Excellency [Sir William Hamilton] is too good to them, and the strong language of an English Admiral telling them plain truths may do good."

It did so much good that Naples was presently induced to declare war upon France, although the Emperor had made it clear to Ferdinand that Austria was not ready to co-operate. Numerically the Neapolitans were greatly superior to the French forces opposed to them. They had "thirty thousand healthy looking troops" under arms, and more to come. Mack, the Austrian general who commanded them, described them as *"la plus belle armée d'Europe,"* and Nelson, when he spurred the King's ministers into war, was bound to take Mack's word for it. The French retired before Mack's advance, and he occupied Rome without resistance. Nelson, for his part, put out from the bay and went north and captured

Leghorn, thus interrupting the enemies' supplies. But alas! — no sooner did Mack's "beautiful army" find itself committed to a battle with the French, who had turned at bay, than the greater part of it faded away into the surrounding countryside, and Mack, with a small remnant, was obliged to make an undignified bolt southward. It afterwards appeared that the ranks were full of traitors; some of the principal regiments had actually been raised by a French artillery officer.

Nelson hurried back to Naples. There he soon heard that the enemy had crossed the frontier and were advancing unopposed on the capital. It became apparent that the King and his Court would have to fly to Sicily, with the assistance of the English fleet, if they wished to avoid capture. But the situation was exceedingly delicate. The *lazzaroni* of Naples, as already indicated, were fanatically loyal to the throne, and no sooner did they realize the true state of affairs than they began to hold demonstrations outside the palace, calling upon the King to remain at his post and lead them against the invaders. Such a course of action would have been suicidal, and the King, who had the greatest tenderness for his own skin, had no intention of adopting it, whatever might happen to the *lazzaroni*.

But he dared not say so. He and his wife — or rather his wife and he, for she was the leading spirit — began to plan their escape secretly. Lady Hamilton was the intermediary; she got in touch with Nelson, and arranged for all the luggage from the palace, including many boxes of gold and jewellery, to be consigned to her, and afterwards transported by night to the *Vanguard* out in the harbour. She had so long been in the habit of corresponding privately with the Queen, that no one thought anything of the messages that were constantly going to and fro. And as Nelson pointed out at the time, and always insisted upon afterwards, it would have been impossible for Sir William Hamilton or himself to have appeared in the matter. Lady Hamilton's assistance was extremely valuable.

In later life she was wont to assert that all the arrangements were left in her hands, and that, but for her, the royal family could never have got clear away. But by that time also she believed — and Nelson too had somehow come to believe — that she had rendered all sorts of valuable services to her country: for instance, that, but for a letter which she had obtained from the Queen, the English fleet, on the last lap of its race after the French before Aboukir, would not have been allowed to water at Syracuse. Nelson, in the famous codicil to his will, wrote that his fleet "could never have returned the second time to Egypt, had not Lady Hamilton's influence with the Queen of Naples caused letters to be wrote to the Governor of Syracuse that he was to encourage the fleet being supplied with everything should they put in to any port in Sicily." He added: "We put into Syracuse, and received every supply, went to Egypt and destroyed the French fleet."

But it is well known that Nelson, in this codicil, was commending Lady Hamilton to the nation — he was making out a case for her — and Lady Hamilton's own story of this "talisman" letter formed part of a statement of her services which she drew up and presented to the Regent after Nelson's death, with the object of obtaining financial assistance. All the other evidence tends to show that her "talisman" was not so important as she thought, and as Nelson came to think. His own letters, written from Syracuse during that visit, though in one of them he thanks the two Hamiltons for their help, suggest that what chiefly influenced the Governor was a shrewd perception of what his own Government would really like him to do, coupled with a wholesome fear of the British guns. Politics, as a matter of fact, were not Emma's natural field of action. If they had been, she would never have attracted Nelson.

And so, though Lady Hamilton's assistance was of the greatest value, we must not assume that the royal family could not have escaped from Naples in December 1798 without her. For about a week beforehand the portmanteaux and boxes had been arriving surreptitiously at the British Embassy, and were being carted down to the boats, where the English sailors, with their dry humour, and their unconcealed insular contempt for this "dago" King, were waiting to take them off to the *Vanguard*. No one knows what was the extent of the treasure which the King took with him; it has been the subject of fantastic rumours. Nelson guessed that it was worth two and a half million sterling. The only thing certain is that he had enough to live on in luxury at Palermo for many months. As for Sir William Hamilton, he had to abandon his furniture, for to have removed it would have been too obvious, but he packed up his valuable collection of Greek vases and other objects of artistic and antiquarian interest, and sent them home on H.M.S. *Colossus*. The *Colossus* was unfortunately wrecked, but about two-thirds of the collection was rescued, and taken to London, where most of the vases found a resting-place in the British Museum.

It may be noted, incidentally, that Hamilton's intelligence as a collector was as remarkable as his stupidity in affairs of the heart. He was the purchaser of the famous Portland Vase. He was the first Englishman to appreciate the intrinsic beauty of Greek vases; but he thought that their chief value was as models for modern manufacturers, and much of Wedgwood's most successful work was based upon copies from the Hamilton collection. He made a special study of Vesuvius in all stages of eruption, employing an artist to make sketches, and ascending to the crater himself more than twenty times. He allowed £100 a year to Father Antonio Piaggi (the monk who was working on the Herculaneum papyri) to supply him with weekly reports. He was much more interested in these matters than he ever was in politics, and, having got his precious collection away on the *Colossus,* he seems to have left all the other arrangements to his wife.

She had arranged for the royal family to reach the shore, where Nelson would be waiting with the boats, by means of a subterranean passage from the palace. The King was hesitating to move. Every day the atmosphere got worse. The mob was out of hand, and people suspected of Jacobin sympathies were chased through the streets and killed. One corpse was dragged by the heels to the palace gates, and displayed under the King's windows. December 20 had been agreed upon with Nelson as the date of the flight. At the last moment the King postponed it for another twenty-four hours. Lady Hamilton was due at a party given by Kelim Effendi, the Turkish envoy, on the evening of the 21st. To have stayed away would have aroused suspicion. She went to the party but, when the gaiety was at its height, she slipped away through a back door, and, leaving her carriage and servants waiting among those of the other guests, and drawing a thick veil over her pretty face, she hurried through the streets to the palace, and was soon escorting the King and Queen to the beach, where Nelson's boats were waiting for them. Nelson himself accompanied the royal party, and by 9 P.M. had them all on board the *Vanguard*.

There followed the usual anticlimax, which is the mark of the true story. They had to remain for two dreary nights and days at anchor in the bay, while the English residents and prominent Neapolitan royalists (who could not be notified before, owing to the secrecy of the proceedings) were embarked with their goods. There were about two thousand fugitives in all. On December 23, the squadron, led by the *Vanguard*, with the *Archimedes*, a Neapolitan seventy-four, and the *Samnite*, a corvette commanded by Francesco Caracciolo, put out to sea, followed by the merchant ships and transports, carrying the main body of the refugees. It was a fine night at first, but just as they had cleared the island of Capri the wind suddenly chopped from east to west, and was soon blowing a gale. Rain fell in torrents, and at 1.30 a violent squall tore most of the *Vanguard's* sails to ribbons. In a letter to Lord St Vincent Nelson says that it blew harder than he had ever known it all the time he had been at sea.

The royal party were in the great cabin, for Nelson and his officers had given up their quarters to them. They were prostrate with fear and sea-sickness. But Lady Hamilton was a good sailor (a great accomplishment this in a pretty woman), and she now rose nobly to the occasion. Taking in her arms the younger of the royal children, she soothed them with kisses and put them to bed. Next she attended to the Queen, who lay like one dead, upon a bed firmly screwed to the floor in the centre of the cabin. After that, Sir William — who could not be found for some time, but was eventually discovered in his cabin with a loaded pistol in each hand, having, as he told her, determined that when the ship sank he would blow out his brains rather than endure death by drowning with the "guggle-guggle-guggle of the salt water in his throat." In fact no landlubber on board was of the slightest use except Lady Hamilton, and it may be guessed that it was during this unpleasant voyage that she laid the foundation of her extraordinary popularity with every officer and man in Nelson's fleet.

On the morning of Christmas Day, just as the storm was abating, the youngest of the royal children, little Prince Albert, aged seven, was taken really ill. The nature of his complaint is a little difficult to discover, but it was accentuated by seasickness. He died in Lady Hamilton's arms. On the following morning, at five o'clock, the fleet anchored off Palermo, and the royal party went ashore with the Hamiltons, where, in spite of their dejection after this terrible voyage, they could not fail to be cheered by the enthusiastic welcome which they received. Their people were loyal to the core. Only the gross incompetence and corruption of the Court had made it possible for the French to win such an easy victory.

As Nelson had long ago perceived, the revolutionist movement in Naples and Sicily was not a popular uprising, but an agitation engineered by a few disgruntled aristocrats. It was only a question of time before the Neapolitans, lazy and unwarlike as they were, would turn upon the French invaders and throw them out. Meantime the French had occupied Naples, and, while scattering high-sounding pamphlets about the equality of man and the wickedness of the upper classes, had made a bloody massacre among the loyal *lazzaroni* who attempted to oppose their progress. They were now busy confiscating the estates of all who adhered to King Ferdinand. And among those officers who applied to him for leave to go back to Naples to arrange some accommodation with the invaders in regard to their property was the Admiral, Prince Francesco Caracciolo.

The King took up his residence at the royal palace at Palermo, and Nelson went ashore and lived with the Hamiltons in the house which they had hired.

CHAPTER XIII

MARKING TIME

WE NOW enter on a period during which Nelson is often accused of having relapsed into a slothful life of ease and luxury, under the influence of his Delilah. Undoubtedly there were gay doings ashore at Palermo. The King, as we have seen, had taken care to leave Naples with well-filled pockets. He had been bitterly disappointed at the failure of his army, and showed his disgust by deposing the Queen from her position as his chief adviser on foreign politics and taking control into his own hands. But he still found plenty of time for gaiety; while the Queen and Lady Hamilton, being less occupied with politics, entered with zest into the social life of the exiled Court.

Of the many gossip-writers who have left records of this period of Nelson's career the most entertaining, though by no means the most reliable, is a certain Lieutenant Parsons,* who was a midshipman at the time on the *Foudroyant,* Nelson's new flagship. He describes, amusingly enough, the scene in the midshipmen's mess, when, the officers being asked to yet another party on shore, a desperate search for clean linen would take place, accompanied by much chaff and horse-play. He tells of a ball given in Nelson's honour, and of an extraordinary scene in the "illuminated garden" of the palace, when a statue of the English Admiral was unveiled. The warm-hearted Nelson, according to Parsons, was so much moved that he had to use his handkerchief; and the irreverent middy did the same — to stifle his laughter! Another great

---

* G. S. Parsons, *Nelsonian Reminiscences* (London, 1843).

occasion was the marriage of the Minister, old Acton, to his own niece — according to Parsons a child of twelve! He says that Lady Hamilton was immensely popular in the fleet, and often interceded with the Admiral to save men from punishment, so that what with this and Nelson's "known aversion to flogging," the "Jacks" had an easy time. The midshipmen, on the other hand, were often in trouble on shore, thanks to their irrepressible spirits and their healthy contempt for the young men of Palermo, and were punished by being refused shore leave.

But it is only necessary to glance at the volume of Nelson's correspondence at this time to realize that, though he may have been enjoying himself, he was very far from idle. Affairs in Naples needed careful watching. The French occupation had been accepted sullenly, but the people only required a little encouragement to rise against the invader. In the interior of the country guerrilla bands were out. Nelson was trying to do so many things at once with his squadron that it was not until March 1799 that sufficient force was collected, under Troubridge, to blockade Naples. Troubridge took possession of the islands off the coast, and found the inhabitants "perfectly mad with joy, and asking for their beloved monarch." Ruffo was making head against the French, and Castellamare and Salerno were recovered for the King.

But at this critical moment the blockade of Naples had to be abandoned, on receipt of news from Lord St Vincent that the French fleet had escaped from Brest, where they were blockaded, and had passed through the straits of Gibraltar and were sailing east. Nelson at once called in his ships, giving up the blockade of Malta and leaving only a frigate to watch Naples, and took station off Maritimo at the westernmost point of Sicily, so as to cover Palermo. He had a small Portuguese squadron with him, and in actual numbers was not greatly inferior to the Brest fleet, under Admiral Bruix; but he placed no reliance on the Portuguese, and awaited further news of the French with some anxiety. It was at this juncture that Lord Keith was sent out to succeed Lord St Vin-

cent — a change which did not please Nelson. At the same
time he was irritated by the presence in the eastern Mediterranean of the gallant but bumptious Sir Sidney Smith, who
always got on his nerves and was now ruffling it in Egyptian
waters with some vaguely worded commission from the Admiralty which practically amounted to an independent command. And it was annoying about Naples. But Keith followed Bruix so closely that the latter was forced to bolt for
safety into Toulon, without having accomplished anything.

Nelson returned to Palermo, and in June he sailed for the
Bay of Naples, taking with him Sir William and Lady Hamilton to act as interpreters between him and Ruffo, who was
commanding the loyal forces on shore. As he entered the
bay he was disgusted to hear that Ruffo had just signed a
treaty with the French garrisons in the forts, none of which
had any hope of holding out much longer. He at once repudi-
ated the arrangement. Ruffo came on board, and there was a
stormy scene between the two men in the presence of the
Hamiltons, but Nelson, as usual, stuck to his guns (and it
may be added here that when the King arrived a little later,
he entirely agreed with him). Ruffo had no authority to
conclude such a treaty. The crux of the whole matter, of
course, was not the fate of the Frenchmen in the garrisons,
but of the Neapolitan traitors who were serving with them,
and would have been shipped with them to France by Ruffo's
treaty. Among these was Prince Caracciolo, and it was his
subsequent execution, after a court-martial, which has aroused
more bitter and prolonged controversy than any other incident
in Nelson's career. More ink has already been spilled than
the subject deserves, but it is necessary to glance briefly at the
facts.

In 1799 in every European country except France, the feeling against Jacobins of all sorts, and especially against the
home-made article, was something for which we have no
modern equivalent — unless, possibly, the feeling of a White
Russian against the Bolshevists. The Neapolitans were a
loyal people, and in their case the horror with which the
N

whole world had read of the excesses of the Parisian mob was accentuated by the fact that their King was a Bourbon and that the unfortunate Marie-Antoinette was a sister of their Queen. The behaviour of the French in Naples had fully confirmed their worst anticipations; and their rage can be imagined when they saw members of their own upper classes and many officers in the King's army going over to the invader. They were now crying out for vengeance, and it may be said at once that, when Ferdinand got back to the capital, he did not fail to satisfy their thirst for blood. In these sentiments the English officers of Nelson's squadron fully shared. Jacobins to them seemed hardly human. We know Nelson's extravagant hatred of everything French. When Troubridge was in command off Naples, some one on shore sent him as a present a Jacobin's head, and Troubridge, so far from being indignant, wrote flippantly to Nelson about this "jolly fellow" in his cabin. Whenever Troubridge captured a Neapolitan rebel he handed him over to the civil arm for punishment without mercy or hesitation; he even declared that until eight or ten of them had been hanged there could be no real progress. He himself tore the epaulettes from one traitor's shoulders, and the cockade from his hat, and threw them overboard, before sending him to a court-martial. But even he drew the line when the local magistrates applied to him for a hangman from among his crew. "I positively refused," he says.

It was in these circumstances that the famous scene of Caracciolo's execution took place in Naples Bay. After his return to Naples, as recorded above, on the pretence of looking after his estates, Caracciolo had immediately joined the French, and had been put in command of their few ships of war. The English officers who knew him well (he had served with Nelson under Hotham) at first thought he might be acting under compulsion, but it soon became apparent that he was one of the leading spirits on the Republican side. Troubridge had written to Nelson months before that he was at Castellamare inspiring the Jacobins to resist. Now when Caracciolo saw

that, by Nelson's intervention, the fort in which he was serving would presently have to surrender to the King's mercy,
he escaped and fled into the country in disguise. But he was
recognized and arrested by two peasants, who brought him
bound to the seashore on the morning of June 29. From
thence he was conveyed on board the *Foudroyant*.

When Nelson heard of this he sent a message over to the
Neapolitan frigate *Minerva* which lay near him in the bay,
requesting her commander, Count Thurn, to assemble a court-
martial of Neapolitan officers without delay. It should be
added that Nelson held King Ferdinand's commission as
Commander-in-Chief of the Neapolitan navy. At noon the
members of the court-martial assembled on board the flagship,
and Caracciolo was brought before them. A sturdily built
man of forty-seven, he held his head up and answered de-
fiantly. It has been suggested that Count Thurn had a personal grudge against him, but there seems to be no scrap of
evidence for this. It did not take long to find the prisoner
guilty, and, in the usual brisk way of settling such matters in
those days, Caracciolo would have been hanged about three
o'clock. Nelson, however, extended the time to five, and at
that hour precisely the body of the unfortunate Admiral
dangled from the *Minerva's* yard-arm.

At that moment Nelson was having dinner in his cabin
with the Hamiltons. He has been violently denounced for
this, and it is possible that some people, in the circumstances,
might have preferred to change their dinner hour. But knowing what we do of Nelson's views about treason and mutiny,
we may guess that he even found his appetite unimpaired.

These are the plain facts. The more picturesque and pa-
thetic version, favoured by Southey, Parsons, and others, begins by making Nelson go back on a treaty already in force,
so that the enemy were betrayed and at his mercy; it then
transforms Caracciolo into a bent and grey-haired old man of
seventy-four, who, after a lifetime spent in his King's service,
reluctantly felt himself compelled by his Liberal principles to
transfer his allegiance to the other side; it turns the court-

martial into a group of the Admiral's personal enemies, ille-
gally summoned to form a court; it suggests that the execution
was carried out with indecent and unprecedented speed; and
it makes Nelson and Lady Hamilton, after a hearty dinner,
get into a boat and row round the bay "to have another look
at poor Caracciolo." As a last grim touch (for which there
seems to be rather better authority) the body of the Admiral
is made to bob up in the water beside the *Foudroyant* three or
four days later, and remain there, a dreadful, accusing figure,
with its "white hair" floating on the waves.

All this time Ruffo sulked in his tent; so Troubridge was
sent ashore with a force of mixed seamen, to reduce St Elmo,
the only fort which had not already surrendered. Later he
marched twenty miles inland with his men, and laid siege to
Capua — a strange occupation for seamen, but it got Troubridge a baronetcy. But now that troublesome French fleet
from Brest once more intervened. They had broken out from
Toulon, and Lord Keith was afraid that they might attack
Minorca. He sent an urgent order to Nelson to dispatch reinforcements to that end of the Mediterranean.

Nelson was in a difficulty. He himself felt every bit as
jumpy about Sicily as Lord Keith did about Minorca. Before this order arrived he had already written to Lord Spencer,
pointing out that if it came to a choice between the Kingdom
of Naples and Minorca, he (Nelson) would probably decide
for the former, whatever Lord Keith might think. On the
very same day that his letter was dispatched the order from
Lord Keith arrived. Nelson promptly decided to disobey it.
But twelve days later came an even more urgent demand, accompanied by a private letter in which Keith explained the
situation, and ordered Nelson to come himself or send Commodore Duckworth (from Malta) at once. Again he refused,
respectfully but firmly, at the same time passing on the correspondence to the Admiralty. Another ten days and a third
order even more strongly worded — with the intimation that
Lord Keith himself was leaving the Mediterranean for home,
but relied on Nelson to carry out these last instructions. This

was not to be refused, and Duckworth was sent west with three ships of the line and a corvette.

This was not the first nor the last time in his life that Nelson had disobeyed his superior officer. As usual, he was right in his decision — not right in the sense that Sicily was in any danger, but right in the sense that neither he nor Duckworth was needed at Minorca, and that they were much better employed where they were. He always *was* right when he committed these startling acts of disobedience which occur at intervals throughout his career. And no doubt it was that confidence in himself, that certainty that he would be right — amounting to a kind of inspiration — that led him on big occasions to take his own way, regardless of the consequences. He often used to say that, if things had gone wrong at St Vincent — to take the most famous example — he would probably have been "broke" for turning out of the line without orders. He seemed almost to pride himself on having taken such a risk for his country's good: it was an act of self-sacrifice, entirely laudable from the patriotic point of view. The professional point of view seems to have troubled him curiously little.

It would not be difficult to multiply instances in his relations with those under him in which he showed the same tendency to let an officer make up his own mind, on the facts before him, without regard to the strict letter of his instructions. Quite a humble example, but worth quoting in this connexion, is the case of Lieutenant Walker, whose escapades may be traced through some of the earlier volumes of Nicolas's collection of Nelson's letters. In September 1796, when Nelson, on the *Captain,* was gingerly approaching Castiglione, not knowing whether it was yet in French hands, and "totally ignorant of the navigation," he says that he "ordered Lieutenant Walker [who was in command of the *Rose* cutter] to keep by me," but he "thought proper to part with me the next night." A day or two later he writes to Elliot: "Lieutenant Walker just in sight off Ferrajo: I am very angry with him." And the month before he had written: "Lieutenant Walker, I

hear from Captain Dixon, did not make the best of his way off
Bastia, but chased and took possession of a Danish brig from
Amsterdam — if so, I shall most probably try him by court-
martial." But he never was tried, apparently. One trembles
to think what would have happened to him under Jervis!
Nelson is merely "very angry" — as with a naughty child.
From other letters we gather that Walker was an excellent
man in a "scrap." In a skirmish on shore at Capraja he conducted himself "very much to my satisfaction." In fact, we
get a picture of a kind of reckless young Midshipman Easy —
only to discover that this wayward Mr Walker was a much
older man, having served under Nelson as master on the *Hinchinbroke* in 1779.

The point is that Nelson seems to have allowed to his jun-
iors very much the same sort of latitude that he claimed for
himself. The Admiralty, however, took another, and, no
doubt, a sounder view. They politely informed the hero of
the Nile, in a letter dated August 20, that they could not discover "sufficient reason for your having disobeyed the orders
which you received from your commanding officer"; and,
putting their finger upon one of the principal causes why Nelson would not (indeed, could not) move from Naples, they
observe that to send a thousand of his best seamen twenty
miles inland (to Capua) for the purpose of conducting a siege,
was a most unusual proceeding, and "I have their Lordships'
commands to signify their directions to your Lordship not to
employ the seamen in like manner in future." Nelson took
these official snubs very much to heart. He replied plain-
tively, in a letter which is worth quoting, as an example of his
muddled reasoning in these matters. He wrote:

> I have to request that you will have the goodness to assure
> their Lordships that I knew when I decided on these important
> points, that perhaps my life, certainly my commission, was at
> stake by my decision; but, being firmly of opinion that the
> honour of my King and country, the dearest object of my heart,
> was involved, and that to have deserted the cause and person of
> His Majesty's faithful ally, His Sicilian Majesty, would have

been unworthy of my name and their Lordships' former opinion of me, I determined at all risks to support the honour of my gracious sovereign and country, and not to shelter myself under the letter of the law, which I shall never do, when put in competition with the public service.

The Admiralty had sugared the pill by appointing Nelson Commander-in-Chief in the Mediterranean during Lord Keith's absence. At the same time King Ferdinand bestowed upon him the Dukedom of Bronte, with an estate supposed to be worth £3000 a year — though Nelson appears to have got next to nothing out of it.

Nothing much happened. The blockade of Malta dragged on; Capua and Gaeta surrendered to Troubridge, and Nelson remained at Palermo, directing affairs from there. Poor Captain Miller of the *Theseus* was killed by the accidental explosion of some shells. There was a first-class row with the Victualling Board in London, to whom a letter was written by Nelson, dressing them down in true quarterdeck style. In December Keith returned — to Nelson's vexation, for he had hoped to get the post. But a cheering event was about to happen.

Intelligence was received that the French were fitting out a small squadron for the relief of Malta, and Keith and Nelson arranged to intercept them. It was understood that among the ships of the relieving squadron was the *Généreux*, one of the two French line-of-battle ships which had escaped from the battle of the Nile (the other, the *Guillaume Tell*, was bottled up in Malta harbour). It will be remembered that the officers and crew of the *Généreux* had subsequently disgraced themselves by their treatment of the *Leander* prisoners. Nelson was eager for revenge. And, as always, the game came in his direction. Giving his usual elastic interpretation to Keith's instructions, he found himself, on February 10, 1800, cruising off the west coast of Sicily, with the *Alexander,* three English frigates, and a corvette also in sight, all engaged in the same pursuit. What followed has been vividly described in perhaps the very best "close-up" portrait of Nelson in action that has come down to us. We have to thank young Midshipman Parsons, of the *Foudroyant,* for it; and all his former sins as an irresponsible scribbler of gossip and a shameless "writer-up" of the Caracciolo affair are easily and immediately forgiven him as soon as our eyes light upon this priceless little pen-picture. Parts of the dialogue, we must suppose, are imaginary, but the whole thing carries the hall-mark of truth. From another source we learn that Nelson had a slightly nasal voice, and that hint, combined with Parsons's indication of his pronunciation and so forth, enables the intelligent reader of the following dialogue almost to hear the great man speak:

"Deck, there! the stranger is evidently a man of war — she is a line-of-battle ship, my Lord, and going large on the starboard tack."

"Ah! an enemy, Mr Stains. I pray God it may be *Le Généreux.* The signal for a general chase, Sir Ed'ard, [the Nelsonian pronunciation of Edward] make the *Foudroyant* fly."

Thus spake the heroic Nelson; and every exertion that emulation could inspire was used to crowd the squadron with canvas, the *Northumberland* taking the lead with the flagship close on her quarter.

"This will not do, Sir Ed'ard; it is certainly *Le Généreux* and to my flagship she can alone surrender. Sir Ed'ard, we must and shall beat the *Northumberland.*"

"I will do my utmost, my lord; get the engine to work on the sails — hang butts of water to the stays — pipe the hammocks down, and each man place shot in them — slack the stays, knock up the wedges, and give the masts play — start off the water, Mr. James, and pump the ship."

"The *Foudroyant* is drawing a-head, and at last takes the lead in the chase.

"The Admiral is working his fin, (the stump of his right arm) do not cross his hawse I advise you."

The advice was good, for at that moment Nelson opened furiously on the quarter-master at the conn.

"I'll knock you off your perch, you rascal, if you are so inattentive. Sir Ed'ard, send your best quarter-master to the weather wheel."

"A strange sail ahead of the chase," called the look-out man.

"Youngster, to the mast-head. What! going without your glass, and be d——d to you? Let me know what she is immediately."

"A sloop of war, or frigate, my lord," shouted the young signal-midshipman.

"Demand her number."

"The *Success,* my lord."

"Captain Peard; signal to cut off the flying enemy — great odds though — thirty-two small guns to eighty large ones."

"The *Success* has hove-to athwart-hawse of the *Généreux,* and is firing her larboard broadside. The Frenchman has hoisted his tri-colour, with a rear-admiral's flag."

"*Bravo, Success, at her again!*"

"She has wore round, my Lord, and firing her starboard broadside. It has winged her, my lord — her flying kites are flying away altogether. The enemy is close on the *Success,* who must receive her tremendous broadside."

The *Généreux* opens her fire on her little enemy, and every person stands aghast, afraid of the consequences. The smoke clears away, and there is the *Success,* crippled, it is true, but, bull-dog like, bearing up after the enemy.

"The signal for the *Success* to discontinue the action, and come under my stern," said Lord Nelson. "She has done well, for her size. Try a shot from the lower deck at her, Sir Ed'ard."

"It goes over her."

"Beat to quarters, and fire coolly and deliberately at her masts and yards."

Le Généreux at this moment opened her fire on us; as a shot passed through the mizzen stay-sail, Lord Nelson, patting one of the youngsters on the head, asked him jocularly how he relished the music; and observing something like alarm depicted on his countenance, consoled him with the information that Charles XII ran away from the first shot he heard, though afterwards he was called "The Great," and deservedly, from his bravery. "I, therefore," said Nelson, "hope much from you in future."

Here the *Northumberland* opened her fire, and down came the tricolour ensign, amidst the thunder of our united cannon.

"The signal to discontinue the firing."

And Sir Edward Berry boarded the prize. Very shortly he returned with Rear-Admiral Père's sword, who, he stated, was then dying on his quarter-deck, with the loss of both legs, shot off by the raking broadsides of the little *Success.* This unfortunate Frenchman was under the imputation of having broken his parole, and was considered lucky in having redeemed his honour by dying in battle.

Nelson, of course, was delighted. "This," he wrote to Lord Minto, "makes nineteen sail of the line and four admirals I have been present at the capture of, this war" — and he wonders whether he ought to tempt Dame Fortune any more, and talks rather bitterly of retiring to Greenwich Hospital, now that he is "evidently thought unfit to command in the Mediterranean." But he did not forget to pay proper tribute to the "great judgment and gallantry of Captain Peard of the *Success* in laying his little frigate across the path of the line of battle ship." It was a shot from the *Success* that killed the French Admiral (whose name was not Pĕre but Perré). Nelson was in poor health, and worse spirits. He had now been a year and a half in the hottest part of the Mediterranean, and he probably needed a change — though it is an idea that certainly would never have occurred to him if he had been given the supreme command. Now, when Keith ordered him to take command of the blockade of Malta, he pleaded ill health, and retired to Palermo, where Ferdinand still kept his Court.

But he seems to have left some of his luck behind him with the *Foudroyant*, for on March 29, about a fortnight after his departure, and on the very day on which the *Foudroyant* returned to the station without him, the *Guillaume Tell* came out of harbour in the middle of the night and attempted to slip through the blockade and get away to France. She was seen by the *Penelope* frigate (Captain Blackwood), who followed her closely in the darkness, yawing every now and then, and firing broadsides (as Nelson had done with the *Ça Ira*) partly with the hope of bringing down a mast or spar, and partly to attract the attention of the other English ships. This plucky action had the desired effect. The *Guillaume Tell* dared not wait to destroy her puny antagonist, and, since the frigate was the better sailer, she could not be shaken off. The Frenchman's only chance was to outdistance the English line-of-battle ships before daylight came; and this last hope disappeared when the *Penelope* succeeded in bringing down her main and mizzen topmasts. The *Lion* (64) came up and engaged her, broadside to broadside; but the *Guillaume Tell* with her eighty guns, which were stoutly served, beat off this attack, and it was left to the *Foudroyant,* which arrived on the scene about sunrise, to make an end of this last survivor of Admiral de Brueys's ill-fated battle line.

Nelson, when he heard of it, wrote a special letter to Captain Blackwood, praising him as he deserved. He was full of enthusiasm at the conduct of every one concerned. But he ought to have been there himself. That was the plain fact apparent to all. Either there, or on sick leave in England. Troubridge wrote privately to expostulate with him, and if no one else dared to follow that example, it is certain that there was a good deal of gossip in the fleet at this time. There was the usual talk of a life of self-indulgent ease, and the fatal influence of a beautiful woman upon a man of action. If Oscar Wilde had been alive then, they might have adopted his saying: "Women are always inspiring us to create masterpieces, and always preventing us from doing it."

Such talk was exaggerated at the time, and has been even more exaggerated since. Nelson disliked Palermo, and was every day urging the King to return to Naples. He was disgusted at the almost daily executions of rebels — "the heads of a whole kingdom cannot be cut off, be they ever such rascals." And he felt no call to action, so long as Lord Keith was in command; in fact he came as near as he ever did in his life to sulking. All these points have to be taken into consideration and given their due weight before we agree that another influence, which undoubtedly helped to keep him at Palermo, was the presence of the beautiful Emma, entertaining him to dinner on shore, or striking her "attitudes" on the quarterdeck. It is a question of balancing these different influences; and, on the whole, and taking into consideration what Nelson had accomplished during the last eighteen months, it is fair to conclude that the presence of Keith in the Mediterranean was at least as strong a narcotic as the presence of Emma Hamilton.

But neither explanation is particularly creditable to Nelson. It is at this moment in his career that we see him at his worst.

A bright spot was his cordial letter of congratulation to Sir Sidney Smith on his triumph at Acre. He disliked gas bags and "climbers," but he knew a brave man when he saw one. And in this conflict of feelings, he wrote, with his usual *naïveté*:

> Be assured, my dear Sir Sidney, of my perfect esteem and regard, and do not let anyone persuade you to the contrary; my character is that I will not suffer the smallest tittle of my command to be taken from me; but with pleasure I give way to my friends, among whom I beg you will allow me to consider you.

The situation had been somewhat altered by the recall of Sir William Hamilton, who was now about seventy years of age, and evidently regarded by the Foreign Office as a little past his work. His successor was already on his way out. And now that the Hamiltons had to leave the Mediterranean, Nelson too began to feel a longing for home. In April he had taken another look at Malta. He had recalled the *Foudroyant,* and made the trip in her, taking the two Hamiltons with him. Off Valetta harbour long-range shots from the French forts passed over his ship, and one of them is alleged to have passed so close to Lady Hamilton as to "part her hair." The Admiral, we are told, was greatly alarmed, and insisted upon her going below. But she herself showed not the slightest uneasiness — much to the admiration of the adoring junior officers. The *Foudroyant* was removed to a safer distance, and the voyage ended at Palermo, after what was really no more than a pleasure cruise. Back in Palermo, Nelson received a letter from Lord Spencer, which is worth quoting, as an example of official tact:

> It is by no means my wish or intention to call you away from service; but having observed that you have been under the

necessity of quitting your station off Malta on account of the state of your health, which I am persuaded you could not have thought of doing without such necessity, it appeared to me much more advisable for you to come home at once, than to be obliged to remain inactive at Palermo, while active service was going on in other parts of the station . . . I believe I am joined in opinion by all your friends here that you will be more likely to recover your health and strength in England than at any inactive situation at a foreign court, however pleasing the respect and gratitude shown to you for your services may be, and no testimonials of respect and gratitude from that court to you can be, I am convinced, too great for the very essential services you have rendered it . . . I trust that you will take in good part what I have taken the liberty to write to you as a friend.

However politely stated, the meaning of this communication was not in doubt. Nelson definitely decided to return to England with his friends. He applied to Lord Keith for the use of the *Foudroyant*, and by doing so laid himself open to yet another gentle snub. Keith was short of line-of-battle ships, and he wrote Nelson a friendly but firm private note, in which he offered him the frigate *Seahorse,* or any troopship, to convey his party back to England, but not a ship of the line. This was no use to Nelson; the accommodation in a frigate was limited, and there was his dignity to be considered; and though Lady Hamilton was a good sailor, poor old Sir William might suffer severely in so small a vessel while crossing the bay. He and the Hamiltons decided to return overland together, travelling with the Queen of Naples as far as Vienna, whither she was going on a visit. The starting-point was to be Leghorn, and, on June 10, 1800, the *Foudroyant* took on board the Queen and her family, Sir William and his lady, and Miss Knight; and, with Nelson walking its quarterdeck for the last time, set sail for that port. As a fitting conclusion to this rather drab episode in the hero's career, they had an abominable passage, which occupied five days, and they were two more days in harbour before it was possible for the passengers to land.

If Nelson felt any regrets we have no record of it; but, in any case, he must have felt cheered by a letter from the crew of his barge, handed to him as he went ashore, in which the simple sailormen expressed their "extreme grief" at losing him, and "most humbly begged" to be allowed to go to England and serve him in any ship he might command, at the same time asking pardon for "the rude style of seamen, who are but little acquainted with writing."

CHAPTER XIV

THE SENTIMENTAL JOURNEY

WE HAVE before had occasion to remark how easy it would be to write a comic life of Nelson. His theatricality, the absurd legends that have grown up round his name, his weakness with women, and his strange association with that ill-assorted couple Sir William and Lady Hamilton — all this aspect of his life has its humorous side, and might be dealt with from that point of view alone. Such a book would make excellent reading, and, if published after a discreet interval from the date of his death, would undoubtedly have commanded an enormous sale — for the nineteenth century keenly appreciated this form of humour.

Its central feature would be this overland journey, now to be described, — this triumphal procession, roses all the way, from Leghorn to Vienna and Dresden and Hamburg; and from thence to Yarmouth, and its cheering crowds, and finally to London — and a certain disillusionment. The leading lady in the farce would be at least as important a character as the leading man. Poor Emma! The brutal truth is that she was beginning to put on weight. She was beginning, as that type does, to indulge a little too freely in the pleasures of life. She was not the sort of woman who would deliberately starve herself in order to preserve her figure, and plumpness, unfortunately for her, was almost as unfashionable then as it is now. Her passion for gambling had grown upon her. Lady Minto has left us an extraordinary picture of a card party at Palermo, Nelson sound asleep in his chair with a bag of gold on the table in front of him, into which Lady Hamilton dipped her hand as occasion required. Gossip said that she often lost

£500 at a sitting; but it is certain that she cannot have done that often with Nelson's money, for we know what he had at the time. She was a bit of a tomboy — like the famous Miss Stuart of Charles II's Court, whose character, in many points, resembled hers, and whose most famous "attitude" has been immortalized in the figure of Britannia on our coinage. We can believe that she laughed a little too loud. And it was obvious that, during her residence abroad, she had got into the habit of drinking rather more champagne than was usual among ladies in England at that time.

The party consisted of the Queen of Naples, Nelson, Sir William, Emma, Miss Cornelia Knight, Mrs Cadogan (Emma's mother), and the members of the Queen's suite. They turned their backs upon the sea without regret. The Queen had been deprived of any voice in the councils of Naples by her husband, and felt herself in disgrace; and since Lord Keith had refused her the *Foudroyant* she had spent most of her time in tears. Nelson and the Hamiltons were longing for England. At Vienna there was a sentimental parting, and the English people went on alone to Prague, where they got a wonderful reception. They happened to arrive on Nelson's birthday, September 29, and the Archduke Charles gave a fête in honour of the occasion. The next stage took them to Dresden, and it was here that they met the lady who, in her diary,* has held them up to the ridicule of the world in as amusing and malicious a piece of gossip-writing as we have in the language. Mrs St George was a young Irish widow, still in her early twenties. She was staying in Dresden, and had made great friends with the British Minister, Hugh Elliot, brother of Lord Minto, Nelson's old friend, but of a very different type. Mrs St George disliked the elder brother, of whom she complains that he was "like a ghost, and will rarely speak till spoken to"; and she goes on to tell some unkind little stories about his absent-mindedness — how he would ask people to dinner and forget all about it, and so forth. But Hugh Elliot, who was a

---

* Mrs M. St George, *Journal kept during a Visit to Germany*, 1799-1800, (London, 1861).

typical young Whig exquisite, suited her exactly. The two of them found the Nelson-Hamilton *ménage* vastly entertaining.

Obviously such a woman would take a dislike to Emma on sight, and obviously Emma, in her good-natured, forthcoming way, would be particularly anxious to win this society lady's affection. It is this clash of personalities that makes Mrs St George's journal so extraordinarily interesting. Though she does not know it, she makes herself and Hugh Elliott at least as ridiculous to the modern reader as the two people of genius whose behaviour in their moments of relaxation it is her object to lampoon. Indeed, it is so easy to separate the dross from the gold of truth, that no biographer of Nelson need hesitate to quote these illuminating entries in full. Here is the first, and the best:

Oct. 3. Dined at Mr Elliot's with only the Nelson party. It is plain that Lord Nelson thinks of nothing but Lady Hamilton, who is totally occupied by the same subject. She is bold, forward, coarse, assuming and vain. Her figure is colossal, but, excepting her feet, which are hideous, well shaped. Her bones are large, and she is exceedingly *enbonpoint*.* She resembles the bust of Ariadne; the shape of all her features is fine, as is the form of her head, and particularly her ears; her teeth are a little irregular, but tolerably white; her eyes light blue, with a brown spot in one, which, though a defect, takes nothing away from her beauty and expression. Her eyebrows and hair are dark, and her complexion coarse. Her expression is strongly marked, variable and interesting; her movements in common life ungraceful, yet not disagreeable.

Lord Nelson is a little man, without any dignity. Lady Hamilton takes possession of him, and he is a willing captive — the most submissive and devoted I have seen. Sir William is old, infirm, all admiration for his wife, and never spoke to-day but to applaud her. Miss Cornelia Knight seems a decided flatterer of the two, and never opens her mouth but to show forth their praise; and Mrs Cadogan, Lady Hamilton's mother, is what one might expect.

After dinner we had several songs in honour of Lord Nelson, written by Miss Knight, and sung by Lady Hamilton. She puffs

---

* Lady Hamilton's daughter Horatia was born less than four months after this.

o

the incense full in his face, but he receives it with pleasure and
snuffs it up very cordially. The songs all ended in the sailor's
way with "Hip, hip, hip, hurra" and a bumper with the last drop
on the nail, a ceremony I had never heard of or seen before.

That sneer, in the last sentence, is characteristic. It is typical
of this period that, while English people would become
maudlin over sloppy sentimental songs about hearts of oak,
the sailors who were saving the nation were habitually and
openly sneered at for their uncouth manners by novelists and
society wits. Mrs St George's thrusts at Lady Hamilton —
though there is always a grain of truth in them for which we
can never be too grateful to her — must be read in the light of
what she has to say about Nelson — that "little man without
dignity." The very next entry in her diary, dated October 5,
relates how she went to see him in his full dress, before going
to a reception at the King of Saxony's Court. After describing
all the decorations that he wore she sums up acidly: "In short
Lord Nelson was a perfect constellation of stars and orders."
She could write like that of the rewards given to this heroic
little cripple for the wounds he had received in the service of
his country! His appearance as he stood there with his "fin"
(as he called the stump of his right arm) and his blotted out
eye, and the great scar across his forehead — no doubt preen-
ing himself like a bantam cock before the looking-glass —
moved this fellow-countrywoman of his only to laughter and
contempt. In later entries she suggests that he drank too much
— which we know to be untrue:

Oct. 9. Lady Hamilton, who declared that she was passionately
fond of champagne, took such a portion of it as astonished me.
Lord Nelson was not behindhand, calling more vociferously
than usual for songs in his own praise, and after many bumpers
proposed the Queen of Naples, adding: "She is my Queen; she is
Queen to the backbone." Poor Mr. Elliot, who was anxious the
party should not expose themselves more than they had done
already, and wished to get over the last day as well as he had
done the rest, endeavoured to stop the effusion of champagne,
and effected it with some difficulty; but not till the Lord and

THE SENTIMENTAL JOURNEY   201

Lady, or, as he calls them, Anthony and Moll Cleopatra, were pretty far gone.

This is entertaining eighteenth-century spite. One feels that Mr Hugh Elliot would rather lose the battle of Trafalgar than "expose" himself in any way. He supplements Mrs St George's account by telling us that the evening concluded with more songs by Lady Hamilton, Nelson frequently interrupting with cries of "Mrs Siddons be damned!" while old Sir William — or "Sir Willum" as Emma called him — was "hopping round the room on his backbone, his arms, legs, star and ribbon all flying about in the air." And he ends with this final piece of venom, after he has got them on to the river-boat for Hamburg:

> The moment they were on board, there was an end of the fine arts, of the attitudes, of the acting, the dancing and the singing. Lady Hamilton's maid began to scold in French . . . Lady Hamilton began bawling for an Irish stew, and her old mother set about washing the potatoes, which she did as cleverly as possible. They were exactly like Hogarth's actresses dressing in the barn.

But it is to be noted that even Mrs St George — this woman without a heart, who would have admired Charles Greville while jeering at Horatio Nelson — has too much intelligence to dissent from the universal opinion about Emma's "attitudes."

> Oct. 7. Breakfasted with Lady Hamilton, and saw her represent in succession the best statues and paintings extant. She assumes her attitude, expression and drapery with great facility, swiftness and accuracy. Several Indian shawls, a chair, some antique vases, a wreath of roses, a tambourine, and a few children are her whole apparatus. She stands at one end of the room with a strong light to her left, and every other window closed. Her hair (which by the bye is never clean) is short, dressed like an antique, and her gown a simple calico chemise, very easy, with loose sleeves to the wrist. She disposes the shawls so as to form Grecian, Turkish, and other drapery, as well as a variety of turbans. Her arrangement of the turbans is absolute sleight of hand, she does it so quickly, so easily, and so well. It is a beauti-

ful performance, amusing to the most ignorant, and highly interesting to the lovers of art. It is remarkable that, though coarse and ungraceful in common life, she becomes highly graceful, and even beautiful, during this performance.

Then Emma sang to this woman's accompaniment, who is again compelled to praise her voice, but remarks disparagingly that it lacked the fashionable "shake." She tells us frequently that Emma loaded her with "demonstrations of friendship," but all in vain — "she does not gain upon me." In short this trivial, fashionable, little Mrs St George was incapable of appreciating a simple, affectionate soul like Emma's; she despised her for her great qualities of heart while reluctantly compelled to admire her as a born artist. "She will captivate the Prince of Wales, whose mind is as vulgar as her own," said the witty Mr Elliot, "and play a great part in England." Wherein, once again, he was wrong.

Against all this ill-natured gossip we have the great mass of the evidence of practically everybody else who knew them. Lord Minto, who disapproved of Lady Hamilton, because he thought she was damaging his friend's career, yet found her a charming woman; and the worst he could say of her at this period is that her manners were "very easy, though not with the ease of good breeding, but of a barmaid." Lady Malmesbury, who was a great lady, held that she "behaved incomparably," and again "quite wonderfully, considering her origin and education." As for her little tableaux display, "you never saw anything so charming." Nor will the theory that Lady Hamilton interfered with Nelson's career bear much examination. Within three months of this time, when he was supposed to be already completely spoiled by adulation and self-indulgence, he was at sea, on his way to the victory of Copenhagen. The truth is that he lived so furiously when he was on active service that he needed his moments of relaxation. And it is not a little nauseating to think of people of the type of Mrs St George and Mr Hugh Elliot sniggeringly noting down his harmless gambols.

AN EXAMPLE OF THE 'ATTITUDES'
Lady Hamilton as the Dancing Muse.
From a drawing by Friedrich Rehberg, in the British Museum.

But we must return to the Hamburg boat — and the Irish stew. It is a safe guess that they enjoyed this part of the journey, freed from the worry of dinner parties and Court ceremonial, and the frigid smiles of polite society. They lived as they liked, and laughed when they felt inclined. And at Hamburg they took ship, and arrived at the port of Yarmouth, in Nelson's native county, on November 6, 1800. He had been away from England more than eighteen months. This was the first that England had seen of him since the battle of the Nile. When he landed with his party, the Mayor and Corporation were there to greet him, and behind them a great crowd of cheering people who took the horses from the shafts and drew the carriage through the streets to his hotel, the Wrestlers' Inn. Lady Hamilton sat beside him, plump and smiling, and shared in his triumph. He was told that Lady Nelson and his father were waiting to greet him in London.

The enthusiasm of the citizens knew no bounds: he was at home now, among his own people, and it was clear from the beginning that they had taken him — yes, and Emma also — to their hearts. They gave him the freedom of the city and an address of welcome, and provided a body of cavalry to escort him from the town. This was something different from the adulation of foreigners. It stirred him deeply. And the welcome of Yarmouth was only the beginning of a succession of similar scenes all the way along their road to London. But before leaving the port Nelson found time to sit down and write to the Admiralty that "my health being perfectly re-established, it is my wish to serve immediately; and I trust that my necessary journey by land from the Mediterranean will not be considered as a wish to be a moment out of active service."

Lady Nelson was waiting in London, with his father. She has been blamed for this, but it is difficult to see what else she could have done. Certainly she could hardly have been expected to grace Lady Hamilton's triumph. She has also been blamed for not going out to Nelson in the Mediterranean, as soon as she heard of his victory and his wound; but it is clear

from one of his letters that she had suggested doing so, and
that he himself vetoed the proposal (he said that it was impossible to set up an establishment, and that if she came to
him he would simply have to strike his flag). So there she
was in London, and surely in no very pleasant mood. Josiah
had told her all about it. Her first meeting with Emma Hamilton was probably a shock to her fastidious taste. But Nelson
wore an air of innocent geniality, and seemed to take it for
granted that she would be prepared to set up house-keeping together with the Hamiltons. This had been his idea for a long
time past, and the extraordinary thing is that he seems to have
been genuinely hurt and astonished that his eminently ladylike
and self-respecting wife should have refused from the outset
to enter into a competition in complaisance with Sir William.
She did, however, make an effort to appear in public with him;
but the only result was a distressing scene at the theatre, when
Nelson and Lady Hamilton stood together in the front of the
box to receive the plaudits of the pit — until it was discovered
that Lady Nelson had fallen in a faint behind them.

Miss Cornelia Knight, a woman of no great intelligence, at
one time prejudiced in Emma's favour, but afterwards es-
tranged from her, has summed up* the situation during these
few painful months in London with a judicial impartiality
and shrewdness, though quite without humour, which is in
striking contrast to the irresponsible gossip of Mrs St George.
After the incident at the theatre she says:

Most of my friends were very urgent with me to drop the
acquaintance, but, circumstanced as I had been, I feared the
charge of ingratitude, though greatly embarrassed as to what to
do, for things became very unpleasant. So much was said about
the attachment of Lord Nelson to Lady Hamilton that it made
the matter still worse. He felt irritated, and took it up in an unfortunate manner, by devoting himself more and more to her, for
the purpose of what he called supporting her. Mischief was made
on all sides, till at last when he was appointed to the command
of the squadron in the Downs, which was to sail for Copenhagen

---

* Miss Cornelia Knight, *Autobiography* (2 vols., London, 1861).

—his brother and sister-in-law, with Sir William and Lady Hamilton being with him at Deal—he wrote to Lady Nelson, giving her credit for perfectly moral conduct but announcing his intention of not living with her any more.

This was certainly not in his thoughts before he returned to England, for I remember his saying, while we were at Leghorn, that he had hoped Lady Nelson and himself would be much with Sir William and Lady Hamilton, and that they would all very often dine together, and that when the latter couple went to their musical parties, he and Lady Nelson would go to bed. Even at Hamburg, just before we embarked, he purchased a magnificent lace trimming for a court dress for Lady Nelson.

When Emma wrote to tell Nelson of Miss Knight's final desertion her letter found him at sea again. It is not to be supposed that she spoke too kindly of Cornelia; and moreover, in this same letter, she had to record the falling away of more than one fair-weather friend. Nelson answered irritably, and rather coarsely: "What a b—— that Miss Knight is! As to the other I care not what she says." The scandal had been growing, of course, and these frequent reminders of what people in his own class thought of his behaviour were getting on his nerves.

To go back a little. Nelson and his wife managed to maintain a joint establishment, without open rupture, from November 9, 1800, when he arrived in London, to December 9 of the same year. There were plenty of social distractions. On the night of the 9th, for instance, Sir William and Lady Hamilton dined with them—though that would not, perhaps, do much to relieve the tension; and on the 10th Nelson was at the banquet given to him by the Lord Mayor, when the gold sword already mentioned was presented to him on behalf of the city for his victory at Aboukir. The mob who, here as everywhere, adored him, took his horses from the carriage and dragged it triumphantly from Ludgate Hill to the Guildhall, while every balcony and window was filled with ladies waving their pocket-handkerchiefs. On the next day the Nelsons dined with the Hamiltons—and that, again, may have been a little difficult—and on the day after occurred that unfortunate scene at the theatre. More invitations followed, and Lady Nelson, being only human, must have noted with a grim satisfaction that Lady Hamilton was doubtfully received at Court, and was beginning to be looked at askance in less exclusive circles, and that this was distressing Nelson.

In the meantime he had plenty of other things to attend to. He saw the Duke of Clarence, he was in and out of the Admiralty, and he took his seat in the House of Lords. There were consultations with Davison, his confidential agent (the same who had saved him from an unfortunate marriage at Quebec) about his private affairs. And, above all, there were Sir William Hamilton's money troubles, real or imaginary. The old man believed himself to be hard pressed, and that curious eccentric, "Vathek" Beckford (who now comes into our story for the first time) was proposing to advance a considerable sum of money if Sir William, on his part, could arrange to get Beckford a peerage.

Sir William very properly rejected this proposal. He did, however, accept an invitation for himself and his wife and Nelson to go down to Beckford's place at Fonthill, and spend Christmas with him there. Nelson joined the party with alacrity, and his wife found herself left alone in the London lodgings, after a bare six weeks of her husband's society. The journey westwards resolved itself into another triumphal procession. Mounted yeomanry escorted the carriage, and the country folk lined the roads. Coming out of Salisbury Town Hall, after receiving the city's freedom, Nelson recognized among the onlookers a sailor who had been with him at the battle of the Nile, and, characteristically, hailed the man as one comrade to another, stopping the procession that he might talk to him, to the huge delight of the crowd. At Beckford's door there was a guard of honour of the local volunteers, and the band played *Rule, Britannia* and *God Save the King*.

Emma had been here before. In those far-off days when she was plain Emma Hart, and Romney was going off his head about her — that is, in 1791 — there had been a memorable house party at Fonthill, and lurid stories had been told about the goings-on there. Evidently Emma, with her habitual honesty, felt no shame at these memories, or she would scarcely have brought her husband and Nelson there. Again the visit was a great success. Emma sang songs and went through her "attitudes" every night. But there was one significant difference: for reasons which one would have thought would by this time have been obvious to everybody, but of which only she and Nelson were apparently aware, she could not dance.

The party returned to London on December 29. Lady Nelson received her husband coldly. It is the familiar, miserable story. One morning at breakfast, while Nelson was gushing about Emma in his usual manner, his wife rose abruptly from the table, announced "I am sick of hearing of 'dear Lady Hamilton' " — and so walked out of the house and out of his life, for she never lived with him again. It is not certain that she meant quite that at the time. But she had made this gesture in the presence of a lawyer, Haselwood, who happened to be breakfasting with them, and to do that is an insult which husbands — even guilty husbands — find it extraordinarily difficult to forgive. Nelson took it just as one would expect. He had been prattling away — a cheerful conversation on indifferent subjects, says Haselwood — when he happened to introduce that unfortunate reference. At his wife's outburst he pulled up abruptly. "Take care, Fanny," he said gravely, "what you say; I love you sincerely but I cannot forget my obligations to Lady Hamilton, or speak of her otherwise than with affection and admiration." That was her last chance — if she had wanted it. Probably she realized that the case was hopeless. Anyhow she gave him no look nor answer, but went out, says Haselwood, "muttering something about her mind being made up." As for him, he already knew — as we know now — that there was a reason why it was no longer possible for him to think of giving Emma up.

It is frequently suggested that this was the only "scene" that the dignified Lady Nelson permitted herself to create. It seems much more likely that it was the culmination of a long series of scenes. Months afterwards, when formally intimating his desire never to set eyes on her again, Nelson wrote to Davison: "Sooner than live the unhappy life I did when I last came to England, I'll stay abroad for ever." It must have been a cat-and-dog life — it cannot have been anything else — but Lady Nelson was too much of a lady and Nelson was too naturally chivalrous to have left any record of it. Or, as Harrison puts it, with that mixture of pomposity and bad taste peculiar to him, "without introducing the reader behind the sacred veil of the connubial curtain," we may opine that Nelson used to go to bed late and get up early. We can only guess at most of what happened during these two or three unhappy months. They were undoubtedly a turning-point in Nelson's domestic affairs. But they were comparatively unimportant in the professional career which — in spite of all the sentimental nonsense that has been written about him — was always first in his thoughts. Lady Hamilton is a significant figure in Nelson's life only because she gave him that feminine sympathy and encouragement which he needed, perhaps more than most men, and — from the biographer's point of view — because it is in his relations with her that he displayed most clearly that softer side of his character which always needs to be taken into account.

Yet one says good-bye to Fanny with a feeling akin to shame.* She was so obviously honest and well meaning. She might have made an ideal wife for the typical eighteenth-century man of affairs, who never forgot to treat his lady with a proper deference, but looked for love elsewhere. Nelson was not of that type: in spirit, perhaps, he was nearer to this present age. Theirs was a typical twentieth-century problem. At any rate he treated her with his habitual generosity in money matters, allowing her an annual income of £1200,

---

* She died in 1831. Her friend Sir William Hotham says that "she continually talked of him [Nelson] and always to palliate his conduct towards her, was warm and enthusiastic in her praises of his public achievements, and bowed down with dignified submission to the errors of his domestic life."

which was wealth in those days, and considering the demands
that Emma was beginning to make upon him was a good deal
more than he could comfortably afford. It would appear, also,
that he went and took formal leave of her before starting on
January 13 to join his ship. He had solemnly assured her:
"I take God to witness there is nothing in you or your conduct I wish otherwise." And that night at Southampton he
scribbled her a little note which must surely have been intended as a peace offering — "My dear Fanny: we are arrived
and heartily tired, and with kindest regards to my father and
all the family, believe me, your affectionate *Nelson.*" She
never answered.

The attitude of Nelson's own relations is a little difficult to
follow. When he hoisted his flag again in January his brother
and sister-in-law were with him on board, and, presumably,
shared with Sir William and Lady Hamilton the ample supplies of champagne which Nelson had ordered from London
for the occasion. His sisters, Mrs Bolton and Mrs Matcham,
though on affectionate terms with Lady Nelson, treated
Emma with every respect. His father, on the other hand, apparently continued to live with Lady Nelson, and it is noticeable that Nelson begins to speak of him as my "poor father"
and my "mistaken" father. What they all thought about his
relationship with Lady Hamilton at this period is difficult to
discover. Both she and Nelson were still resolutely maintaining an appearance of a merely Platonic friendship; and Sir
William Hamilton — so far as he counted at all — was os-
tentatiously accepting that view of the situation.

At some time between January 29 and 31, at No. 23, Piccadilly, Sir William's town house, Emma Hamilton gave birth
to a daughter, who was afterwards named Horatia. It was
given out that she was confined to her room with a cold.
Just at that time Nelson had to go down to Plymouth to join
Lord St Vincent's command. He was terribly anxious: they
had arranged some elaborate camouflage, under which he
was to write to her on the subject of herself and the child as
though he were talking about a mythical Mr and Mrs Thomp-

son, whose messages he and Emma were charged to convey. We have only his end of the correspondence, because as he (or rather Mr Thompson) said: "I burn all your dear letters, because it is right for your sake." * But when the child is safely born, he says: "I believe poor dear Mrs Thompson's friend will go mad with joy." Sometimes the man was a husband, sometimes a friend: sometimes all pretence is forgotten, and Nelson is to Emma, "for ever, ever yours, only yours." The birth of this child had sealed their relationship. He pours out his love in letter after letter, with a simple sincerity which cannot fail to warm the heart of the most sophisticated reader, even today. There is no need to quote these letters.

As for Sir William, he was writing round to his friends politely explaining that Lady Hamilton was indisposed. He was living in the same house when it happened, but he never appeared to know. And whether he was a fool or a knave, or both, is a question that will probably never be answered now. He does not really matter much.

It only remains to be stated that when the baby was less than a fortnight old, it was smuggled out of the house, and taken to Little Titchfield Street, Marylebone, and left there in the charge of a certain Mrs Gibson. And there, when he returned from smashing the Danes at Copenhagen, Nelson would visit his child, and play with her for hours, sitting on the nursery floor.

---

* It has been alleged — rather shabbily — against Emma that she kept his letters (against his wish) because she foresaw the future value of a Nelson autograph. But she had plenty of money at this time and was the last woman in the world to think of such a thing. In disobeying her lover on this particular point, she only did what any woman in love would do.

CHAPTER XV

THE NORTHERN ADVENTURE

IT WAS, therefore, a harassed and anxious man who went down to Plymouth in January 1801, with orders to hoist his flag on the *San Josef* (the former Spanish three-decker), and join the fleet under Lord St Vincent at Tor Bay. Lady Hamilton's condition, and the elaborate precautions which he and she were taking to conceal the real facts of the case, must have preyed upon his mind; and now he was afflicted with an attack of ophthalmia in his one remaining eye. "My eye is like blood," he says; he can see only "from the corner farthest from my nose." His doctor ordered green eye-shades, and Nelson wrote to Lady Hamilton, "Will you, my dear friend, make me one or two?" But even with so much on his mind he must have found it an interesting experience to be once again upon that quarterdeck where he and Edward Berry, tumbling down from the mizzen shrouds, had received the surrender of the surviving Spanish officers on St Valentine's Day, 1797.* He joined the Channel fleet at the end of January — just about the time when Horatia was born. Lord St Vincent had been appointed First Lord of the Admiralty, and was leaving the fleet, and a few weeks later he was directed to shift his flag to the *St George,* and proceed to Yarmouth to join Admiral Sir Hyde Parker, who was going to the Baltic.

Before sailing for this new station Nelson obtained a few days' leave, and hurried up to London, where he got a glimpse of the child. Apparently Emma did not expect the visit to be so short, for she wrote to Mrs William Nelson, the parson's

_____
* See p. 119.

wife (to whose friendship she clung desperately, believing that this was the one member of the Nelson family who might take her to her heart): "Oh, my dearest friend, our dear Lord has just *come in* — he goes off to-night, and sails immediately — my heart is fit *to Burst* quite with greef." The italics and spelling are hers.

Returning to Portsmouth, he sailed with a squadron of seven ships of the line and reached Yarmouth on March 2. From there he addressed to his wife a final letter of dismissal: "Living I have done all in my power for you, and, if dead, you will find I have done the same. Therefore my only wish is to be left to myself." That sounds decisive enough; yet she wrote to him after Copenhagen, expressing thankfulness at his safety, and again, some months later, definitely suggesting a reconciliation. The only response was the curt reply conveyed to her by Davison, and quoted in the previous chapter. In the business arrangements connected with the separation Nelson was represented by this same Mr Davison, who had prevented one of his marriages and now had the task of breaking up another. A curious person, this Davison, an adventurer not quite in the best sense of the word, a man who knew what the inside of a prison looked like — and not from the visiting justices' point of view! But he served Nelson faithfully.

Aften ten days at Yarmouth the fleet set sail for the Baltic. Sir Hyde Parker's orders were about as vague as any ever given to a British admiral. He was sent on a delicate and dangerous mission such as Nelson, it is true, would have delighted in. But Sir Hyde Parker was an oldish man with an undistinguished career; this was his first important fleet command, and he also expected it to be his last; and his one idea (like Hotham's) was to get through it somehow without disgrace and subside into a comfortable retirement. In these circumstances he was, perhaps, unlucky in being given a Nelson as his second-in-command. The clash of personalities was inevitable — and the result equally so.

The situation he had to deal with was roughly as follows.

The proclamation of armed neutrality by the northern states, Russia, Denmark, and Sweden, was causing grave anxiety to the British Government. For the moment this armed neutrality meant little more than the denial of the right of "visit and search," which England had always insisted upon. But the mad Emperor of Russia, who was the leading member of the confederacy, had laid an embargo on English shipping in his ports. Moreover, the French were putting increasing pressure on Denmark and Sweden, so that at any moment they, as well as Russia, might be forced to use their not inconsiderable fleets against England. The Government had rightly come to the decision that it was necessary to show, by some decisive action, that those sea Powers which were not for England were against her. It was a question of what step to take — whether to destroy these potential enemies before they had time to strike, or to rely upon the presence of a British fleet in the Baltic and a little blustering language.

For purposes of negotiation Sir Hyde Parker had a representative of the Foreign Office, a Mr Vansittart, on board. Nelson did not like this. "I hate your pen and ink men," he wrote to Lady Hamilton, "a fleet of British ships of war are the best negotiators in Europe." He disliked the whole idea of negotiation. He had a characteristic scheme of his own, of which we shall have more to say in a moment. "Your Nelson's plans," he wrote to Emma, "are bold and decisive — all on the great scale." His letters to her at this time make exhilarating reading. This was just the sort of adventurous voyage, with the future all in doubt, and its leader invested with the power of making history, that appealed to his very soul, and stirred him to a mad impatience to act. He felt himself capable of anything. "It shall be my study to distinguish myself," he wrote to his beloved, "that your heart shall leap for joy when my name is mentioned."

But how to get at Sir Hyde? The latter never saw Nelson — seemed to avoid him. "Sir Hyde is on board sulky." "Sir Hyde has not told me officially a thing." Unless the old man could be talked to for a few minutes he would inevitably adopt some policy of negotiation and marking time. Yet Nelson could not force his way into the Admiral's cabin. He paced the quarterdeck of the *St George* in an unusually silent mood.

It was then that one of his lieutenants, named Layman, who knew those seas well, chanced to remark that on the Dogger Bank some years before, at the very point the fleet was now passing over, he had one day caught a remarkably fine turbot. To his surprise, Nelson showed the liveliest interest in this obscure feat of angling. "Do you think *we* could catch a turbot?" he asked. Layman said they could try. Lines were got out, and after a time, sure enough, a small turbot was duly hauled on board. Upon which Nelson at once proposed sending it to the Admiral (and it was then that Layman, remembering Sir Hyde's weakness for the pleasures of the table, suddenly saw light). But it was now night time, and the waves were high, and this was respectfully pointed out to Nelson. He would not even listen. A boat was ordered out, and, with great peril, conveyed the turbot across the dark waters from the *St George,* to the Admiral's flagship, the *London.* When it came back it bore a grateful note of thanks, couched in the most cordial terms. And a day or two later Nelson was invited to the flagship to a conference. "Now we are sure of fighting," he wrote to Emma, "I am sent for."

Lest this version of events should seem trivial and unconvincing it may be added that years later, when Nelson and Layman met again, the latter accused the Admiral of having won the battle of Copenhagen through the assistance of a turbot, and, according to him, Nelson laughingly admitted it. It is certain that, from this moment, he more or less took charge. The fleet anchored in the Kattegat on March 20, and the conference on the flagship took place on the 23rd. It fell to the duty of Lieutenant Layman to steer Nelson's boat across from the *St George*, and even he could not help observing that "on board the *London* the heads appeared very gloomy." As a matter of fact, they had already practically decided to remain in the Kattegat, and open negotiations from there. A glance at the map will show that a fleet so situated would be

powerless to enforce anything: it must pass through the Sound
— a narrow passage, a mile or two wide, Danish on one bank,
Swedish on the other — before it could get within striking distance of Copenhagen.

Nelson soon altered all that. His prestige, his popularity,
his driving-power were not to be resisted by a man of Parker's
calibre. Colonel Stewart, who commanded the marines, has
left us the picture of Nelson striding restlessly up and down
the Admiral's cabin, while the others remained seated round
the table. Some one remarked upon the unexpected strength
of the Danes. "The more numerous the better," he snapped.
The Russians were formidable — "so much the better." The
fact is that these reports of the enemies' numbers and pre-
paredness had seriously alarmed Parker, in the absence of
Nelson. He had further to consider that, if he entered the
Sound, the Swedes might open fire upon him from the
northern bank, as the Danes were certain to do from the south,
and he might find himself running a very unpleasant kind
of gauntlet — as Duckworth did at Constantinople a few years
later. It is a question whether, in the absence of Nelson, he
would ever have moved out of the Kattegat.

But Nelson bore all before him. Returning to his ship,
when the meeting had broken up, he embodied his views in a
really masterly memorandum, which should be read by every
one who has fallen into the habit of thinking of him as a mere
swashbuckling hero. Needless to say he advocated an immediate offensive as the best method of defence. His first and
favourite scheme was to leave a squadron to watch the Danes,
and hurry northward and surprise the Russians in Reval.
"The measure may be thought bold," he admits, "but I am
of opinion the boldest measures are the safest"; and no less
an authority than Mahan holds that, if this proposal had been
adapted, the Northern Confederacy must immediately have
fallen with a crash — for the Tsar was its base. The other
plan was to attack and destroy the Danish fleet at Copenhagen — good enough in its way, but, as compared with Reval,
rather like lopping off the branches at the top of a tree, in-

P

stead of slashing through the trunk. This memorandum, which took the form of a letter addressed to the Admiral, represented perhaps the best use Nelson ever made of his pen.

Sir Hyde Parker, of course, preferred the second plan. He could not face the risk of sailing north to Reval, with an undefeated enemy in his rear. And an enemy the Dane was, for Mr Vansittart had been ashore, and had returned with a firm refusal of the British demands. Another conference was held on the 31st. Nelson, seeing that he could never spur the Admiral into the Russian adventure, concentrated upon persuading him to attack the Danes at once. And Sir Hyde Parker, by this time, as Nelson says to Emma, had "found out the worth of your Nelson and that he is a useful sort of man in a pinch," never took another important decision without consulting him. In the meantime the fleet had safely passed through the Sound. The Swedes, who were evidently waiting to see which way the cat would jump, had not fired a shot from their bank, and, by steering well to the north, the English ships had been able to keep out of range of the Danish batteries, which nevertheless wasted a lot of ammunition. They were now anchored six miles from Cronenburg, detained by contrary winds. When they could get a little nearer, Nelson and Parker together personally reconnoitred the Danish defences.

The enemy's position was so strong that it is impossible not to sympathize with Parker's hesitations. Copenhagen could not be approached from the north because of the powerful Crown battery. Southwards from the battery was anchored a row of hulks, nearly four miles in length, which were well enough armed to be called floating batteries, though a line-of-battle ship was believed to be stronger than any one of them. Immediately in front of the town was a shoal, called the Middle Ground, which closed the direct approach. An enemy must therefore advance in single file, either past the Crown battery on the north, or wriggling in between the hulks and the shoal at the southern end. This was the situation that the senior English officers had to consider at the conference of the 31st. And it was then that Nelson offered to take twelve of the lightest ships of the line, with all the frigates, and try to get at the enemy through the difficult and shallow channel to the south, while the Admiral, with the rest, made a demonstration against the Crown battery from the north. He had shifted his flag from the *St George* to the much lighter *Elephant* (74) commanded by his old friend Captain Foley, who had led the line at Aboukir. This plan was officially adopted, and as there was no time to be lost Nelson weighed anchor, and, though it was late in the afternoon, led his squadron round the Middle Ground, until they reached the south-eastern end of the shoal, and cast anchor at the entrance to the channel through which they must pass next day to make their attack.

It was now getting dark. As usual before going into action, Nelson was in that mood of feverish excitement which next day would harden into cold steel. He was in high spirits at dinner in the great cabin of the *Elephant* to which he had invited Captains Foley, Hardy, Fremantle, Riou (in command of the frigates), and Rear-Admiral Graves, who was his second-in-command. They all drank to a leading wind next day, and the confusion of the King's enemies. Nelson and Riou then went out and reconnoitred the channel, taking careful soundings, and they were confirmed in their opinion that it was possible for the squadron to slip through and anchor by the stern, in line ahead opposite the Danish hulks. Afterwards they sat up with Foley in the after-cabin preparing the plans. Nelson never made an attack that had not been carefully thought out beforehand; but these orders for battle at Copenhagen were by far the most detailed he ever wrote, simply because the situation was already fixed, and he had, therefore, several hours in which to prepare them. By comparison with Copenhagen, the Nile and Trafalgar were mere guesswork, though every effort was made to anticipate every possible situation. Nelson was a great improviser, and he never thought better than when he had to do it quickly. But it is only at Copenhagen that we see his tactical ideas, so to speak, in full dress and worked out at leisure. That is what gives the battle its unique interest.

He walked up and down the cabin, as his habit was, dictating these orders to his secretaries, and the night was already far advanced and daylight near when his old servant, Tom Allen, that rough, faithful watchdog, insisted upon his going to bed. Even then he did not rest, calling out continually from his cot to know how the copyists were getting on. There must be a fair transcript of the orders in every captain's hands before breakfast. It is an interesting scene — and not its least interesting feature is that the southernmost ships of the Danish line were less than two miles away, so that it seems certain that, with a little more enterprise, and a little less attention to purely defensive preparations, they might have advanced some of their mortar-boats, and thrown shells over the tip end of the shoal into the midst of the English squadron! They did not do so. The English, on the other hand, continued making soundings all night, and Captain Hardy is even alleged to have reached the leading Danish ship and had his boat rowed round her while he tested the depth of the water with a long pole.

Day dawned with a fair wind from the south, and nothing to prevent the carrying out of Nelson's orders if the seamanship of his fleet was equal to the occasion. The plan was for the three leading English ships, having passed through the channel and rounded the shoal, to anchor opposite the fifth, sixth, and seventh in the Danish line. The fourth and fifth English ships were to tackle the first and second Danes, while the rest went farther north, taking stations successively opposite the enemy line. The idea in this somewhat complicated arrangement was that the first two Danes would be battered by the first three English as they passed, and would therefore be disposed of quickly by their true opponents, the fourth and fifth English ships, who would then immediately cut their cables and drift north, so as to bring overwhelming force against the next section of the Danish line. And to make this more certain the *Desirée* frigate was ordered to anchor across the bows of the southernmost Dane, as soon as she was fully engaged, and rake her.

It was the old idea of bringing battering-ram strength against one point in the line. Nelson could not, as at the Nile, obtain this result by an enveloping movement, because there was not enough water between the Danish ships and the shore. So he produced this kind of sectional or kangaroo attack as an ingenious substitute. The English bomb vessels were to anchor behind the line, near the shoal, and throw bombs over their own ships at the Danes — and this they duly did, but without much effect. The frigates under Riou were kept in reserve. Each ship of the line towed a flat boat full of soldiers, who were intended to be set ashore to storm the Crown battery, if, after the destruction of the enemy fleet, the British peace terms were not agreed to. As it turned out, they were not required; but posterity may feel grateful to them for being there, since it was their commander, Colonel Stewart, who wrote the best and fullest account of the battle that we possess. This chapter is based upon his admirable narrative.

That was the plan. But almost immediately things began to go wrong. To begin with, when the pilots were called on board the *Elephant* between eight and nine o'clock in the morning to receive their orders, they began with one accord to disclaim the responsibility of leading the fleet through the channel. Most of them had served on merchant ships in those waters; they knew them well enough, they said, to follow another man through, but not to lead. At last the master of the *Bellona,* a Mr Brierly, solved the difficulty by offering to go on board the *Edgar,* the leading ship, and pilot her through. At half-past nine the signal was given to weigh in succession, and the *Edgar* proceeded through the channel "in a most noble manner," until she reached the fifth ship in the enemy line, when she anchored and began to exchange broadsides. But the next in line behind her, the *Agamemnon* (Nelson's old ship), failed to weather the shoal and never got into action; and two other ships of the line, the *Bellona* (deprived of Brierly's services) and the *Russell,* though they rounded the shoal, kept too close to it and ran aground before they could reach the enemy. Only two bomb vessels reached their station by the shoal, and they, with the *Bellona* and the *Russell,* continued to fire over the English ships at the enemy throughout the action.

That reduced the English strength from twelve ships of the line to nine. The others, following the *Edgar,* did their best to conform to the situation: the *Elephant,* for instance, anchored opposite the Danish flagship, and the others disposed themselves so as to fill up the gaps left by the three ships aground, and cover the Danish line as far as possible. But the northernmost of the fifteen or sixteen Danish hulks were left without any opponents, and no one was firing a shot at the Crown battery, which it had been intended to engage at the same time. Riou therefore took his frigates (except the *Desirée,* which had got across the bows of the southernmost Dane as arranged) to the northern end of the line, and very gallantly plunged into the conflict against some of the enemy's heaviest metal. The English, as we have seen, had anchored by the stern, their sails loose but clewed up, the wind still blowing fresh from the south.

There began a ding-dong struggle, yard-arm to yard-arm — a mere slogging match, so to speak, with none of the art and the rhythm and the decisive finish of the Nile. The Danes fought valiantly, and they kept reinforcing their crews with boatloads of men from the shore, so that, for a long time, the issue hung in the balance. Nelson had never had his ships so badly knocked about before, and his casualties were terribly high — though, curiously enough, this was the only first-class engagement he was ever in without getting hurt himself. The Danes were losing even more heavily; their decks were covered with dead and dying; most of the officers were down, but they continued obstinately to bring off fresh men from the shore to work the guns, so that it really seemed that this bloody contest might go on for ever or until even the stamina of the English seamen gave way.

Admiral Sir Hyde Parker, from his station in the northern channel, was watching the progress of the battle with increasing anxiety. He was out of range of the Crown battery, which was spitting fire at Riou's frigates, the nearest British ships in his line of vision, and obviously doing considerable execution among them. Beyond he could see the long double line of Nelson's seventy-fours and the Danish hulks swaying in their desperate struggle. He could not get near to help — for it would have been suicide to attempt the northern channel under the battery's guns — and it is to his credit that his helplessness exasperated him. He does not appear to have appreciated that the real reason why this hammer-and-tongs exchange of broadsides had gone on so long, without any decisive result, was that the English ships were anchored at a full cable's length from the enemy, being afraid to go closer because of the shallow water. That is another reason why this action often seems a little "out of character" in Nelson's record. Speed, his characteristic quality, was absent — being unnecessary in the preparation and impossible in the execution. But Admiral Sir Hyde Parker did not grasp all this. He could see that it was touch-and-go — or so it seemed to him — and he did the inevitable thing that such a man would do in such a situation: he made the signal to discontinue the action.

Admiral Lord Nelson was walking the quarterdeck of the *Elephant* with his quick, eager step. He was talking to Colonel Stewart. A round shot knocked a piece out of the main-mast and the splinters flew round them. "He observed to me, with a smile," says Stewart, "it is warm work, and this day may be the last to any of us at a moment,' and then, stopping short at the gangway, he used an expression never to be erased from my memory, and said with emotion, 'but mark you I would not be elsewhere for thousands.' " The *Elephant* was warmly engaged with the *Dannebrog,* the enemy flagship, and two other floating batteries. One or two hulks had ceased fire; but most of them — and notably those at the southernmost end of the line, which it had been intended to silence quickly — were still fighting vigorously and upsetting

Nelson's calculations. (Indeed the *Isis* (50) and the *Polyphemus* (64), the two southernmost British ships, had suffered very severely, and but for the plucky conduct of Captain Inman of the *Desirée,* who kept his frigate across the bows of these great hulks throughout the action, raking them vigorously, the little *Isis* must have been entirely destroyed.)

At this moment the signal lieutenant of the *Elephant* reported to the Admiral that the signal to discontinue action was flying from the flagship. Nelson appeared to take no notice, but continued his walk up and down the starboard side between the gangway and the after-cabins. But the lieutenant, a conscientious officer, met him at his next turn, and inquired whether the Commander-in-Chief's signal was to be repeated to his squadron. "No," said Nelson, "acknowledge it" — that was all. But as the officer climbed the ladder to the poop he shouted after him to know whether the signal for close action was still hoisted from the *Elephant,* and on being told that it was, he added, "Mind you keep it so." He said no more at the moment, but as he continued his walk, Stewart noticed that he waved the stump of his right arm, a sure sign of agitation with him. Suddenly turning to the soldier, he asked him if he understood the Admiral's signal, and explained what it meant. "Leave off action!" he kept repeating indignantly, "now damn me if I do!" A few more steps, and he suddenly turned with a broad grin to Captain Foley, who was on the quarterdeck, and exclaiming that with only one eye he had a right to be blind sometimes, he clapped his glass to his right eye, and directed it towards the flagship. "I really do not see the signal," said Nelson; and with that he dismissed Sir Hyde Parker from his mind, and turned his attention to the matter in hand — the victory of Copenhagen.

A few minutes later Captain Otway came on board. He had come from the Admiral with a message for Lord Nelson. Sir Hyde Parker explained that, if Nelson saw a prospect of victory, he might disobey the last signal, but that if he felt he should break off the action, there was his authority. There has been much argument about this incident. On the strength of a statement by Dr A. J. Scott, who was Parker's secretary (and afterwards Nelson's at Trafalgar) that it was "arranged between the Admirals" for the signal for retreat to be made, in order "to give Lord Nelson the option of retiring if he thought fit," it has been suggested that everything had been *previously* arranged, and, in fact, that the business with the glass was mere pantomime and playing to the gallery — a pastime from which Nelson was not entirely averse. But it is obvious that Otway, on this theory, need never have been sent; and in fact he only arrived with his explanation after the signal had been disobeyed. It is clear that Nelson disobeyed first and was authorized to do so afterwards. This view of what happened reconciles all contemporary evidence, and accounts for Nelson's later remark that he was acting contrary to orders, and "might perhaps be hanged."

But the most conclusive argument against any previous arrangement is to be found in the action of the other English commanders. The nearest of these to the flagship was Riou; behind him Graves, with the northernmost English ships of the line; and beyond him again Nelson, towards whom Captain Otway was being rowed in his gig. Mark what happened. As soon as Riou saw the signal he repeated it to his frigates, and his whole squadron, which was being rather badly mauled, drew off from the enemy. As Riou's ship, the *Amazon,* showed her stern to the Crown battery as she turned away, she was raked, and Riou and many others were killed. Graves took a line of his own; he acknowledged the signal and repeated it to his ships, but at the same time he kept the signal for close action flying, and never made a movement to break off. Surely the confusion caused by this unhappy signal is sufficient proof that it had never been discussed beforehand.

But now at last the Danes began to crack. At two o'clock in the afternoon most of the hulks had ceased to fire. The *Dannebrog* and one or two others were in flames and had struck their flags. But to make your opponent strike was one thing; it was quite another, in this unusual kind of sea-fight, to take possession of him. For just as the British boats were approaching more Danes would arrive from the shore, and would hoist the flag again, and fire on the boats, to the great indignation of the English. One can easily understand how it happened; most of the officers were killed, or had gone ashore, or removed themselves to other ships, as the Commander of the *Dannebrog* had done; and, in their absence, the more warlike spirits among the men would rally round some petty officer and renew the fight. This was what happened when Nelson's boats attempted to take possession of the opposing flagship. He was enraged beyond measure. Hurrying into the stern gallery of the *Elephant,* he took paper and wrote his famous letter to the Danish Crown Prince, which began, "To the brothers of Englishmen, the Danes," and ended with the plain threat that unless all firing ceased at once, he would burn every prize he had taken, with their crews on board of them. He has been blamed for using such a threat; but it undoubtedly saved the lives of large numbers of Englishmen and Danes — which was precisely its object.

We must remember the horror which these violations of the rules of warfare would inspire in a professional sailor; nor could we expect him, in the heat of the moment, to pause and consider that half the men at the Danish guns were landsmen who knew nothing of these rules. The strength of his feeling on the subject may be judged by the indignation with which he afterwards read the official report of the battle by Commodore Fischer, commanding the *Dannebrog,* in which the writer tried to represent the result as a draw, exaggerated the strength of his opponents, and spoke of two English ships striking their flags. Nelson, in reply, wrote to the Danish Adjutant-General, accusing Fischer of cowardice in deserting his ship, and of dishonourable conduct in going on board another ship which was continuing the fight, when he had already struck his own flag. Lindholm, the Adjutant-General, who was Nelson's personal friend, replied soothingly, and the matter dropped.

It was at this difficult moment, when the battle, though

practically over, kept breaking out again unexpectedly here and there (for instance, the *Elephant* had ceased firing, but the three ships ahead of her were still actively engaged), that the boat from the *Elephant,* with its flag of truce and Nelson's letter, reached the shore. The Crown Prince was found near the sally-port, encouraging his people to renewed efforts, but as soon as he had read Nelson's letter, he returned a civil reply asking for a more detailed proposal of terms. In the meantime Nelson had sent for Fremantle from the *Ganges,* and with him and Foley, was discussing the possibility of bringing up his least damaged ships from the south, and making a united attack upon the northern hulks and the Crown battery, which was the only part of the Danish line where there was still any serious resistance. Two ships from the Commander-in-Chief's division had succeeded in approaching, and with their help something might be done; but it looked like the beginning of a second battle, with victory again in doubt.

It is no reflection upon the ardour of Nelson, or his two captains, to suggest that the arrival of the Crown Prince's conciliatory reply must have been a relief. In answer he offered to cease hostilities, and to send all the Danish wounded on shore, while he collected his unwounded prisoners and burned his prizes. On these terms a truce of twenty-four hours was arranged. And Nelson, after giving orders that the British ships were to remain at their stations all night, had himself rowed out through the channel to the *St George* and went to his own cabin, where he managed to scribble a few lines to Emma — "9 o'clock at night, very tired after a hard fought battle" — and threw himself exhausted on his cot.

Thus ended the battle of Copenhagen, of which it has been said, with some justice, that, as regards its political importance, it was second to none among Nelson's victories; while as regards the difficulties to be overcome, the strength of the resistance, and the ill luck which upset his plans in many details, it was the most critical battle he ever fought. The English lost nearly a thousand killed and wounded, the Danes at least twice as many. The boats were busy all night collecting the prisoners, and taking the wounded Danes ashore. Early in the morning Nelson was back on the *Elephant,* directing operations — the refitting of the English ships and the securing of the ten or more Danish prizes, in regard to some of which it was a disputed question as to whether they had surrendered or not.

In the meantime notes were passing between Sir Hyde Parker and the Crown Prince, and about noon Nelson was instructed to go ashore and interview the latter with a view to arranging an armistice. Without hesitation he stepped into his barge, and was pulled into the landing place, where was assembled a great, murmuring crowd of the citizens of Copenhagen, their feelings about equally divided between hatred and admiration. He was totally unconscious of all that. He sprang lightly ashore, and, with his sunny smile, began to push his way through the people in the direction of the palace. It is difficult to say which of his two outstanding qualities, his vanity or his indifference to danger, was most conspicuous at this moment. Perhaps the former, for, in his own account of the incident, he says that "the people received me as they always have done; and even the stairs of the palace were crowded, huzza-ing, and saying, 'God bless Lord Nelson.'" And it is certain, from contemporary accounts, that there was something so disarming about him that this Danish crowd did actually raise a cheer. Incidentally, it was a tribute to their sportsmanship. For our own purposes it is important as one of the best illustrations in Nelson's career of his unconscious power over the mob.

He saw the Crown Prince. There was a number of Danish officers present, and the discussion, on the whole, was amicable, as between opponents who knew each other's worth. Nelson demanded an armistice of fourteen weeks, which, as he very frankly told them, would give him time to go to Reval and deal with their allies, the Russians, and come back again. Some of the Danes objected to this, and one of them said something about a renewal of the battle of the morning. Nelson knew just enough French (the language of the conference) to understand this threat, and he turned like a flash and exclaimed to Colonel Stewart: "Tell him we are ready at a moment; ready to bombard this very night." In the end he got his terms, and so dropped the curtain on the last armed conflict that has ever taken place between Englishmen and Danes. The Danish prizes were burned and sent to the bottom, with all their guns, and the English ships moved out again through the channel.

On April 12 the fleet once more entered the Baltic, but the *St George,* with her great draught, found it impossible to pass the straits and had to be left behind temporarily, with Nelson on board. The fever of battle was still upon him. He was longing to make an end of England's other enemies in the north. The news of the assassination of the Tsar, and the consequent change in Russian foreign policy, had not yet reached the fleet. But as he sat fuming on the *St George,* there was a sudden rumour (a false one, as it turned out) that the Swedes were at sea, and that an engagement might be expected at any moment. Nelson had tasted blood and was mad for more. "We have reports that the Swedish fleet is above the shallows, distant five or six leagues," he wrote. "All our fellows are longing to beat them, and so do I, as great a boy as any of them, for I consider this as being at school, and going to England as going home for the holidays, therefore I really long to finish my task."

That was to Lady Hamilton, of course. What he did was to get into one of the *St George's* boats, without food or any proper wraps against the cold, and set out forthwith on a six-hours' row against wind and current to join the British fleet. He would not miss a fight. The officer in charge of the boat offered him his great-coat, but Nelson refused. "No, I am not cold." It was midnight when he reached the fleet and climbed on board the *Elephant,* once more hoisting his flag there. Of course he caught a severe chill, and had to go to bed, where, for the moment, we will leave him — only noting that he was somewhat recovered by the end of May, though, as he wrote to Emma, "emaciated more than you can conceive."

CHAPTER XVI

FRUSTRATION

WE HAVE said that it was a worried and harassed man who set out on the northern adventure. It was a worried and harassed man who returned from it. With our modern preoccupation with sex-problems it is natural to ascribe all Nelson's nervousness and obvious unhappiness at this time to his more or less clandestine love affair, to his enforced absence from his mistress and her child, and, above all, to the terrible fits of jealousy which now began to assail him. The remarkable series of letters in which he reveals these tortures of the heart have only recently been made public — another reason, no doubt, why modern writers are inclined to overemphasize them. But whatever we may think of their real importance in Nelson's life, they require to be noticed and taken into consideration.

The trouble began with the Prince of Wales. That shrewd official, Mr Hugh Elliot, had already prophesied of Emma (p. 202): "She will captivate the Prince of Wales whose mind is as vulgar as her own." For a time it seemed likely that this prophecy would come true, and the handsome young voluptuary, who was afterwards to ascend the throne as George IV and bequeath Buckingham Palace and Brighton to the nation, was, at the moment, comparatively heart-free. He had long ago forgotten the unfortunate affair of Perdita Robinson, and had survived so many later fancies that it now required something more than mere beauty and wit — something more dramatic and sensational — to appeal to his jaded palate. He had overloved as he had overeaten, and was suffering from the effects of both. In these circumstances, the arrival in London of the famous Lady Hamilton, whose graceful "attitudes" were the talk of the town, whose portraits by Romney and Reynolds and others he must have seen a dozen times, whose native wit and diplomatic skill were said to have held Naples to the allied cause, and who now trailed the popular hero of Aboukir in her train like a captive must have seemed to him in the nature of a challenge.

He did nothing for the first few months; but after Nelson had left London, to hoist his flag on the *San Josef*, he wrote to the Hamiltons and invited himself to dinner. Not much in that, to the modern mind; but the way in which Emma's two protectors, her husband and her lover, took it, is an amazing revelation of one of the essential differences between 1801 and 1931. Nelson first heard of it from Sir William, who wrote him a letter in which he vainly tried to conceal the panic he was in. From every point of view this letter was such an extraordinary communication that it deserves to be quoted. The husband wrote:

> We have been drawn in to be under the *absolute necessity* of giving a dinner to the P. of Wales on Sunday next. He asked it himself, having expressed a strong desire of hearing Banti's* and Emma's voices together. I am well aware of the dangers . . . not that I fear that Emma could ever be induced to act contrary to the prudent conduct she has hitherto pursued; but the world is so ill-natured that the worst construction is put on the most innocent actions. As this dinner must be, or he would be offended, I shall keep strictly to the musical part, invite only Banti, her husband and Taylor; and as I wish to show a civility to Davison, I have sent him an invitation. In short, we shall get rid of it as well as we can, and guard against its producing more meetings of the same sort. Emma would really have gone any lengths to have avoided Sunday's dinner. But I thought it would not be prudent to break with the P. of Wales; who really has shown the greatest civility to us when we were last in England, and since we returned: and she has, at last, acquiesced to my opinion.

---

* The operatic singer.

The man might almost be apologising to Nelson! The latter was appalled at the news. After a night of agony he seized pen and paper, and scribbled off the following half frantic effusion, not to old Sir William, but to Emma herself:

> You are too beautiful not to have enemies, and even one visit will stamp you . . . the thought so agitates me that I cannot write. I had wrote a few lines last night, but I am in tears, I cannot bear it . . . forgive me, Emma, oh forgive your own, dear, disinterested Nelson . . . I am so agitated I can write nothing. I knew it would be so and you can't help it. Do not sit long at table. Good God! He will be next to you and telling you soft things! Oh, God! that I was dead.

He even so far forgets his loyalty as to refer to the Prince of Wales as a "serpent." And, "as to letting him hear you sing, I only hope he will be struck deaf and you dumb, sooner than such a thing should happen." The writing stumbles a little. His left hand — his only hand — is strangely unsteady; and his sight, as he tells her, is dimmed by tears. His frail figure is shaken cruelly. Now that he has found his love at last — cannot he even now be *sure*?

In the end there was rather a feeble anticlimax. Lady Hamilton was taken ill, and the dinner party was abandoned. "I am so unwell," she wrote to Mrs William Nelson, "that we cannot have His Royal Highness to dinner on Sunday, which will *not* vex me." Nor is there any reason to doubt her word.

The effects of this, no doubt, highly ridiculous incident — it is always so easy to laugh at lovers' fears — are to be seen in the letters which Nelson wrote to Lady Hamilton before and after the battle of Copenhagen. He made an effort to forget all about it. Before the actual date of the dinner party he was writing:

> Your letters have made me happy to-day; and never again will I scold unless you begin, therefore pray never do; my confidence in you is firm as a rock.

And in May, soon after the battle, this wonderful confession of faith:

GEORGE, PRINCE OF WALES

Gillray's caricature entitled *A Voluptuary under the Horrors of Indigestion.*

As truly as I believe in God do I believe you are a saint . . . and may God's curse alight upon those who want to draw you, my dearest friend, from a quiet home into the company of men and women of bad character; and I am one of those who believe that in England the higher the class, the worse the company.

From some of his letters, one might suppose him to be entirely in her power:

Mr S. is quite right that through the medium of your influence is the surest way to get my influence . . . for you never ask anything that does not do honour to your feelings as the best woman, as far as my knowledge goes, that ever lived.

Yet we note that his "private feelings" are "fixed ever on you and about you *whenever the public service does not arrest my attention.*" A rather prosaic version of—"I could not love thee, dear, so much." And, a few months later when, as we shall see, he was in command of the Channel defences, and Emma wrote to him (for she was almost as much in love as he was) begging him not to leave harbour on dangerous expeditions, he replied quite definitely that "even if I was to forfeit your friendship, which is dearer to me than all the world," he could make no such promise. "For I go out; if I see the enemy and can get at them, it is my duty; and you would naturally hate me if I kept back one moment."

We must not fall into the habit of thinking of Nelson as though he were a character in a modern novel. It is no more than a simple fact, which anyone with a balanced mind, a slight acquaintance with history and with his fellow-men will immediately recognize, that there were at least a dozen reasons, every one of them as important as his love affair, to account for Nelson's state of mind at this time. All the circumstances in which the Baltic campaign was fought were of the sort to drive a man of his fiery genius to distraction — the delays, the vacillations of his chief whom he served so loyally but could never believe in, the difficulty of persuading people to allow him to act, as he said himself, "on the great scale." And now, when the victory was won, and Sir H. Parker had

Q

been recalled — for, though Nelson never said a word against
him, his whole conduct, and especially that unhappy signal,
was more than the Admiralty could stomach — and when
Nelson had been made Commander-in-Chief in his place, and
been raised to the rank of Viscount, and had been thanked by
everybody, and was more than ever a national hero — even
now things were not right; there was a sense of frustration.
Why had the city of London done nothing? He afterwards
estimated that this Baltic campaign cost him personally
£2000; and no doubt he had calculated upon some material
reward, such as had been voted to him after Aboukir. He was
a poor man. Worst of all, nothing was done for the gallant
officers and men under his command. No medal was issued.
He knew what was the real opinion of anyone who mattered.
Lord St Vincent had written to him privately: "Your Lordship's whole conduct, from your first appointment to this
hour, is the subject of our constant admiration: it does not
become me to make comparisons; all agree there is but one
Nelson." But as First Lord of the Admiralty he had con-
curred in the half-hearted approval coldly accorded to the
terms of the armistice obtained by Nelson after Copenhagen:
and Nelson knew in his heart, as we can see, that these terms
were good, and could only have been got by a Nelson.

So here was the newly created Viscount, shivering amid the
ice and frost under the leaden northern skies which his poet's
soul had always hated; and his small invalid body shrunk
from doing dull routine work, still in the neighbourhood of
Copenhagen, with no hope left that the Swedes or anybody
else would fight him. And then he gets a letter from his old
friend Troubridge, now Sir Thomas Troubridge of the Admiralty, actually congratulating him upon having succeeded
to the command. "Does he take me for a greater fool than
I am," remarked Nelson irritably — and his affection for
Troubridge sensibly cooled.

But I go back to that word *frustration*. It is as though
Nelson, the man of destiny, knew, with some inner conscious-
ness denied to lesser men, that his time was getting short.

From the victory at Copenhagen to the final scene at Trafalgar was but four and a half years. That was all he had left to finish his work in. And with that strange instinct of his, amounting almost to a gift of prophecy, which we see manifesting itself at short intervals throughout his career, he may have known that only a portion even of those few years would be given to him — he may have felt the approach of the Peace of Amiens more distinctly even than the diplomatists who negotiated it. I do not mean simply that he had a presentiment of death, and wanted to get all he could out of life; I mean, what is almost exactly the opposite, that he wanted to write *finis* to his work and make it an artistic whole. And here he was kicking his heels in the Baltic.

Yet he kept that fleet in apple-pie order. If the Swedes had harboured any thoughts of taking hostile action (which is doubtful), they forgot them now that Nelson was in command. The British fleet, having tasted battle, was greedy for more, and, as in all fleets commanded by Nelson, every one from powder-monkey to Admiral was "on his toes." And this he did without the slightest appearance of being a martinet. He hated punishments. Ferguson tells us that Nelson "was more miserable and unhappy during the execution of a sentence than the culprit himself" — a variation of the familiar schoolmaster's theory that a cane hurts him more than it does his victim, but in this case probably true. It is in connexion with this particular voyage that we hear of his pleasant practice of calling tired young midshipmen off the watch to have breakfast with him at four or five o'clock in the morning — his usual hour of rising — and of how he would enter into their boyish jokes with them, so that he must have known more of what went on in the midshipmen's berth than any admiral before his time or since. He was not a martinet, but, as Ferguson says, "he understood mankind and could lead them where he pleased."

If Nelson now began to pull the strings, in order to secure his return to England, no one can say that he was deserting in the face of the enemy, for there was no enemy to face; and if he gave as his reason for asking for leave that his health had suffered from the rigours of the northern climate, no one who has studied his career can doubt that it was true. He wrote a number of letters, and Lord St Vincent replied privately that he quite agreed Nelson ought to come home, and that they were sending out his friend, Admiral Pole, to replace him. His second-in-command, Graves, had also been ill and in bed. On May 24 he heard of the death of his elder brother, Maurice, and became more than ever anxious to get back and attend to family affairs.

At last, on June 13, arrived the Admiralty's formal sanction of his leave, and suddenly everything began to look brighter. Accompanying the Admiralty's letter were instructions to Nelson to confer upon Rear-Admiral Graves the Order of the Bath, in the name of the King, and in recognition of his services at Copenhagen. It was the only recognition accorded to anyone below him; and it involved precisely the kind of ceremony that Nelson delighted in. All the officers of the fleet were assembled on the quarterdeck of the *St George,* and even the cold Baltic sun was doing its best to shine, when Nelson, in full uniform, wearing all his decorations, drew his sword with a flourish and gave Graves the accolade. Afterwards he made an animated speech to the assembled company. A few days later Pole arrived. Nelson was so excited that he declares to Emma that he could not sleep. An hour or two's conversation with his successor was all that was needed, and he set sail for England, turning his back for ever upon the northern snows.

Nelson landed at Yarmouth on July 1, 1801, and the first thing he did was to repeat his visit to the hospitals — which were now filled with the wounded from Copenhagen. The volunteer cavalry again escorted him from the town, and he made his way once more to London, amid the acclamations of the people. Arrived there, he went straight to No. 23, Piccadilly, where the Hamiltons were then living, having sold most of Emma's jewellery in order to pay the rent. But this was early July, and London was empty and dull and dusty.

So they went, all three, and stayed for a few days at Box Hill with Nelson's clergyman brother, William, and then they moved on to the Bush Inn at Staines, which they made their headquarters during this all too brief leave.

We can know nothing of what happened between them, except that Nelson now stated his wish to have a country place of his own, to which he might retire with these two friends if there should be a peace with France, and that he authorized Lady Hamilton, who was clever at that kind of thing, to find such a house for him, and make all the arrangements. He seemed to know it would be his last chance. He was suffering the inevitable penalty of popularity. "Oh, how I hate to be stared at!" he wrote about this time; and when strangers came to call on him he passionately refused to "be shown about like a beast." There is a marked change here from the attitude of the professional national hero. Emma seems to have been more in love with him than at any time since Naples. As soon as he had left them she began to write him letters showing jealousy not only of his "aunt" (as they called Lady Nelson between them), but of every woman he ever mentioned. He replied vigorously: "You need not fear all the women in this world, for all others, except yourself, are pests to me."

It was not to be supposed that Nelson could rest yet. By the Peace of Lunéville, between France and Austria, signed on February 9 of this same year, 1801, war had ceased all over the continent of Europe. Only England still stood out. And Napoleon — that greatest master of publicity and propaganda in the whole history of a not too reputable art — had determined to frighten England, the only one of his enemies that he had not been able to chastise, into a disadvantageous peace. He proceeded to do so by the simple and inexpensive method of setting up an enormous paper army at Boulogne and Flushing and all the Channel ports, ostensibly designed for the invasion of London or the southern counties. England was seriously alarmed. Those were the days when the name of "Boney" was used to frighten naughty children with; and now the British Government, fearful for its popularity, was looking round for a name equally potent to set against it as a sedative.

Obviously Nelson's! Appoint him to command the southern coast defences, or at any rate the most important section of them, and public confidence would immediately be restored. We have had nothing like it in our time, except the influence of Lord Kitchener's name in 1914, when the Liberal Government very properly made him Minister for War. In 1801 the wealthy merchants of London, the fishermen and agriculturists of the southern coasts were all agreed about one thing — that if Nelson were there the French could do them no harm. Had he not said himself that "the only way to deal with a Frenchman was to knock him down?" — and had he not shown that he was the man to do it? If the name of Boney frightened idle children into wakefulness, the name of Nelson soothed the good ones to sleep at night. He was accordingly asked to take command of the fleet of frigates and smaller vessels which had been assembled for the defence of the coast between Orfordness in Suffolk and Beachy Head. He immediately accepted, and on July 27, less than four weeks after his landing in England, he went to Sheerness and hoisted his flag on the *Unité* frigate. A few days later he transferred to the *Medusa,* the frigate on which he spent most of his time during the succeeding months in the Channel.

He found himself in rather a delicate position, for it had been specially provided that he should be independent of the admiral commanding in the Downs, and this was just the kind of situation which in those, or any other times, might be expected to lead to friction. But the admiral in the Downs happened to be his old friend Lutwidge; and Nelson — though alas! he had lost much of his former sunny radiance and no longer laid himself out to capture the heart of every man he met — was still a person impossible to quarrel with unless he himself desired it. Lord St Vincent wrote to both officers, explaining very frankly the Admiralty's reasons for dividing the command, and to Nelson he added that he relied on "the delicacy you have already shown to senior officers." He was not disappointed; relations between Nelson and Lutwidge continued perfectly cordial to the end. It need hardly be said that from the moment of Nelson's arrival at Sheerness events began to move. He drew up an elaborate memorandum, in which he examined in detail the possibilities of a French attack at different points on the coast, and came to the conclusion — quite unwarrantably — that they would probably divide their forces and strike at London and the Sussex coast at the same time. And having done this, he set sail himself and went and had a look at the French ports — and in less than a fortnight was able to assert confidently that there would be no invasion at all! This time he was right.

Any other commander finding himself in such a situation — and any other man as desperately in love as Nelson was, so that he was writting to Emma, "our separation is terrible, my heart is ready to flow out of my eyes"—would surely have been content now to mark time, and allow his name to act as a soothing syrup for the public, which was all that the Admiralty really asked of him. But though he was tired and unhappy and longing for home, he at once set to work to see what could be done against the French, since it was clear that nothing would be done by them. The fleet, as always, had caught his spirit. "In my command," he wrote to the Admiralty, "I can tell you with truth that I find much zeal and good humour; and should Mr Bonaparte put himself in our way, I believe he will wish himself even in Corsica." But he adds significantly that he hopes whatever happens will take place before the autumn, "for my stamina is but ill-suited for equinoctial gales and cold weather." His health was indeed wretched — we note the recurrence of the old feverish attacks — but, as usual, though he had so much to say about it in his letters, it was not allowed to impede his activities. Edward Parker, a young officer whom Nelson had taken a great liking to in the Baltic — much as he had to young Hoste in the Mediterranean — was again serving with him in this

Channel adventure, and has left us a brief account of Nelson's way of doing things when he first hoisted his flag on the frigate at Sheerness. "He is the cleverest and quickest man, and the most zealous in the world," says Parker. "In the short time we were in Sheerness, he regulated and gave orders for thirty of the ships under his command, made everyone pleased, filled them with emulation, and set them all on the *qui-vive*."

Yet even he had found a difficulty in manning his ships. Men had come forward in fair numbers from Suffolk and his own Norfolk, but the seafaring population of Kent and Sussex were definitely tired of the war, and, in particular, chary of entering the King's service. Nelson asked the Admiralty to authorize him to give assurances that the men would be returned to their homes when the danger of invasion was past; but, in spite of every promise, he found them "always afraid of some trick." And no wonder. Any man who, on a homeward voyage after years of active service, had found himself suddenly transferred to an outward-bound ship, as described in a previous chapter, might well be suspicious of the King's service for the rest of his life. So the "fencibles," as they were called, hung back, and it was with difficulty that the fleet was manned. The result of all this was an interesting memorandum on the subject of recruiting for the Navy, which Nelson drew up many months later, when on leave in England, and forwarded to the Admiralty. In the meantime he had got his men somehow, and good men too. And he was particularly pleased to find that his old knowledge of the waters at the Thames mouth had not left him, so that he was still a useful pilot there—an unusual quality in an admiral, but very valuable just now.

Looking at the French coast, he asked himself characteristically, "Why not stir them up in Boulogne itself, where the bulk of their forces is assembled? Why not strike for the vitals?" Flushing would perhaps have been better—Nelson always called it his "grand object," for if there was any embarkation at Flushing, it would be aimed at London—but the difficulties there were too great. At Boulogne, on the other hand, there was a string of twenty-four hostile ships moored across the mouth of the harbour; and Nelson thought that he could get in close enough to send in his boats by night, and capture or burn the greater part of these. "I have been looking at Boulogne this morning," he wrote on August 2. He took an artillery officer with him on that occasion, and, as a result of their observations, the English bomb vessels were brought close in on the morning of the 4th and took potshots at the French line, as though at a target, damaging several vessels. "Boulogne," says Nelson, "was certainly not a very pleasant place that morning." It seems to have been rather a futile demonstration, and effected nothing except to give warning to the French.

For some days Nelson hesitated. No doubt he remembered Teneriffe. He even took the course, unique in his career, of writing to Lord St Vincent to obtain his approval before taking action. "I own," he wrote, "that this boat warfare is not exactly congenial to my feelings." Yet as soon as he got his old friend's concurrence, he settled down to prepare the attack. It was timed to take place on August 15, and on the night of the 12th-13th he was laid low by fever, but was up again next day, giving detailed orders to the leaders of the expedition. He proposed to send in his boats in four divisions, under the command of Captains Somerville, Cotgrave, Jones, and Parker — whom we have already met. "Little Parker" as Nelson always called him, had obviously obtained this early promotion through the favour of his admiral. As at Teneriffe, each division of boats was roped together to prevent them from scattering in the darkness; and again, as at Teneriffe, they all assembled near the flagship, and at the fixed hour, 11.30 P.M., pulled away in dead silence towards the enemy. The only difference was that Nelson remained behind. It would have been obviously absurd for the admiral in command of the coastal defences from Sussex to Suffolk to have engaged in a cutting-out affair in Boulogne harbour; yet it rankled in his mind, and he told St Vincent afterwards that nothing would induce him ever again in his life to order out a boat expedition in which he did not personally take part.

In the meantime all he could do was to hang over the bulwarks, staring through the darkness in the direction of Boulogne. He could see nothing: indeed it was darker than anyone had anticipated. At last he heard the sound of firing: it grew in volume, as he stood there listening, and then unaccountably died away. A few minutes later it broke out again in the same way, and then again, and again. To the trained ear there was something miserably inconclusive about it. What had happened? By this time the flames from the burning French ships should have lit up the sky.

And then the English boats began to return, one by one, very slowly; and he learned that the expedition had failed. It was the second defeat of his career, and both had been boat attacks. What had happened was briefly this: the divisions of boats had lost each other in the darkness, and had also encountered unexpectedly strong tides against them; so that instead of arriving simultaneously at the line of French ships across the harbour-mouth, they had arrived one at a time, and had been cut up in detail; they had got on board several of the Frenchmen, and had tried to cut them out from the line, but had found that they were all tied together, not by ropes but by iron chains — and before they could do anything more, before they had time even to set fire to a single one of their prizes, so heavy a fire of musketry had been opened upon them from both banks, as to kill and wound above a hundred of them (and also a great many among the French crews), and force the rest to retire to their boats again. Parker had got his division there first, and was gallantly leading his men when he was shot through the thigh, and desperately wounded. Many other officers were down.

As soon as Nelson understood the extent of the disaster he wrote to Lord St Vincent taking all the blame upon himself. The "most astonishing bravery" was evinced by his officers and men:

Captain Somerville, who I never saw till a few days ago, showed all the courage and good conduct which was possible, and succeeded completely in the fighting part of the business. Cotgrave and Parker also distinguished themselves. Indeed all behaved well, and it was their misfortune to be sent on a service which the precaution of the enemy rendered it impossible to succeed in. Of course, if they had been so lucky as to arrive all at the same moment, it might have been different; but I knew the difficulty of the undertaking, and no person can be blamed for sending them to the attack but myself.

But it was a blow to his pride, though Lord St Vincent was sympathetic, and no one in authority ever blamed him. He must have been severely tempted, when an enthusiastic officer, Captain Owen, came to him with a plan for attacking Flushing. But Nelson could see at once that his subordinate's zeal had made him overleap sandbanks and tides and laid him too easily aboard the enemy; and though he admired and sympathized with the spirit displayed, he flattered himself he could still "discriminate between the impracticable and the fair prospect of success."

There was really nothing to be done, and he arranged for the Hamiltons to come and spend a week or two with him at Deal. It was not a very happy holiday. A blackmailer, who signed himself Hill, wrote to Nelson threatening to arraign his conduct at Boulogne in the public press, unless he received a cheque for £100 by return of post. Nelson, who was like a child in such matters, instead of ignoring the letter, or replying briefly in the words of a famous contemporary "Publish and be damned!" wrote at some length admitting sadly that he was probably unfit for his command, and hoping that the Government would have no difficulty in finding "an officer of greater abilities" to succeed him. "But," he concluded with a little more spirit, "I have not been brought up in the school of fear, and, therefore, care not what you do." What hurt him, it is quite clear, was that even this despicable Hill should be his enemy. And then there was some "vagabond" who was turned out of the town of Deal by the Mayor for making speeches against Nelson — who actually goes to the trouble of reporting to Lord St Vincent an incident which any other man in his position might have forgotten to mention to his wife. There were other attacks of this kind and, worst of all, there was poor little Parker in hospital at Deal, and now evidently dying. Nelson was assiduous in his attentions, but it was too late to save him, and, soon after the Hamiltons left Deal, young Parker died. Nelson, overwhelmed with grief, went to the funeral, but could hardly get through the ceremony. "Thank God, the dreadful scene is past," he wrote to Lady Hamilton. "I could not suffer much more and be alive." In this black mood he returned to his ship in the harbour. "I came on board, but no Emma." Since the birth of their child he had hardly seen her — and was in fact to live with her for only eighteen months before his death.

He put to sea again on September 20, and there was some vague talk of running a fire-ship into Boulogne. The Channel was very choppy, and he suffered terribly from seasickness in his frigate, as he always did in a small ship. It was notorious that peace negotiations were in progress. Why did the Admiralty keep him there? And then, on October 4, the French Ambassador arrived in London, and was given a great reception by the mob. "I am mad to read that our damned scoundrels dragged a Frenchman's carriage," wrote Nelson indignantly. "I am ashamed for my country." He was not the last man to be irritated by this sentimental English habit of rushing to embrace their enemies almost before peace is signed.

Yet when terms were finally agreed upon, he could write quite sincerely to Lady Hamilton, "Thank God, it is peace." Peace meant Emma and Merton, the house that she had bought for him in the country. Peace meant rest for body and mind. He had endured much. His flimsy constitution had been severely tested. He had suffered the snubs of society, directed not against himself, but against his lady-love, and therefore unforgivable in his eyes, and he was beginning to lose faith in his old friends, St Vincent and Troubridge —

especially Troubridge, who had become so "great" and so "fat" and cared not a button what happened to Nelson. Even now, when the peace was signed, they kept him another fortnight at sea — even now, when the only home he was ever to know was waiting for him, "a warm room," as he wrote to Emma, "with a good fire and sincere friends."

But at last, on October 20, the order came and he hurried ashore and took post to Merton. He could hardly have endured the Channel another day.

CHAPTER XVII

INTERVAL FOR REFRESHMENT

"IT WOULD make you laugh to see Emma and her mother fitting up pigstyes and hencoops," wrote Sir William Hamilton to Nelson, while the latter was still tossing uncomfortably in the narrow seas. He was referring to the new house at Merton, in Surrey, only "one hour's drive from Hyde Park," which Nelson had authorized Lady Hamilton to buy for him.

It is a pleasantly bucolic picture thus conjured up, and no doubt Emma played her part very gracefully, and Mrs Cadogan as though to the manner born. Happily there was no Mrs St George peering over the garden wall, making notes of the furniture that was carried into the house and of the fact that the stream at the bottom of the garden was called "the Nile," as a compliment to the hero. It was a happy household. All the arrangements had been left in Lady Hamilton's hands. "I entreat I may never hear about the expenses again," Nelson had written to her. It was she who had found the house. It had to be of a certain size, and at a certain distance from London, and Sir William (who was to live there too, of course) had at first been sceptical about it. But when he saw the place he wrote enthusiastically to Nelson, assuring him that he could not fail to be pleased. Nelson formally approved of the transaction in a letter dated August 20, two months before he landed. He was so short of money at this time that he was forced to accept a loan from Davison in order to complete the purchase.

So here, at last, was that "little country cottage" he had so often talked of: not quite a cottage in the modern sense, for it was bigger even than Roundwood — but still the cottage of his dreams. It stood near the high road in the little village of Merton, five miles east of Kingston, and only eight miles from Westminster Bridge. It was a plain brick building, but two stories in height, and with barely sufficient accommodation for the family and staff, until Nelson built two cottages at the bottom of Abbey Lane for his coachman and gardener. A mulberry-tree he planted in the cottage garden is still to be seen.

The pleasure grounds were on both sides of the road, and were connected by an underground tunnel. On the farther side from the house were the stables, and not far from them a grass mound surrounded by trees, and surmounted by a summer house, where Nelson and his friends would sit in the cool of the evening, during the summer months of 1802. It should be added that the house was almost surrounded by a wooden verandah, covered with climbing roses, woodbine, and honeysuckle, and that it turned its back upon the road and faced due south, as though seeking sunshine and privacy. The grounds had been laid out under Lady Hamilton's personal supervision; the artificial stream which she called the Nile was her own idea; her personality must have expressed itself in every detail of the arrangements, indoor and out. It was Nelson's house, but it was her home — the home she had prepared for her hero. And there he came to anchor for the most tranquil months of his life — a bare eighteen of them!

Of the interior of the house, and of the kind of life led by the oddly assorted trio who inhabited it, we get, as usual, conflicting accounts. One thing is certain — that there were many visitors, for both Nelson and the Hamiltons were hospitable to a fault, and that the housekeeping was conducted upon a lavish scale. It was nothing uncommon for as many as fourteen places to be laid for dinner, and we know that the weekly bills (which Nelson and Sir William shared between them) amounted sometimes to as much as £100. Among the guests were Nelson's old sailor friends, Hood and Troubridge, Ball and Saumarez; Lord Minto, who strongly disapproved of the Hamilton connexion, but could not desert his old friend; the famous Dr Burney, who borrowed Nelson's night-cap (having left his own behind) and accidentally dropped it into his bedroom fire*; and flocks of Nelson's relations. Some of these guests appear to have supposed that the Hamiltons were simply living on Nelson, which is not quite fair to Sir William, who shared in the expenses and also had to keep up his town house, at No. 23 Piccadilly, where Nelson would stay during his visits to London. Portraits of Lady Hamilton and of Nelson, with representations of his victories, pieces of plate presented to him, the flag-staff of the *Orient,* and other trophies are said to have covered "not only the rooms, but the whole house, staircase and all," in a vainglorious display. Lady Hamilton is described as "in high looks but more immense than ever," and ladling out "towelfuls of flattery" to Nelson.

On the other hand, Nelson's nephew Mr Matcham, nearly half a century later, published in *The Times* a description of the household at Merton, which leaves a much pleasanter taste in the mouth, and is specially valuable as being the recollection of a youthful visitor, who, when he went to Merton, would be too young to be prejudiced by any moral objection to the *ménage* there. Mr Matcham's immediate object was to refute Mrs St George's insinuation (then recently made public) that Nelson would occasionally become boisterous in his cups (p. 200). He says "it would have formed an amusement to the circle at Merton, if intemperance were set down to the master of the house who always so prematurely cut short the *sederunt* of the gentlemen after dinner." He remembers Nelson as a quiet little figure, sedate and unobtrusive, clothed always in "a plain suit of black." Although he was a sailor, and of "a warm and generous disposition," he was very far from being "a rude and boisterous captain of the sea." Mr Matcham

---

* Dr Burney carefully collected the charred remains and returned them to Nelson with the following lines:

> *Take your night-cap again, my good lord I desire,*
> *I would not detain it a minute;*
> *What belongs to a Nelson, wherever there's fire,*
> *Is sure to be instantly in it.*

THE HOSTILE VIEW OF LADY HAMILTON

Gillray's brutal caricature, entitled *Dido in Despair*. Unpaid bills strew the floor. Through the window Nelson's fleet is seen putting to sea. The reference is to his departure from England to take over the Channel command in 1801.

"never heard a coarse expression issue from his lips." "At his table he was the least heard among the company, and so far from being the hero of his own tale, I never heard him voluntarily refer to any of the great actions of his life." He goes on to recall the simple pride with which Nelson once told him that when he called upon Mr Pitt, that great statesman had done him the singular honour of rising from his chair and accompanying him to his carriage.

That, I think, is the true picture: a quiet little gentleman in black, with powdered hair, his thin face burned yellow like old parchment, but his one blue eye as bright as ever, and his quick smile ready for every one he met. His vicar's daughter has told us — and who should know better? — that he dispensed his charity among the villagers with a generous hand, and attended regularly at church. For if Nelson's private life was not, in every respect, quite all that the Vicar of Merton might have desired, there is no doubt that he was a loyal Churchman, and with a strongly religious side to his character. He walked in the grounds, and talked to his guests, but the ordinary pursuits of a country gentleman would, for the most part, be denied to him: he is said to have fished on the river Wardle, but even that must have been difficult with only one arm.

He wrote a certain number of letters. He had not, for instance, forgotten his grievance against the city of London, for failing, as he considered, to give proper recognition to the victory of Copenhagen. Nothing had been done for the officers and men in the squadron under his command. For himself, as he stated bluntly in a letter to Davison, he expected "a sword from the City of London and their thanks, and the freedom in a gold box to Admiral Graves." In response to various invitations to dinner and so forth he wrote long and perfectly polite letters, explaining that he would accept no honour (it was proposed to pass a vote of thanks to him for his services in the Channel), nor would he dine with, nor appear in public with, the Lord Mayor until they made amends

R

for the injustice of Copenhagen. And from that attitude he never wavered.

On his rare visits to town ("I seldom go to London," he wrote) he would put up, as we have said, at the Hamiltons' house in Piccadilly. And since there was, at that time, no club much used by naval men, we may assume that he was a frequent visitor at Fladong's Hotel in Oxford Street, where the officers of the senior service nightly foregathered, so that it would be positively dangerous for a civilian, and still more for a soldier, to appear in the coffee-room. The streets of London must have been full of sailors at that time. In the last year of the war England had something like a hundred and forty thousand seamen and marines afloat, and the Peace of Amiens had thrown about half of these out of employment. The competition for such jobs as were still going was correspondingly keen, and the officials of the Admiralty were kept busy dealing with applications from active young officers and well-tried veterans who deserved something better of their country than to be pushed casually on to the shelf at half pay until their services were again required. Their mahogany countenances and their quarterdeck gait would look strangely out of place among the London bucks in St James's Park; and the emptiness of their pockets would not tend to improve their tempers during this period of enforced inaction.

It is to be feared, too, that their relations with the soldiers were not always too friendly. In John Davis's *The Post Captain*, published in 1805 — that remarkable repository of naval slang and naval manners in Nelson's time — we get an entertaining little glimpse of the hero, Captain Brilliant, and his junior officer, Lieutenant Echo, walking arm-in-arm down the Strand towards Temple Bar:

"Bestow your charity, my noble sea officers," cried a one-legged sailor to our heroes, "Bestow your charity upon poor Jack, who is hove to under a storm-stay-sail!"

"Here, ship-mate," cried Brilliant, "is half-a-crown for you."

"Here I come, Sir," cried Jack, redoubling his agility, "here I crowd all the sail I have left!"

"And there's another half-crown," said Echo. "Luff, boy, luff! And catch it in your hat."

"God Almighty bless you both!" cried Jack, "I could tell you were seamen by the peak of your mizzens. I might have begged of the red-jackets till all was blue again. Huzza! Huzza! Huzza!"

At Fladong's Nelson would meet old friends like Collingwood and Foley, Hardy and Troubridge. It may have been after conversation with them that he decided to put on paper his ideas about the manning of the King's ships, a subject which had been in his mind ever since he had come up against the difficulty of obtaining crews for the frigates under his command in the Channel. Nelson, whose name had always been sufficient to draw hundreds of seamen to the quay-side as soon as it was known that he had hoisted his flag; Nelson, who, at the outset of every voyage was embarrassed by a flood of applications from the parents of midshipmen barely in their teens, from petty officers and officers of all ranks who considered their fortunes made if only they could sail with him; Nelson, the popular hero, had suddenly, for the second time in his life, been brought face to face with the strong distaste of the average English seafaring man and the average inhabitant of the coastal districts for service in the King's Navy. He had known it well enough when he was young. He had even shared it, as we saw in Chapter II. And, to the day of his death, there was something in his easy, human relations with his men, his instinctive appeal to their affections rather than their fears, which suggests that he never quite forgot the bitter talk of old John Rathbone, as they walked the decks of that merchant ship on the way to the West Indies in the year 1772.

There was probably not an officer in the King's service who had made less use of the press-gangs than Nelson had. From the first he had been recognized as a rising star; and we have already seen that when he wanted a crew he made a point of posting his notices in the East Anglian ports, where his family was known, and his name held in honour. Yet in 1801, when he was in command in the Channel, he had found the greatest difficulty in obtaining crews for the captains of his frigates.

Not a man had come forward in Kent or Sussex. This distressed him deeply, and, in forwarding his suggestions to Sir William Scott at the Admiralty, he remarked, with feeling, that "something should be attempted at these times to make our seamen, at the din of war, fly to our navy, instead of flying from it." He proposed to introduce a system of certificates for seamen (it is extraordinary that nothing of the kind existed) giving their length of service, characters, and so forth; and also that every seaman who had an unblemished record of five years' service should receive once a year the sum of two guineas, and for eight years' service four guineas, exclusive of any wound pension.

But the most difficult problem was the prevention of desertion. Nelson declares that "whenever a large convoy [of merchantmen] is assembled at Portsmouth, and our fleet in port, not less than 1000 men desert from the navy; and I am sure that one-third of this number, from loss of clothes, drinking, and other debaucheries, are lost by death to the Kingdom." He discloses another scandal. A ship would clear from Gravesend for Portsmouth, with her papers all in order, including the names and particulars of her crew. But every member of the crew would be a "ticket-man" — which is to say that he would hold some paper exempting him from being seized by the press-gangs. And at Portsmouth, every one of these "ticket-men" would go ashore, and their places would quietly be taken and their names adopted, by deserters from the King's ships then in harbour. As a remedy, Nelson vaguely suggests a new Act of Parliament, but does not attempt to give its terms. The truth is, of course, as Rathbone had once convinced him, that something was wrong with the conditions of the service. It is too complicated a question to take up here; but when Nelson mentioned pensions for wounded men, he put his finger on one of the weak spots.

On April 26, 1802, Nelson's father died. He was then in his seventy-ninth year, and his intelligence — never, so far as we can judge, a particularly bright one — was dimmed by age. He had continued to live with Lady Nelson — a fact which does credit to both of them, but naturally prevented him from seeing very much of his son. He had visited Merton in the previous October, and had then gone on to Bath for the winter, as was his custom, and had quietly died there. In that same October he had written to Lady Nelson suggesting that, in the spring, he might once again take up his abode with her for the warmer months; but she, very properly, had advised him not to, since it prevented him from seeing his children. He had rather thrust himself on his daughter-in-law in the first instance, as we saw in Chapter X; but Lady Nelson, having once accepted the responsibility, applied herself so conscientiously to the task of looking after the old gentleman's comforts, that he was now unhappy with anyone else — which fully accounts for his whole attitude.

In July of that same year Nelson and the two Hamiltons started on a tour of Wales and the west country. The main object was to visit Milford Haven and view the harbour improvements which Charles Greville, Hamilton's nephew, was carrying out there. Greville had been pressing with his invitations. He was, as usual, short of money, and he was becoming daily more interested in the state of his uncle's health. He was confident enough about his place in the will, but — well, you never know, and he had behaved like a cad to Emma years ago. Emma, he was told, was getting plumper, but even more generous and easy-going than before. She ate and drank a little too much: that type always did after forty. She never gave a thought to money. Still, he would like to get this celebrated trio down to Milford Haven, and entertain them a little, and get his position, so to speak, regularized. So they started off, and went first to Oxford, where the university conferred upon both Nelson and Sir William the degree of D.C.L., and the former was also made a freeman of the city. At Blenheim, the Duke of Marlborough's residence, there was an unpleasant incident. The Duke, instead of inviting them to a meal, sent refreshments out to them in the park. Nelson returned them, untouched, and proceeded on his journey, with his feelings bitterly hurt. One of the most kindly, sensitive men that ever lived, he had unfortunately got himself into a position where he was always liable to suffer such slights as this — and the fact that they were on Emma's account, not his, made them only harder to bear.

That, however, was the only untoward incident of a highly successful tour. The Matchams, sister and brother-in-law, and the son whose recollections are quoted above, joined them at Oxford and went on with them to Gloucester, where all the church-bells were set ringing, and the mounted yeomanry came out to meet them, and the carriage was drawn through the streets by willing hands, under triumphal arches, while the populace shouted themselves hoarse. The bigwigs joined in; never after Blenheim did they get another rebuff. At Ross, and Monmouth, and Brecon it was the same story. At Milford Haven there was the elegant Charles to meet them, with his perfect manners, and that smile that Emma remembered so well. She could estimate him more accurately now, and there is no evidence that he made any strong impression upon any member of the party. Then to Swansea, Hereford, Ludlow, Coventry, they pursued their primrose path, fêted and adored wherever they went, even the country roads lined with cheering yokels — and so back to Merton in September, as the autumn leaves began to fall.

But not to peace. Old Sir William was becoming troublesome. He rather enjoyed that Welsh tour: old as he was he played his part with characteristic dignity. But he was beginning to feel neglected. He understood — it is impossible for any modern reader to doubt for a moment that he must have understood — his precise position in that triangle. He had bought Emma from Greville as one would buy a horse, and he had treated her always more as a daughter, or as a favourite niece, than as a wife. It is not without significance that in the private correspondence of Nelson and Emma he is invariably referred to as "Uncle" (as Lady Nelson is always "Aunt"). That is the true guide to the sex relations of these people. Old Sir William, with so much dignity and so little real pride, had been willing to close his eyes to the presence of a distinguished lover, and one for whom he felt a personal affection. But he was determined to have his socks properly darned. And he resented those continual dinner parties, in the cost of which he was compelled to share.

There began a series of undignified quarrels — "altercations" he called them. Hamilton instinctively hated this kind of thing. He wrote that in spite of "the nonsense I am obliged to submit to here [Merton] to avoid coming to an explosion," he was still inflexibly "determined that my quiet shall not be disturbed, let the nonsensical world go on as it will." To Emma he wrote pathetically (in a memorandum, summing up his grievances) "let us bear and forbear for God's sake." Nelson, for whom he thought himself neglected, is still, however, "the best friend I have in the world." It was all smoothed over in the end, and apparently without much difficulty. Nelson and Emma were naturally generous and considerate, and the old man hated rows. There is a rather disconcerting reference, in one of Nelson's earlier letters, to the fact that "God Almighty can, when he pleases, remove the impediment," by which he must have meant poor Sir William; but in the meantime both he and Emma seem to have done their very best to keep the impediment not only alive but happy.

But the sands were running low, and the winter of 1802–03 was just too much for him. On April 6, 1803, Sir William Hamilton died, very peacefully, "in Lady Hamilton's and my arms." They sat, one at each side of the bed, supporting him. Nelson adds that "the world never never lost a more upright or accomplished gentleman." And Lady Hamilton wrote, "unhappy day for forlorn Emma; ten minutes past ten dear blessed Sir William left me." Whatever else we may think of him, it must be admitted that he played the game to the end. The famous codicil to the will, so often quoted, ran as follows:

The copy of Madame Le Brun's picture of Emma, in enamel, by Bone, I give to my dearest friend Lord Nelson, Duke of

Bronte, a very small token of the great regard I have for his Lordship, the most virtuous, loyal and truly brave character I ever met with. God bless him, and shame fall on those who do not say Amen.

It has been rightly pointed out that if Sir William understood the true facts of his domestic situation — as he surely must have done, for he was not a fool — there is a certain nobility in this deliberate attempt to silence malicious tongues after his death. From another point of view it might be regarded merely as a tribute to the personal magnetism of Nelson. In any case, it shows Sir William at his best.

At this point it is impossible not to drop one's pen and reflect upon the triviality and short-sightedness of ordinary men and women, when, through no will of their own, they are caught up in the affairs of great men and great events. Lady Hamilton, obviously somewhat deteriorated, thinking only about how she is to amuse herself during the next hour or two; Greville worrying about his legacy; Mrs St George seeing nothing in it all but a subject for gossip; Sir William exerting himself with his last breath to conceal from posterity certain unpleasant facts, without having the imagination to foresee that posterity would insist upon unearthing every fact even remotely connected with Nelson — you realize with a shock how impenetrably stupid, how purblind all these people were compared with the ordinary mob, the ragamuffins of the London streets, the drunken loafers on the quay-side at Portsmouth, who not only adored Nelson, but seemed to understand that their adoration must know no sense, no limits — because it was something beyond reason — because Nelson stood for something greater than they could ever comprehend.

Only Nelson himself went serenely on his way. He had said that he did not want to hear about the household expenses, and it is extremely unlikely that Emma ever showed him the tradesmen's bills. It is clear, however, that his financial resources were severely strained; for Nicolas prints a letter which he wrote to his agent Davison as early as December

1801, from which it appears that he was at that time trying to sell some, if not all, of the diamonds presented to him by foreign sovereigns — and would have done so if the offer obtained by Davison had been a better one. As it was, he observed bitterly that "I would sooner beg than *give* those fellows my diamonds." We do not know who "those fellows" were, and, apparently, Nelson never gave the matter another thought. The only kind of detail he consented to bother about was that a wire-netting fence should be erected along the banks of the "Nile," so that little Horatia — "my Horatia," as he now frankly called her — who was coming to live at Merton, Sir William being dead, should not fall into the stream and be drowned.

Emma was forty-two when Sir William died. He left her a sum of £800 and an annuity of the same amount, and he paid off all her debts, so far as she had disclosed them to him up to the day of his death. It must be remembered that Nelson allowed her £1200 a year, and free possession of Merton; so that she had really not the slightest excuse for getting into debt again, as she very quickly did. But Emma would have got into debt if her annual income had been not £2000 but £200,000.

And so for one month they lived together as man and wife in this house of their choosing. For one month all "impediments" were out of the way, or could conveniently be forgotten. And the interval was so short that even the busy tongues of society scandalmongers had hardly time to warm to their work. Just one month — and then Nelson was needed again, to save his country.

CHAPTER XVIII

THE LONG BLOCKADE

THE Treaty of Amiens was a farce. It said peace, when there was no peace. Anyone in touch with public affairs, as Nelson was, knew perfectly well that there never could be a lasting peace between England and Napoleon, nor any treaty that was more than a mere respite. No dictator of Europe could get peace from England except by conquest, and Napoleon knew that, and every Englishman (except the inevitable group of pacifist politicians) knew that he knew it and that he would act accordingly.

The interval of peace lasted from October 1801 to May 1803. Napoleon, characteristically, used it to strengthen his resources. England, equally characteristically, used it to effect drastic economies in her fleet. Lord St Vincent, the ruthless disciplinarian of 1795, now appeared as an equally ruthless wielder of what we would call the "axe." He reduced the number of ships in commission to a minimum, and their equipment to the barest necessities. The Mediterranean fleet was the only one kept up to its numbers — which showed St Vincent's clear perception of the realities of the strategical situation. Yet when Nelson arrived there (as we shall see presently) to take over the command, he found that there was an average shortage of no less than a hundred men in the crews of the line-of-battle ships. These economies, it must be added, were dictated not by any feeling of security in regard to the international situation, but purely by the exigencies of party politics at home. St Vincent, as a member of the Government, was instructed to carry them out, and he performed the unpleasant task — once he had reconciled it with his conscience — with his usual efficiency.

In the terms of the Treaty of Amiens Napoleon had scored all along the line. The diplomatic representative of England was Lord Cornwallis, who was distinguished only for having lost North America when he surrendered at Yorktown; and Napoleon found it as easy to get the better of him in diplomacy as the American rebels had in warfare. In fact he made so many concessions and with so little show of resistance, that the French were more than ever confirmed in their distrust of "perfidious Albion." They thought there must be a catch somewhere. The First Consul, for his part, hardly bothered to keep up a pretence of carrying out the terms of the treaty. He would not withdraw his troops from Holland, he reoccupied Switzerland, and he reimposed restrictions upon British shipping as though the two countries were still at war. And when King George's ministers, having made an obviously bad bargain for which they deserved to be impeached, attempted to hold him to its terms, he publicly insulted the British Ambassador in Paris. The French army in Egypt, having surrendered to Abercrombie, was transported to France in British vessels (Nelson, who had marooned them there by his victory of the Nile, always maintained that they should never have been allowed to leave except as prisoners of war); whereupon Napoleon held a grand review at Lyons, under the eyes of the foreign diplomatists, when he welcomed the remnants of Kleber's force as though they were returning conquerors. Every issue of the *Moniteur* was filled with diatribes against England — the first example known of propaganda by the Press on modern lines. England, on her side, refused to evacuate Malta.

It is plain to the most casual student of the diplomatic history of this period that Napoleon never meant to abide by the terms of the Treaty of Amiens. Even the unusually stupid ministers who held office in Whitehall in 1803 could comprehend that much. He simply used the respite which the treaty gave him to build up his plans for the restoration of the French colonial empire. And for that the first necessity was the restoration of the French fleet. By the terms of the treaty he had been able to preserve this empire, almost unimpaired, thanks to the feebleness of Cornwallis; but immediately upon a fresh declaration of war his fleets must retire to their harbours, leaving all the islands of the West Indies and the East at the mercy of the English, who had captured most of them before, but this time might not so easily give them up again. In March 1803 he had only forty-three line-of-battle ships in commission, and, even against the depleted English fleet, these were insufficient. But he had twenty-three more on the stocks, and, by the end of 1804, he might fairly hope to be in a position to engage his opponent on equal terms.

But he ruined everything by his impetuosity. Seeing the day of revenge approaching, as he thought, he bullied and blustered to such an extent that even Addington and his colleagues became alarmed. For more than a year they had endured a policy of pin-pricks with exemplary patience; but now, on May 16, 1803, they suddenly cut short the interminable arguments about Malta and Holland, Sardinia and Lampedusa, with an abrupt declaration of war. It was the best thing they could have done. It was the only dignified, the only possible, answer. Napoleon was genuinely astonished and indignant — not at the declaration of war, which he had fully anticipated, and indeed had provoked, but at the fact that it had arrived some months before he was ready for it. And having taken that strong step, the Ministers, like many other peace-loving British Governments before them, proceeded to get down to the business of war with a promptitude and enthusiasm which startled friends and foes alike. As early as March Nelson had been warned that his services might be required as Commander-in-Chief in the Mediterranean. And now, on May 18, only two days after the declaration of war, he received his commission, and hoisted his flag at Portsmouth on board of his last and most famous ship, the *Victory*.

How eagerly he responded to that promptitude, in which he must have detected the hand of his old friend St Vincent! He was all on fire to be back with the fleet. At Portsmouth there was a delay of forty-eight hours, and it nearly drove him mad. "I cannot sail before to-morrow," he wrote, "and that's an age."

However, on the 20th he got away, and two days later was close to Ushant, looking for Cornwallis, who was supposed to be blockading Brest. But it was "blowing strong, and a heavy sea," and Cornwallis, there being nothing much in Brest to engage his attention at the moment, was cruising some nine or ten leagues off, and Nelson could not find him. Now he had been ordered to leave the *Victory* with Cornwallis, if the latter thought he needed her, and proceed to join the Mediterranean squadron in some smaller ship. This order had vexed him in the beginning. As he pointed out in a letter to the Admiralty, he had put all his personal belongings on board of her before sailing, and they could not easily be moved. "All my things, servants, wines, etc. etc., are ordered to be sent to her, be where she will — even my sheep, poultry, hay, corn, and every comfort [there seem to have been not a few of them] are ordered to her." And now he could not find Cornwallis. He waited wearily two days, and could bear it no longer. He hated small ships, for he was always sea-sick on them; but now he tumbled himself and his whole staff into the frigate *Amphion,* where they were crowded to suffocation, sleeping seven or eight in a cabin, and made sail for Gibraltar, leaving behind him the *Victory,* and a hurried note of explanation for Cornwallis. He reached Gibraltar on June 3, bringing with him the first news of the renewal of war.

On board the *Amphion* with Nelson (having been transferred with him from the *Victory*) was that elegant official Mr Hugh Elliot, whom we have met before at Dresden, where he was so much embarrassed by the arrival of Nelson and the Hamiltons, and entertained Mrs St George by his witticisms at their expense. He was now on his way to Naples to take up the post of British Ambassador there. Whatever may have been his subsequent relations with the Hamiltons, this short voyage had been sufficient to work a startling change in his attitude towards Nelson. It is fair to him to remember that he had never seen Nelson in action before. We now find him deferring, almost reverently, to his opinions; and when the great Admiral finally left the Mediterranean, Elliot wrote despairingly from Naples declaring that he would never have undertaken his mission if he had not felt that he could rely upon the support of Nelson's "pre-eminent talents and judgment." At Gibraltar Elliot was transferred to the frigate *Maidstone,* for direct passage to Naples, while Nelson went on in the *Amphion* to join his fleet. There he presently shifted his flag to the *Victory,* which Cornwallis, on seeing his letter, had immediately sent after him.

Returning to the Mediterranean after more than three years' absence, the new British Commander-in-Chief on the station found things very much altered in favour of the French. He found Piedmont formally annexed, he found no pretence left of neutrality among the remaining principalities of Northern Italy. He found the Papal States enjoying just as much independence as Napoleon (for political and religious reasons) found it wise to allow them. He found a French army corps of 15,000 men occupying the heel of Italy and watching Naples as a cat might watch a mouse. Everywhere the cause of France had advanced, and that of England and her allies had gone back. Yet, from the point of view of the officer commanding on the Mediterranean station, the change was not entirely for the worse. The situation had, at any rate, been clarified. There was no longer any need to respect the alleged neutrality of Genoa, for instance, or to keep British frigates hanging about the coast attempting to co-operate with local armies which invariably ran away at sight of the enemy, when these frigates were urgently needed for service with the main fleet. All Italy, except Sicily, had now plainly adhered to the enemies of King George, and could be treated accordingly.

For Naples alone Nelson retained a special consideration, which was certainly not based on mere sentiment. It is true that he speaks of the place tenderly in one of his letters to Emma, but he showed no desire to revisit it. On the other hand, he was as fussy about the fate of the Kingdom and the royal family as he ever had been when his lady-love lived ashore. During the following months he always kept a line-of-battle ship in Naples Bay (though he could ill spare one) in order that the King and Queen might be promptly removed to Sicily and safety should the French army approach.

In general Nelson's theory of the situation as he found it was somewhat as follows. Napoleon was believed to be planning to invade and conquer England, and he already had, on the shore of the English Channel, an army probably sufficient for that purpose. For reserves he had a population of some forty million to draw on, as compared with the seventeen million inhabitants of the British Isles. But his army could not cross without the support of his fleet, and the latter, since there was no suitable port for it in the Channel, was always absent at the outbreak of war. It must be at Brest, or Cadiz, or Toulon in the Mediterranean. And there, as usual, the English had blockaded it. Cornwallis was off Brest, Collingwood cruised in the bay, and Bickerton, who commanded in the Mediterranean before Nelson arrived, sailed immediately for Toulon at the first rumour of war and locked up the French squadron there. It was the familiar stale-mate.

But Nelson and many others thought that rather than live under the daily and hourly threat of invasion, England should attempt some diversion in Napoleon's rear, on the Mediterranean coasts. Nelson proposed to occupy two fortified harbours, and then invade some selected point in Southern Italy. For that purpose, however, he needed troops. "We never wanted 10,000 men more than at this moment," he exclaims in one of his letters home. It maddened him to think that Abercrombie's gallant little army, fresh from its conquest of Egypt, should only just have been sent back home. It must be confessed that Nelson was as blandly optimistic about what could be done with a small land army as Napoleon was about what could be done with an inefficient fleet. Yet the surprising moral effect of the British victory at Maida a few years later (strategically it was thrown away) does seem to show that the sailor's confidence had more justification than the soldier's. And there was this further excuse for Nelson's suggested "side shows" (we would have called him an "Easterner" in the Great War) that even when Napoleon seemed about to pounce upon the British Isles he always kept one eagle eye turned in the direction of Egypt and India. There nothing stood in his way, except the Mediterranean fleet. That is why Nelson always urged that England must hold Sicily and Malta — because they were stepping-stones on the way to the East — though neither of them was near enough to Toulon to be used as a base for a blockading squadron.

But first Toulon. Nelson had nine ships of the line, and the French squadron he was blockading was of at least equal strength. Obviously he needed a near and suitable base where his ships might refit and return to him quickly. As a first move, therefore, he calmly took possession of the fine anchorage at Maddalena in Sardinia. It is true that the King of Sardinia had declared the island neutral, but that was only because he could not help himself, and bigger issues were now at stake. The local authorities were openly on Nelson's side. So, with this convenient and friendly base behind him, Nelson took his station off Toulon, and began that long blockade that was one of the greatest achievements of his career. Here he must keep the sea in all weathers, year in year out, watching for enemies as strong as himself and infinitely better equipped, who might choose their own moment to make a bolt for it on any day or night in the week. We have seen the same situation before on a minor scale in the course of this history; but here we touch the most ambitious project ever attempted by a blockading fleet — the central achievement, and the summing up, so to speak, of England's whole naval effort in the Napoleonic wars. Nelson and his ships formed the last and southernmost link in a long chain of blockading squadrons which stretched from Brest to Toulon, encircling the coast like a belt of iron, curbing and stifling the great Corsican's designs at every point. As Mahan has said in a well-known passage, it was the relentless, bull-dog grip of those storm-tossed English ships, which the Grand Army never saw, that settled the final issue of the conflict.

For the moment we are concerned only with Nelson's end of the chain. He took over the command off Toulon from

H.M.S. "VICTORY" AFTER RECONSTRUCTION

1. The Quarter deck, where Nelson fell.
2. The Big Gun Deck.

Photos Stephen Cribb, Southsea

Bickerton, on July 8, 1803. For the next eighteen months he maintained a blockade so strict that not an enemy ship slipped past him. He himself never once set foot on shore from his leaving Malta in June 1803 to his arrival at Gibraltar two years later. "If I should miss these fellows," he said, "my heart would break." He began, as we have seen, with only seven ships, and reinforcements seldom reached him. His ships soon became so foul that, even allowing for the magnificent seamanship of Nelson's officers, it seems almost impossible that they should have been kept so long at sea.

But even that is not the most remarkable feature of this amazing blockade. Nelson had once praised Lord Hood as the best "manager" of a fleet in the history of the Navy. He himself, who is too often spoken of as a mere fighting-man, now proved immeasurably the superior of Hood or any other admiral in the more humdrum duties of administration. It is not only that there was no mutiny in this fleet, engaged as it was in exceptionally arduous services. There is no recorded case of mutiny in any fleet commanded by Nelson. The only grumbling he had to contend with was directed against the French for not coming out to battle. Over and over again we get it from contemporary authorities that all the English, from Admiral to powder-monkey, were burning for a fight.

But that again — that splendid fighting spirit of the English — was nothing new. What was entirely new, and has remained probably unequalled ever since, was the clean bill of health in Nelson's fleet. "We are healthy beyond example," he wrote in October 1803, "and in great good humour with ourselves." On the *Victory,* which carried a crew of eight hundred and forty men, there was sometimes one man on the sick-list, often none at all. The figures for the other ships were hardly less remarkable. Even the most spick-and-span modern fleet, carefully clothed and fed on the latest principles of hygiene, would think itself lucky if it could show figures half as good. The truth is that Nelson, having no enemy before him, no diplomatic correspondence on his hands, no woman to make love to, was giving his attention to these things. We have

s

before noticed his sane ideas about the importance of dieting to avoid scurvy, and he now went a little further, and arranged not only a diet, but a carefully thought out scheme of life for his fleet, so as to preserve its health and spirits. Fresh vegetables and fruit, especially onions and lemons, were provided from the islands, with the assistance of the natives, and so regularly that no ship could be entirely without them for long. Nelson had a tremendous respect for onions, as a preventive against scurvy.

But he saw that diet was not everything. He recognized, more clearly than any of the medical experts of his time usually did, the importance of keeping his men cheerful and awake by frequent changes of scene and occupation. He had so few ships that not more than one or two could ever be away at the same time; but he has explained in his letters how he moved them about as much as possible, and when water ran short he would take the whole fleet to Maddalena for a day or two, leaving one ship on the watch. The results we have seen. Of course, as he said, "a sight of the French squadron twenty leagues at sea would cure all complaints." And of course the fact that none of Nelson's men ever went sick without being really ill would react favourably on the statistics. But in the meantime he holds the record for having commanded, on this difficult and wearing service, perhaps the healthiest and keenest British fleet that ever put to sea.

Nelson, at first, was as fit as any of his men. "Not a finger-ache," he boasted. But as the winter came on and the ship tossed outside Toulon he began to suffer from his usual complaint of sea-sickness. Also his eyesight was getting steadily worse, and now, as he walked the quarterdeck of the *Victory* under those grey winter skies, he was never without his green shades which Lady Hamilton had made for him. Nelson was continually straining his one remaining eye by staring through his glass at the entrance to the harbour at Toulon, where the French fleet must one day appear. It was the opinion of many of the doctors who saw him at this time, that within two or three years at the most he would lose his eyesight altogether.

In the meantime it was no use arguing with him. He continued to gaze hungrily at Toulon.

Nor was his temper improved by the silly gasconade of the French Admiral, Latouche-Treville, who, having ventured as far as the outer roads, in the ordinary course of his rather restricted fleet exercises, published a long account in the *Moniteur* of how he had sighted the English Admiral with his squadron and had chased him till nightfall. This Latouche-Treville was a renegade French Royalist, who had annoyed Nelson personally on more than one occasion, and had commanded the French at the disaster of Boulogne. Nelson, always childishly sensitive in these matters, no sooner read the report than he began to rage helplessly. He could do nothing against his enemy, of course; but he carefully kept a copy of the mendacious dispatch, and "by God, if I take him he shall eat it!" The French Admiral escaped this punishment by dying in August 1804 — as the result, observes Nelson bitterly, of walking so often up the hill to the signal-post to look defiance at the British fleet.

On board the *Victory* the days slipped by quickly in the regular routine. According to Dr (afterwards Sir William) Beatty, who served as surgeon, Nelson's health was "uniformly" good, apart from what he calls "accidental causes." He says that Nelson cured the gout, to which he had been subject, "by abstaining for the space of nearly two years from animal food, and wine, and all other fermented drink, confining his diet to vegetables, and commonly milk and water." That "two years" must be an exaggeration. Teetotal vegetarians were so rare in those unenlightened days that if Nelson had practised any such *régime* for more than a few months it is certain that some other writer besides Dr Beatty would have noticed it. Beatty also says that Nelson gave up salt entirely when he first went to sea, "believing it to be the sole cause of scurvy," and this again is difficult to credit. On the other hand we can easily believe that he was studiously moderate at table, "the liver and wing of a fowl and a small plate of macaroni in general composing his meal, during which he occasionally took a glass of champagne"; and that he still kept to the rule of not more than four glasses of claret or port after dinner, which his old servant, Tom Allen (now gone from his service) used so strictly to enforce.

In other respects he was a worry to the doctors. For instance, he seldom got more than two hours uninterrupted sleep — he didn't seem to need it, for, like Napoleon, he had the gift of taking a nap at any time — and the result was that he would often appear unexpectedly on deck in the middle of the night, to see how things were getting on. On these occasions he would never take the slightest precaution to protect himself against the weather, and would not even consent to change his clothes when they got wet. He would usually be wearing light shoes or pumps (he seldom wore boots), and when the water got through to his stockings the most that he could be persuaded to do would be to kick off his shoes, and walk about on the carpet in his cabin, declaring that this was an excellent method of drying his feet and saved the trouble of sending for fresh stockings.

But the best description of daily life on the *Victory* comes from Beatty's predecessor, Dr Gillespie, who has taken us through one whole day from reveille to lights out. "At six o'clock," he says, "my servant brings a light and informs me of the hour, wind, weather and course of the ship, when I immediately dress and generally repair to the deck." It may be added that, as the surgeons' cabins were always in the lower part of the ship, in the immediate vicinity of the storerooms and the various midshipmen's and petty officers' messes with their variegated odours, the fresh air of the quarterdeck must have meant a pleasant change of atmosphere. But he would hardly have time to sniff the salt breeze, and glance round in the darkness for the first sign of dawn, when "breakfast is announced in the Admiral's cabin." Nelson, Hardy (commanding the *Victory*), Rear-Admiral Murray (the Captain of the Fleet), the chaplain, the secretary, one or two other officers, his friends Captain Hallowell of the *Tigre* and Captain Keats of the *Superb*, probably a couple of middies, "and your

H.M.S. "VICTORY": THE STERN VIEW

The windows in the middle row are those of Nelson's cabin. Hardy's are above. The balustrades outside and just below the cabin windows indicate the position of what used to be called the "Admiral's Walk" and the "Captain's Walk" respectively. Nelson, throughout most of his career as a commanding officer, would be accustomed to walk up and down these balconies, admiring the view and watching the other ships of the fleet following in line. But shortly before the battle of Trafalgar these pleasant 'walks' were done away with. The balustrade remained, but was built flush against the stern of the ship, as it is in the above illustration.

Photo Stephen Cribb, Southsea   266

humble servant," Dr Gillespie, would assemble round the hospitable table and breakfast on "tea, hot rolls, toast, cold tongue, etc."

Warmed by this light refreshment (which was all they were going to get till three o'clock in the afternoon) the group of officers, in their blue and white uniforms, would once more climb the short ladder to the quarterdeck, and there walk up and down, or lean against the bulwarks admiring the dawn. Gillespie speaks with genuine feeling of the beauty of the scene, as the East lightened and the pale colours spread themselves delicately over the smooth surface of the Mediterranean. Turning their eyes aft they could see "the majestic sight" of the English ships of the line, the "wooden walls of Old England," following steadily, one behind another, their dark hulls rising and falling with the swell, their tall white sails flushing in the dawn.

Between seven o'clock and two in the afternoon the chief business of the day was transacted. Nelson, as we know from another source, spent a large part of the time walking rapidly up and down the quarterdeck. He would walk for six or seven hours every day. Now and then something would suddenly occur to him — a new order to be issued, a letter to be written — and, almost before you missed him, he would have popped down the ladder to his cabin to commit it to paper.* It should be understood that Nelson's cabin did not open on to the quarterdeck, but on to the deck below. The "poop-cabins" (as they were called, being immediately under the poop) which gave on to the quarterdeck were Hardy's as flag-captain. Nelson, descending the ladder and turning aft, would pass between smaller cabins, occupied by his secretary and chaplain, and so reach his own suite — first the dining-room, which was comparatively small, and then the "grand cabin," a spacious apartment, lit all along one side by the great stern windows of the ship, through which could be seen, across the blue water, the next in line of the British squadron, tossing her bowsprit as

* Beatty.

she followed in the Admiral's wake. In the early morning in these latitudes it must have been a glorious place. Here he could write. Here was his desk and his little portrait of Emma.

Here also he spent many industrious hours with his private secretary, the Reverend A. J. Scott.* (He had in addition a "public secretary," whose name, inconveniently enough, was also Scott — Mr John Scott). Mr A. J. Scott, or Dr Scott, as he was usually called, has left us an amusing description of his and Nelson's methods of dealing with correspondence. Nelson disliked the act of writing, and therefore always supposed (strange delusion!) that any man who took a pen in his hand must have something of value to say. He consequently insisted upon every letter being read, and every pamphlet or article in a foreign newspaper being carefully scrutinized for information, rather to the disgust of little Scott, who was a dreamy, unmethodical sort of man. There were two great black leather arm-chairs in Nelson's cabin, constructed on such ample lines that, when he had occasion, he would lash them together and use them as a bed. In these chairs were roomy pockets for the reception of papers, and into these pockets Nelson and Scott would cram their piles of letters and pamphlets until they were able to deal with them.

Dr Gillespie's morning has soon slipped away. What with "business, studying, writing, and exercise," he has taken us to two o'clock, at which hour punctually "a band of music" salutes our ears. It would be mainly fiddlers, I suppose, for there were always plenty of fiddlers on a man-o-war in those days. At any rate, there would be nothing like the amount of brass that we are accustomed to — and no saxophones! The band would play till a quarter to three, when "the drum beats the tune *The Roast Beef of Old England,* to announce the Admiral's dinner which is served up exactly at three o'clock." It will be noted that this dinner, the principal meal, for which every one must have been ravenously hungry, was taken during the very hottest time of the day, when every self-respecting

* See p. 223.

inhabitant of the Mediterranean coast lands is enjoying his siesta. It consisted of three stout courses, followed by "a dessert of the choicest fruit, together with three or four of the best wines, champagne and claret not excepted."

Coffee and liqueurs closed the meal about half-past four or five o'clock, "after which the company generally walk the deck, where the band of music plays for nearly an hour." Between six and seven there was tea, again in the Admiral's cabin, after which the company would continue to sit about at their ease, chatting in an informal manner with Nelson, "who at this time generally unbends himself, though he is at all times as free from stiffness and pomp as regards to proper dignity will admit." At eight o'clock "a rummer of punch, with cake or biscuit, was served"; after which those officers who were still off duty bade the Admiral good-night and left him. He was generally in bed before nine.

Gillespie amply confirms the general verdict as to Nelson's charm of manner at the dinner-table. Whereas he is supposed to have been too boisterous at Dresden, and perhaps too much subdued at Merton, at sea he was, by general admission, the perfect host. Beatty describes him as "affable and attentive to everyone." Gillespie says that "if a person does not feel himself perfectly at his ease [at Nelson's dinner-table] it must be his own fault, such is the urbanity and hospitality which reign there." The Admiral, who himself played such a poor knife and fork, might have been expected to find the sitting a long one; on the contrary, it was his happiest moment of the day, as he turned from one guest to another with his ready smile, keeping the ball of conversation rolling cheerfully. At this hour he would forget all his worries: the difficulties of his command, Lady Hamilton's health (during this period she gave birth to a little daughter, who survived only a few weeks) and the ever present financial problem — for his expenses, on board ship must have been considerable, though, as he wrote to Davison, "God knows, in my own person, I spend as little as any man."

Apparently he seldom mentioned his private affairs to his

brother officers; but young Parker, a nephew of Lord St Vincent's and a special friend of Nelson's, relates that on one occasion, when all the other officers had left the cabin, and he and the Admiral stood by the table about to say good-night, Nelson suddenly seized a decanter, poured himself out a glass of claret, and drank it off to "Lady Hamilton, my guardian angel."

Over the wine he liked to chaff his secretary, parson Scott — a quaint character, full of humour (much of it unconscious), who adored Nelson. Scott, an excellent linguist, made a point of going ashore in neutral ports whenever an opportunity offered, and wandering about the streets in his apparently absent-minded, inconspicuous way, buying the local papers and often picking up much useful information. It amused Nelson to pretend to think that this "intelligence work" was a mere excuse for enjoying himself ashore in a manner unsuited to his cloth. Also he would incite Scott, who was very voluble, to argue with Hardy or Murray about some matter of practical seamanship. "Ah, my dear Doctor," Nelson would say chaffingly, "give me knowledge practically acquired." Hardy's broad shoulders (he was a great, squat, mountain of a man, with a heart as soft as a woman's) would shake with laughter. Even the quiet, shrewd Murray, who at first had hesitated to join Nelson's command (fearing that no captain of the fleet could serve under so dazzling a genius without either quarrelling with him or being eclipsed) but was now one of Nelson's most devoted friends — even Murray enjoyed the joke.

Nelson, though he found Scott very useful, probably valued him even more highly as an eccentric character. "Dr. Scott," he wrote privately to Emma, "is at times wrong in the head; absolutely too much learning has turned him — but we all go on very well." He liked Scott. But Scott's feeling for him well illustrates that strange power of Nelson's — strange, that is, in a man of action — of evoking a kind of love that is usually given only to saints. "I never knew how much I loved him," wailed Scott after Nelson's death. And again, "When I think what an affectionate, fascinating little fellow he was, I become stupid with grief for what I have lost."

CAPTAIN T. M. HARDY
From a portrait by Robert Evans in the Painted Hall, Greenwich.
By permission of the Lords of the Admiralty   270

Those are words of extraordinary significance. Can anyone imagine the most devoted of Napoleon's followers, for instance, referring to him as "a fascinating little fellow?" These men reverenced Nelson, almost worshipped him. They sprang to obey his slightest command, with such eager emulation that one of his favourite officers complains that it was exhausting being on the same ship with him. Yet the feeling they had for him, and the secret of his power, was primarily, and before everything, not respect, nor fear, nor admiration, but love. In that way he differs from — and should we not say stands above? — every great commander in history.

Every detail of this picture that I have drawn of Nelson in his hours of ease is taken from contemporary authorities. Those were happy days — full of strenuous activity, and unceasing vigilance, with the ever present anxiety as to the enemy's next move hanging over them like a nightmare that might have shattered another man's nerves. But to Nelson and his well-tried companions in arms they were happy days. No doubt Hardy often thought of them years afterwards, when he was Governor of Greenwich Hospital where the Nelson relics are now housed — his sword, his stockings, the very coat he was wearing when he fell at Trafalgar; * and Dr Scott, too, when he took Nelson's body home after the final victory, and sat up with it night after night, praying and weeping.

---

* The very dinner-table over which Nelson and his friends conversed stands, as I write, in his cabin on the *Victory*. It is stated that the owner, a Portuguese gentleman, is about to remove it. Apparently it has not been possible to buy it for the nation. His portrait of Lady Hamilton was there for a time. The glasses from which he and his friends drank their grog may still be seen at Greenwich.

CHAPTER XIX

PURSUIT

ON JANUARY 19, 1805, when the blockade had continued for a year and a half, things suddenly began to move. Nelson, with his fleet, was watering at Maddalena, when a frigate arrived with the news that the French had slipped out on the previous night and were last seen off Corsica, steering south, with a strong north-west wind. Within three hours the English fleet was at sea, south-west of Sardinia, and in such a position that, as a glance at the map will show, the French could not steer for Naples or Sicily without being intercepted.

They were not intercepted. Nelson, therefore, saw two alternatives: either the French had persisted in their southward course, and were making for the north coast of Africa (and so to Egypt); or they had put back to Toulon. With a gale of wind blowing from the north-west, Gibraltar was plainly impossible: if there had been the remotest danger of a breakaway there he would have turned west. As it was he made for Egypt, scattering frigates behind him to look for news. He could not sleep. "Stromboli," he says in his diary, "burnt very strongly throughout the night of the 28th; passed round it at three in the morning. I am in a fever: God send I may find them!" The French were not at Egypt. Struggling back, against the adverse wind, he heard that, as he more than half expected, they had returned to Toulon.

Nelson revictualled at Sardinia. He was so covering the approaches to the eastern Mediterranean that he now felt confident that the French Toulon fleet could not escape in any direction except to the westward through the Straits. To that extent his mind was at ease. But easterly winds were fre-

quent, and he waited eagerly for news so that if Villeneuve *
chose the western route he might be close on his heels. Luck
failed him again — badly this time. Villeneuve, as a matter of
fact, was already under orders to pass the Straits of Gibraltar,
as soon as circumstances were favourable, pick up the Spanish
squadrons at Cartagena and Cadiz, and set sail for the West
Indies, where he was to occupy his time in mopping up English commerce and destroying some of the weak English garrisons there, until he could be joined by the French fleet from
Brest, which was to break out at the first opportunity and follow him. This was Napoleon's pet project, by which he
hoped to assemble a fleet powerful enough to attain at any
rate temporary control — and that was all he asked — of the
English Channel. Anything might happen then.

The first essential move was that Villeneuve should pass the
Straits. *And Villeneuve, though Nelson did not know it, had
already done so.* On March 30, having repaired the damage
suffered by his ships in that north-westerly gale, and the wind
being now in the east, he again slipped quietly out of Toulon,
and stole away westward, keeping close to the coast of Spain.
Nine days later he was through the Straits. He called at
Cartagena for his Spanish allies, but, to his disgust, failed to
induce a single one of them to join him. Hurrying on to
Cadiz, he chased away a small English squadron commanded
by Sir John Orde (Nelson's old enemy) and, picking up six
Spanish and one French ship there, he forthwith made sail for
the West Indies, according to his orders.

Nelson was still cruising between Sardinia and Toulon. For
once his frigates, of which he never had enough, must have
failed him; for it was not until April 4 that he heard that the
French had sailed. Even then he was not sure of their destination, and it was necessary to make quite certain that they had
not got past him to the East, before he passed the Straits and
left the Mediterranean empty of British ships. He had made
up his mind on that point by the second week in April, but

---

* Latouche-Treville's successor at Toulon.

by that time Villeneuve was clean away. And when Nelson turned westwards after him, it was to encounter persistently contrary winds, with never a breath from the East to help him. It was May 6, nearly one month later, before he put in at Gibraltar. All his calculations had been upset. But, though Villeneuve had a long start, Nelson was on his track now, and Nelson's blood was up. The great pursuit had begun.

It is necessary to pause here (I am not attempting to give the operations of 1803–04 in any detail) in order to explain the presence of Sir John Orde. Spain had joined the war on the French side in the latter part of 1804. But Nelson had made formal application for leave, on grounds of health, about the middle of August of that year. He hated doing it. As he said in a letter to Elliot at Naples, "I leave the finest fleet in the world, with every officer and man attached to me." But his health, never robust, was beginning to feel the strain, and he put it up to the Admiralty as a business proposition that "a few months of quiet may enable me to serve next spring." He suggested that Bickerton should be given temporary command until he returned — in plain words, to keep the place warm for him. But the Admiralty responded, with disconcerting promptitude, by sending out Sir John Orde with five sail of the line, to take over the blockade of Cadiz, thus cutting out of Nelson's command (for Orde was senior to him) the section from Cadiz to Cape Finisterre. At the same time they wrote to Nelson granting him leave whenever he liked; but Nelson, unfortunately, did not get the letter until after he had heard of Orde's arrival.

And, in the meantime, he had changed his mind about taking leave. It had become apparent that Spain was about to enter the war. Also Rear-Admiral Campbell was seriously ill (he was succeeded by Rear-Admiral Louis whom we have met before, in command of the *Minotaur*), and Bickerton, too, was on the sick list. On November 6, therefore, Nelson sent off a sloop of war, with letters to the Admiralty, withdrawing his request for leave and explaining why he thought he ought to stay. Off Cape St Vincent, on November 18, this sloop

passed the *Swiftsure* (74), bringing out Sir John Orde. It was
bad luck. The Spanish end of Nelson's command was, of
course, the very point at which rich prizes (the galleons from
the West Indies, for instance) might be expected. And even
Nelson, who never thought of prize money, remarks, rather
wistfully, in a letter to Lord Radstock, that he thinks he
"could have made as good a use of a large fortune as Sir John
Orde, or any other admiral." His references to Orde are contemptuous. "I shall not talk of Sir John Orde, who must be
the richest admiral that ever England saw." "He is sent off
to Cadiz to reap the golden harvest." In fairness to Orde it
should be said that he had been pestering the Admiralty for
an appointment for some time, and that there is no evidence
that he was merely gambling on the galleons (out of which
all the same, he made a pretty haul).

Before he ever began his pursuit of the Toulon fleet which
was to take him first to Egypt, and afterwards to the West
Indies, Nelson had been made to feel the inconvenience of a
British admiral commanding immediately to the north of
him, who was personally hostile and made no concealment of
the fact. His frigates were intercepted and sent away to England by Sir John's orders. "I cannot get even my dispatches
home." In these circumstances, he decided, characteristically,
to short-circuit Sir John, and the result is a curious incident
which is worth recording, as an illustration of sea manners
in those days. Nelson sent for Captain William Parker, Lord
St Vincent's nephew, commanding the frigate *Amazon,* and
handed him his mails for London, with instructions to dodge
round Orde's fleet and dispatch them by land from Lisbon. If
he was stopped by an English ship with an admiral on board,
he was to take that admiral's orders; but to any lesser officers
he was to show Nelson's letter of instructions, and proceed on
his way, whatever they might say. "But remember, Parker,"
Nelson added significantly, "if you cannot weather that fellow, I shall think that you have not a drop of your uncle's
blood in your veins."

Parker accordingly took a wide course after passing the

Straits, hoping to escape observation; but unfortunately he was seen by Orde's fleet, and chased by a frigate, which was a better sailer than the *Amazon,* and eventually overtook him. All the other ships were then out of sight. The Captain of Orde's frigate came on board, probably not in the best of tempers. But what was Parker's relief when he recognized his old friend Captain Hoste, "that charming good boy," whom we last saw sitting blushing in a carriage with Lady Hamilton in the streets of Naples. Parker hurried him down to the cabin, and — if we may believe his own account * — pointed out to him that he owed all his advancement in the service to Lord Nelson and to Parker's uncle, and concluded with the suggestion, "Do you not think it would be better if you were not to meet the *Amazon* this night?" Hoste took the hint, and quietly departed.

It was with these incidents in mind that Nelson, having watered at Tetuan Bay, on the African coast, put in to Gibraltar on May 6, inquiring eagerly for news of the French fleet. What was his disgust to find that Orde had made not the slightest attempt to keep in touch with the flying enemy, nor had he left any frigate or sloop behind to hand on information. Driven from his station, he had merely retired with his whole force to Brest, leaving Nelson to look after himself. Orde was afterwards bitterly blamed in England for not engaging Villeneuve, which, with his five ships of the line, would merely have been suicide. The real charge against him was that he made no attempt to ascertain any of his movements, or to assist Nelson in any way. He soon afterwards resigned his command, and the Navy was rid of a singularly incompetent commander.

As for Nelson, those readers who have followed me so far will understand his state of mind. "One whole month in getting down the Mediterranean, which the French had done in nine days!" he wrote despairingly to the Duke of Clarence.

---

* Sir Augustus Phillimore, *The Last of Nelson's Captains* (London, 1891).

And now, thanks to Orde's failure, he was "as much in the dark as ever" as to the enemy's whereabouts. One of his officers described him as "almost raving with anger and vexation." "I can neither eat, drink, nor sleep," he says. On April 18 and 19 he sits in his cabin writing letter after letter to the officers commanding on the different British stations, describing himself as "broken-hearted," and "half killed," but congratulating Lord Gardner in the Channel on the great chance that may be coming his way, and assuring the Governor of Gibraltar that he will not leave him unprotected, but will "give every comfort to the old Rock." On April 19 he still definitely thought that the French were aiming at Ireland or Brest. On May 4 he was beginning to change his mind, but "I cannot very properly run to the West Indies without something beyond surmise, and if I defer my departure Jamaica may be lost." The situation was becoming desperate. "Disappointment has worn me to a skeleton," he wrote a few days later. He actually had on his desk a letter from the physician of the fleet, "enforcing my return to England before the hot months."

He never answered that letter. He was too busy preparing for his great chase to the West Indies and back. At last he had the news he wanted. Off Cape St Vincent a British officer named Campbell, serving in the Portuguese navy, came out to the fleet at considerable personal risk and gave Nelson the first certain information that the French had gone to the West Indies. (In parenthesis it may be noted that French influence in Portugal was strong enough to get this officer dismissed, and that he died soon afterwards, leaving his family in distress.) Instantly the whole world changed for Nelson. "My lot is cast, I am going to the West Indies." The prospect of immediate action fired his genius as it always did. He believed that Villeneuve had twenty-four sail of the line (in reality he had eighteen). He prepared eagerly to chase him with ten. Jamaica was in danger. If Villeneuve's strength had been even greater than he supposed it was, Nelson would undoubtedly have followed him; for, as he explained later, before the French could have destroyed him they themselves would have been so crippled that their power for mischief in the West Indies would have been practically nil.

There was a military expedition coming out from England, convoyed by Rear-Admiral Knight with two line-of-battle ships, some of the troops being destined for Gibraltar, and some for the Mediterranean. Nelson felt he must wait for them, and see them safely into the Straits. But he could hardly contain himself. His little fleet of eleven ships, weather-worn from their long vigil off Toulon, their crews hardened and tested by experience and inspired by a devoted attachment to their leader, was, without a doubt, the finest fighting instrument that had ever sailed the seas. The health sheets were as wonderful as ever; "not a man sick in the fleet" occurs more than once. Nelson himself describes them as "eleven as fine ships of war, as ably commanded, and in as perfect order and in health, as ever went to sea." They consisted of:

Victory (110). Vice-Admiral Lord Nelson; Rear-Admiral George Murray (Captain of the Fleet); Captain Thomas Masterman Hardy.

Royal Sovereign (100). Rear-Admiral Sir R. Bickerton; Captain John Stuart.

Canopus (80). Rear-Admiral Thomas Louis; Captain Austen.

Spencer (74). Captain the Hon. Robert Stopford.

Leviathan (74). Captain William Bayntun.

Tigre (80). Captain Benjamin Hallowell.

Donegal (74). Captain Pulteney Malcolm.

Conqueror (74). Captain Israel Pellew.

Superb (74). Captain R. G. Keats.

Belleisle (74). Captain William Hargood.

Swiftsure (74).

Active, Amazon, and *Decade* frigates. One store-ship and two sloops.

At noon on May 11 Knight's convoy came in sight. At 4 P.M. the *Martin* sloop left in advance for Barbados, to warn the authorities there, and get in touch with the naval officer commanding on the station. At 6.50 the whole fleet made sail.

Nelson had left the *Royal Sovereign* with Knight, partly because he thought the convoy needed more protection, and partly because her bottom was in such a condition that she would have seriously impeded his pursuit of the French, since the speed of every fleet is that of its slowest member. The *Superb,* commanded by his particular friend Keats, was in hardly better state. She had not been in an English harbour since the early part of 1801. But Keats pleaded so earnestly to be allowed to go that Nelson at last consented — with the rather ironical result that poor Keats missed the battle of Trafalgar, whereas the *Royal Sovereign,* having in the meantime undergone repairs, was present at and took a noble part in that victory. Parker tells us that Keats obtained from Nelson special leave to carry full sail all the time during the westward voyage, even when the other ships had been ordered to shorten sail for purposes of communication. His studding sail booms were kept lashed to the yards. In this way he was often able to get well ahead, so that the fleet was but little delayed. One of the pleasantest incidents of this memorable voyage was a characteristic letter dispatched from the flagship to Keats:

I am fearful that you may think the *Superb* does not go so fast as I could wish. However that may be (for if we all went ten knots I should not think it fast enough), yet I would have you be assured that I know and feel that the *Superb* does all which is possible for a ship to accomplish; and I desire that you will not fret upon the occasion. — Nelson and Bronte.

There is little to be said about the incidents of the voyage; but we may note here some of the reasons given by Dr Gillespie for the exceptionally good health of the fleet. In addition to intelligent victualling (plenty of fresh food, and wine instead of spirits in the hot weather), ventilation of the lower decks, which were kept dry and warm with stoves, and careful nursing of the few cases of sickness which occurred, Gillespie mentions particularly that Nelson encouraged "music, dancing and theatrical amusements," in which the flagship always took the lead. And he adds that "intemperance and skulking were never perhaps so little practised in any fleet as in this"; indeed they were kept so actively engaged that there was little opportunity for such indulgences.

There would be frequent interviews with his captains. Nelson always preferred a friendly *tête-à-tête* on the quarterdeck, or over a glass of wine in his cabin, to any number of formal conferences. He wrote many letters. There is one to Davison, thanking him for "paying the bills for Merton," and hoping to be able to refund the money when he finds out how his accounts stand. There are letters to Lady Hamilton, and his lawyer, Haselwood, about taking little Horatia ("my adopted daughter") out of the hands of Mrs Gibson, and making Merton her home. Mrs Gibson was to have an annuity of twenty pounds a year for life — a reward so completely out of proportion to the services that she had rendered that it is difficult to resist the impression that it must have been intended partly as hush-money. Nelson thought a lot about his little daughter. "Ay, she is like her mother," he wrote, "will have her own way or kick up a devil of a dust . . . I am afraid I should spoil her, for I am sure I would shoot anyone who would hurt her."

The French and Spanish had thirty-five days' start. Nelson gained ten upon them on his voyage out; that left Villeneuve an uninterrupted twenty-five days in which to make hay among the islands and shipping in the West Indies. No wonder Nelson trembled for Jamaica! But he should have known his enemies better. In the first place, Villeneuve's fleet, in contrast with Nelson's, was in a deplorable state of health; he landed 1000 sick as soon as he reached the first French island. In the second place he was — Villeneuve. His only warlike exploit during the whole of this interval was to recapture Diamond Rock, a small islet off the south end of Martinique, which the English had held for some time to the annoyance of the French.

Nelson reached Barbados on June 4; two days later Villeneuve, who had not yet heard of his arrival, was lucky enough to capture fourteen British merchantmen, which had very fool-

ishly set out together from the island of Antigua, hoping to
elude him. From them he learned of Nelson's presence in the
West Indies (with fourteen sail of the line, he was told). He
instantly abandoned the plan he had been preparing for an
attack upon Barbados, and decided to struggle back to Europe.
Nelson afterwards claimed, and with every justification, that
he had saved the West Indies. He did not succeed in bringing
Villeneuve to action; but "I have saved these colonies, and
more than two hundred sail of sugar-loaded ships."

But if Villeneuve remained in the West Indies until after
Nelson's arrival, how was it that he again escaped? The answer is that it was pure luck. It need hardly be repeated that
Nelson, like every man in his fleet, was eager for an engagement, in spite of the odds. When a rumour reached him that
Villeneuve had been reinforced by the Ferrol Squadron, of
fourteen sail of the line (six French and eight Spanish) which,
if the rumour had been true (which it was not), would have
brought his total strength up to about forty sail, Nelson made
this cool comment upon the opposing fleets: "Mine is com-
pact, theirs most unwieldy; and although a very pretty fiddle,
I don't believe that either Gravina or Villeneuve knows how
to play upon it." But almost simultaneously with Nelson's
arrival at Barbados there came an apparently circumstantial
report from the officer commanding the troops at Santa Lucia,
a certain General Brereton, stating that the allied fleet had
passed there going south during the night of May 28-29.
There was no earthly reason to doubt this report. Obviously
the enemy meditated an attack upon Tobago and Trinidad.
Yet Nelson hesitated: some instinct warned him that Villeneuve, now that he knew of his arrival, would either attempt
a more daring *coup* than this or retreat to Europe. However,
he turned south to Trinidad, and, sure enough, found not a
Frenchman there.

He was bitterly disappointed. For weeks after his letters
are full of lamentations — "Oh, General Brereton, General
Brereton!" and, more concisely, "Damn General Brereton!"
He wrote to Davison:

When I follow my own head, I am, in general, much more correct in my judgment than following the opinion of others. I resisted the opinion of General Brereton's information until it would have been the height of presumption to have carried my disbelief further, and now . . . he has lost me the French fleet.

But there might still be time. Villeneuve had waited to transfer some of the soldiers, with whom his decks were crowded, to the garrisons on the French islands. He had then made sail northwards on June 8, and Nelson was at Antigua four days later, and heard of it. What did this new move mean? Prophets were numerous, and they all disagreed. "In this diversity of opinions," said Nelson, "I may as well follow my own," — a highly characteristic conclusion. His own feeling was that Villeneuve had abandoned everything and was returning to Europe. On the next day he staked his whole career upon that opinion, and started once more across the Atlantic under a press of sail. He was right, as he usually was when he trusted his instinct; but he took a more southerly course than Villeneuve's, because he could not be sure of the latter's objective, and he always bore in mind that his was, after all, the Mediterranean fleet, and that his first duty was to guard the Straits. The French passed the Azores on June 30 to the northwards, the British on July 8, a little further south.

On July 18 he fell in with the squadron before Cadiz, commanded by his old friend Collingwood. Nothing had been seen there of the French, and Nelson's temper can hardly have been improved by Collingwood's frankly expressed opinion that Villeneuve had deliberately decoyed him away to the West Indies. Collingwood thought that, having got rid of Nelson by this device, the French Admiral was now picking up his ships from Ferrol and Rochefort, so that he might suddenly appear off the coast of Ireland with a fleet too strong for any British force in that neighbourhood to attack. It was not a cheerful prospect. And when Nelson landed at Gibraltar on July 20, 1805, setting foot on shore for the first time since June 1803, he was in a miserable mood. But the world in general appreciated the great effort that he had made — as no doubt did Collingwood, though that cold reserve of his prevented him from saying so. A letter written by Elliot from Naples, as soon as he heard of Nelson's return, expresses the general view. He wrote:

> After an unremitting cruise of two long years in the stormy Gulf of Lyons, to have proceeded without going into port to Alexandria, from Alexandria to the West Indies, from the West Indies back again to Gibraltar; to have kept your ships afloat, your riggings standing, and your crews in health and spirits, is an effort such as was never realised in former times, nor I doubt will ever again be repeated by any other admiral.

Meantime, as it turned out, Nelson had as effectually circumvented Villeneuve's designs in the north (whether against Ireland or the English Channel) as though he had never lost sight of him. At an early stage of the return voyage he had sent off the *Curieux* brig with urgent dispatches for London; and the *Curieux* had fortunately sighted the French fleet and noted their course, and had hurried on to England, where Captain Bettesworth had made his report. Lord Barham, the new First Lord of the Admiralty, who was seventy-nine years of age, acted with surprising vigour.' Within a few hours he had dictated and sent off his dispatches to the officers commanding the blockading squadrons before Rochefort and Ferrol. So that when Villeneuve arrived there, on a thick and hazy morning, with his fleet now reduced to twenty sail, he found the united English squadrons, amounting to fifteen ships, under Sir Robert Calder, prepared to intercept him. Calder will be remembered as Jervis's Captain of the Fleet, who, at St Vincent, had objected to Nelson's independent tactics and had ever since been generally regarded as one of Nelson's enemies. He now behaved in a strikingly un-Nelsonian manner. In a scrambling engagement with the allied fleets of France and Spain, in which neither commander could see what the other was doing because of the fog, he succeeded in capturing two of the Spaniards; but instead of following up his advantage he retired northwards and joined Cornwallis off Brest. Villeneuve put into Vigo.

That was on July 22. On August 3 Napoleon Buonaparte was at Boulogne, reviewing a line of soldiers said to have been nine miles long. These were the troops for the invasion of England (not Ireland, as Collingwood thought); and often would he turn towards the west and stare through his glasses at that western end of the Channel where he hoped to see presently the sails of Villeneuve's fleet, reinforced from Ferrol and Rochefort, and strong enough at last to give him just a few hours command of the Channel during which he might ferry this irresistible army across. He was never to see those sails. Calder had prevented it. But Calder, because he was content with this and did no more, became the butt of angry criticism in England. "Would Nelson have let the Frenchman go?" they asked, — and the answer was obvious.

Nelson, when he heard that Calder was in trouble, was genuinely sorry for it, though he was the last man in the world to excuse backwardness in the presence of the enemy. He wrote to Fremantle:

> Who can, my dear Fremantle, command all the success which our country may wish? We have fought together, and therefore well know what it is. I have had the best disposed fleet of friends, but who can say what will be the event of a battle? And it most sincerely grieves me, that in any of the papers it should be insinuated that Lord Nelson could have done better. I should have fought the enemy; so did my friend Calder; but who can say that he will be more successful than another? I only wish to stand upon my own merits, and not by comparison, one way or the other, upon the conduct of a brother officer.

And to his parson brother, who appears to have written to him on the subject, he administered this gentle snub: "We must not talk of Sir Robert Calder's battle, I might not have done so much with my small force."

Nelson himself, with his eleven ships, having taken in fresh food at Tetuan, and made arrangements with Collingwood and Bickerton for a proper defence of the Straits should neces-

sity arise, sailed northwards and joined Cornwallis on August
15. He still had in his pocket the Admiralty's letter, which
had reached him in the Mediterranean months before, author-
izing him to proceed to England on sick leave. And now, on
Cornwallis's orders, the *Victory* went on alone to Spithead,
where he landed.

He went straight to Merton. Emma, apparently, had not
been expecting him, and there was a moving little scene when
he arrived at the door. He was to have just a fortnight — no
more — and it seems almost as if these two knew it. It was a
strangely quiet little holiday, with a sort of hush over it all.
There was none of the exuberance we should expect from
emotional Emma, welcoming her hero back from the sea.
Little Horatia was there, and soon his brother and sisters, with
their children, joined him. Lord Minto dined there on August
24, and found quite a family party — Lady Hamilton at the
head of the table and Mother Cadogan at the bottom. Of
Nelson he writes:

> He looks remarkably well, and full of spirits. His conversation
> is a cordial in these low times. Lady Hamilton has improved
> and added to the house and place extremely well, without his
> knowing she was about it. He found it already done. She is a
> clever being, after all. The passion is as hot as ever.

There were several visits to London — four to be precise.
Lord Barham, the First Lord, was much impressed by Nelson's journal, when it was handed to him, and still more by
the little hero's personality. Not only were Nelson's opinions
on the actual situation listened to with the deepest respect, but
he was also expected to prophesy. He always did so, with
his usual confidence, though, as he flippantly remarked to
Keats (who was present at some of these interviews), "If I
make one wrong guess, the charm will be broken." Lord
Barham handed over his private secretary to Nelson, telling
him to dictate his own orders and choose his own officers and
such ships as he wanted in addition to his own squadron when
he next put to sea. This was flattering enough, but the adula-

tion of the populace when he appeared in the London streets was positively embarrassing. They would not leave him alone. "I met Nelson in a mob in Piccadilly," writes Minto, "and got hold of his arm, so that I was mobbed too — it is really quite affecting to see the wonder and admiration and love and respect of the whole world . . . it is beyond anything represented in the play or in a poem of fame."

It was on one of these visits to London (somewhere between the 10th and the 13th, for he left on the latter date) that Nelson had his only meeting with Wellington in the waiting-room at the Colonial Office. Wellington's account of that curious encounter is quoted in Chapter I. It is a pity that no more is known of the meeting between these two great little men: one so dry and dapper and self-contained, the other so warm-hearted, love-compelling, emotional, that they must either have become devoted friends or have despised and misunderstood each other to their dying days. They considered each other like two fencers. Wellington fell back on his natural pose, the defensive. Nelson, no doubt, was in one of his moods of nervous exaltation. It is plain that throughout this holiday he felt instinctively that some great crisis was impending. How that may have affected him at any given moment it is impossible to say. Anyhow, Wellington was won over.

But in trying to picture this fortnight our thoughts turn always back to Merton. There he spent every moment that could be snatched from public affairs. There, in "Paradise Merton," as Emma called it, he spent those last few golden days of peace and content. There, with his mistress and his child, he could momentarily forget — just for that last fleeting hour — the destiny that claimed him. Yet he never really forgot it. The presentiment that was to grow so much stronger in the succeeding weeks is already apparent in the letters that he writes about this time. And when, on September 2, his old friend, Captain Blackwood — being then on his way up to London with the urgent intelligence that Villeneuve was out again — stopped at the gates of Merton at five o'clock in the morning, it was to find Nelson already up and dressed. There was no need to tell his news. "I am sure," said Nelson, before he could speak, "I am sure you bring me news of the French and Spanish fleets." And he added, "I think I shall yet have to beat them."

We need not linger over Harrison's and Southey's accounts of how Nelson at first refused to go, saying that others might take the risk for once, and of how Lady Hamilton persuaded him. "Brave Emma!" he is said to have exclaimed, melting into tears, "If there were more Emmas, there would be more Nelsons." The story is untrue, of course. It never happened except in the imagination of Lady Hamilton. But it is not quite so silly as it sounds. There is in everything Nelson wrote and said at this time a strange reluctance quite foreign to his usual behaviour on the eve of a campaign. "I hold myself ready to go forth whenever I am desired," he wrote, "although God knows I want rest; but self is entirely out of the question." Here is a spirit of sacrifice very different from the old, eager fire.

But he did not hesitate — it is preposterous to imagine such a thing. Even his apparent reluctance is curiously mixed with a fierce determination to complete his work. And that Emma played her part like the gallant woman she had often shown herself we have no reason to doubt. On August 13, 1805, after saying a prayer by his little daughter's bedside, and bidding his love farewell, Nelson drove away for the last time from the gates of Merton — "dear, dear Merton" — and went down to Portsmouth and to the sea again.

CHAPTER XX

VICTORY

Six o'clock in the morning, at the George Inn, Portsmouth, on September 14, 1805. The *Victory* swung at anchor in the harbour. Nelson sat at breakfast with some of his officers, for he was up early, as his habit was, and he intended to hoist his flag before noon. Through the windows came the sound of cheering. A great crowd of the common people had assembled before the hotel, even at that hour, and were clamouring for a sight of their hero.

They got Nelson away by a back door and hurried him through side streets to the harbour, where his barge was waiting for him, every member of the crew an old *Victory,* every face beaming a welcome. But the people of Portsmouth were not to be denied. The news of his having left the hotel soon got about, and the cheering crowd turned and followed him. And there they were, kneeling bare-headed in the narrow road-ways as he passed, and again on the beach as his boat was pushed off, crying down blessings upon him, weeping and praying for his safe return. There are people who will call this hysteria. God help them! God help anyone who can hear the story of Nelson without being moved to tears.

As Nelson was stepping into the boat, he waved his hat to the English people he was never to see again, and turning to Hardy, deeply stirred, he said: "I had their huzzas before, I have now their hearts." It is as though he felt suddenly awed at what he had done. For he had won the heart of England — and he has it still.

He was on board at 2 p.m., and next day at 8 o'clock in the morning the *Victory* got under way. The winds were con-

sistently adverse. She had struggled as far as Plymouth on
the 17th, where two other line-of-battle ships joined her. On
the 20th, south-west of the Scilly Isles, Nelson met his old
friend Bickerton, who was on his way home from the Mediterranean ill. He heard that Villeneuve was back in Cadiz. On
the 28th, on the eve of Nelson's forty-seventh birthday, the
Victory joined Collingwood's fleet off Cadiz, then numbering
twenty-nine sail of the line, and Nelson took over the command. But, like everybody else, he understood very well the
effect that the news of his arrival would have upon the French.
Villeneuve, skulking in harbour, yet anxious to save his reputation by doing something definite before it was too late,
might well be influenced in his final decision by the presence
or absence of Nelson in the opposing fleet. He might risk an
engagement with Calder, if Calder was still there, or even,
perhaps, with Collingwood or Cornwallis; but Nelson had an
unpleasantly well-established reputation for fighting to a finish. So a frigate was sent ahead to Cadiz, warning Collingwood that, when the *Victory* appeared, no salutes were to be
fired nor even colours shown if the fleet was in sight of port.

The *Victory!* The news went through the fleet like light-
ning. Codrington says that there was "a sort of general joy."
Every admiral and captain, every junior officer who could find
a decent excuse, came crowding on board her, not just to pay
the usual formal visits to an admiral, but more like schoolboys
welcoming a hero returned from sick leave on the eve of the
decisive match of the term. Nelson says:

> The reception I met with on joining the fleet caused the
> sweetest sensation of my life. The officers who came on board to
> welcome my return, forgot my rank as commander-in-chief, in
> the enthusiasm with which they greeted me. As soon as these
> emotions were passed, I laid before them the plan I had pre-
> viously arranged for attacking the enemy.

It was a plan distinguished by the daring simplicity of genius.
We shall have more to say about it presently. In the meantime let us try to picture the scene in the Admiral's cabin on

the *Victory*. It has been painted on canvas (quite unconvincingly) more than once. Here was Nelson at the centre table, turning quickly from one to another, as he outlined his scheme in his eager, high-pitched voice. Here was the circle of veterans, with their hard, weather-beaten faces, hanging upon Nelson's words — Collingwood, cold and precise as ever, yet adoring Nelson in his heart, and every other one of them secretly rejoicing that the warm-hearted little hero had come to take the place of the conscientious martinet. "Some may be Judas's," wrote Nelson, rather unfairly, "but the majority are certainly much pleased with my commanding them." And when he had finished expounding his plan, "when I came to explain to them the *Nelson touch*" (his own expression) it was, as he wrote simply to Emma, "like an electric shock." An extraordinary scene followed. They crowded round the table, shedding tears. "Some wept," says Nelson, "all approved." They said it was so "singular," so gloriously "simple," it *must* succeed. And when, after a glass all round, they went off back to their ships, they were inspired, every one of them, with an enthusiasm and a certainty of victory which was solely the work of the genius and personal magnetism of that one crippled little man, now left sitting alone in his chair, with the thought of Merton in his heart, and the presentiment of death upon him.

This is the opening paragraph of the plan of attack as he wrote it:

The business of an English Commander-in-Chief being first to bring an Enemy's Fleet to Battle, on the most advantageous terms to himself (I mean that of laying his ships close on board the enemy, as expeditiously as possible;) and secondly, to continue them there, without separating, until the business is decided; I am sensible beyond this object it is not necessary that I should say a word being fully assured that the Admirals and the Captains of the Fleet I have the honour to command, will, knowing my precise object, that of a close and decisive Battle, supply any deficiency in my not making signals; which may, if extended beyond these objects, either be misunderstood, or, if waited for, very probably, from various causes, be impossible for the Com-

LORD COLLINGWOOD
From the painting by H. Howard in the National Portrait Gallery.

mander-in-Chief to make: therefore, it will only be requisite for
me to state, in as few words as possible, the various modes in
which it may be necessary for me to obtain my object . . .

He goes on to detail the methods by which he would break
the enemy's line and overwhelm one end of it (for that was
always his central idea) when approached from different angles,
and with the wind in different quarters. For the benefit of
his captains he added carefully drawn plans. And in a memorandum dated October 9 he further elaborated his views.

> The whole impression of the British fleet must be to overpower
> from two or three ships ahead of their Commander-in-Chief,
> supposed to be in the centre, to the rear of their fleet. I will
> suppose twenty sail of the enemy's line to be untouched; it must
> be some time before they could perform a manoeuvre to bring
> their force compact to attack any part of the British fleet engaged,
> or to succour their own ships . . .
>   Something must be left to chance; nothing is sure in a sea
> fight beyond all others . . . but, in case signals can neither be
> seen nor perfectly understood, no captain can do very wrong if
> he places his ship alongside that of an enemy.

There we have as clear an exposition as this unhandy writer
ever penned of the Nelson theory of tactics; and in the last sentence a delightfully complete epitome of what is meant by the
expression the "Nelson touch." No captain can do very wrong
if he places his ship alongside that of an enemy!

Nelson had been keeping his fleet out of sight of land, hoping
to deceive Villeneuve as to his own presence and the number of
ships in his command. It is unlikely that Villeneuve was
hoodwinked. The British force, as a matter of fact, was dwin-
dling rapidly. Rear-Admiral Louis, much against his will, was
sent with a small squadron to guard Gibraltar; and now Nelson still further weakened his fleet for a reason which does
more credit to his heart than his head. Sir Robert Calder had
joined Collingwood from the Bay of Biscay before Nelson arrived to take command, and it was now the new commander's
unpleasant duty to inform his brother officer of the Admiralty's

orders that he should shift his flag to a frigate and proceed to England for court-martial. Calder, though he himself had asked for an inquiry when the general dissatisfaction at his failure to annihilate Villeneuve first made itself heard, was terribly upset at the order to transfer to a frigate. He clearly thought that he was about to be shot like Admiral Byng (as a matter of fact he got off with a well-deserved reprimand) and appealed pathetically to Nelson to allow him to go home in his own flagship and take some of the officers of the fleet with him as witnesses. Nelson hesitated; he could ill spare either the ship or the men, and I cannot help thinking that only a little earlier in his career he would have refused emphatically. But there was a strange softness about him during these last few weeks of his life. "I have had, as you will believe, a very distressing scene with poor Sir Robert Calder," he wrote to Lady Hamilton. He granted all Calder's requests, and did his best to advise him, "as to my dearest friend." Calder was one of the two or three enemies he had made in his life. Moreover, Nelson, in his heart, could see no decent excuse for his failure. But, "he is in adversity, and if he ever has been my enemy, he now feels the pang of it, and finds me one of his best friends . . . God send him a good deliverance!"

So Calder went home in the *Prince of Wales,* a ship of ninety guns, and Nelson's fleet was reduced, one way and another, to only twenty-three sail of the line. "But I trust," he wrote to the Admiralty, "that I shall be considered to have done right as a man, and to a brother officer in affliction — my heart could not stand it, and so the thing must rest." Four ships joined him within the next few days, bringing his numbers up to twenty-seven. One of the four was the *Agamemnon,* which he had himself commanded for so long, now in the capable hands of his friend, Sir Edward Berry. Remembering her sailing qualities, he sent her to join his frigates (with which, as usual, he was ill supplied) and Berry and Blackwood between them managed to watch the French closely while maintaining rapid communication with their own fleet.

For some days past Villeneuve had been in the outer harbour, as though he might, at any moment, venture forth. Nelson, fifty miles away in the Atlantic like a hovering hawk, was waiting for the signal. Though Nelson did not know it, Villeneuve was already under orders from Napoleon (with a threat of dismissal behind them) to leave Cadiz and make for Toulon. The plan of sweeping the Channel clear and invading England had failed, through mistiming and the pusillanimity of the French Admiral. It was temporarily abandoned. A new menace had arisen in the East, where Austria, Prussia, and Russia were combining against France, and in that direction Napoleon's eyes were now turned. Villeneuve must get back through the Straits to Toulon and carry help to the troops in Italy, even if he had to fight on the way; or some one else would be found to do it. The appointment of Admiral Rosily to succeed him was already in contemplation. It was now or never with Monsieur Villeneuve.

A lot depended on the weather, which is never more unreliable in the Gulf of Cadiz than at this time of year. On October 18 Nelson noted in his diary that the weather was clear, wind easterly: "The combined fleets cannot have finer weather to put to sea." He was not to know that within the next forty-eight hours the wind would shift to the west with heavy showers of rain, and would hardly allow time for the great battle to be fought before it blew a gale. Nor did the French and Spaniards know. On the contrary, Villeneuve thought he saw his opportunity at last, and at daylight on the 19th the combined fleet began to move out of harbour with the wind behind them. And before evening the wind failed, leaving twelve ships becalmed outside and the rest still within. But at half-past nine in the morning Blackwood's frigates had seen them, and already the signal, passed from mast-head to mast-head, had reached Nelson's flagship. His moment had arrived. The enemy was out. On the following morning the rest of the French left harbour, and, the wind being now in the south-west, the whole fleet stood out from the land in line to the north-west to gain sea room before turning south for the Straits of Gibraltar. There was no mistaking their intention, and Nelson, though he had not yet set eyes upon them, immediately made signal for his own fleet to move in the opposite direction, that is the south-east, to protect the entrance to the Mediterranean.

At noon Nelson went down to his cabin. There could be no doubt now. Within forty-eight hours at the most one of the decisive battles of history would have been fought, and he, Horatio Nelson, would have fulfilled his destiny. His plans were all perfected. There was nothing more to be done. He sat down at his desk and wrote two letters:

My dearest beloved Emma, the dear friend of my bosom, — the signal has been made that the Enemy's combined Fleet are coming out of Port. We have very little wind, so that I have no hope of seeing them before to-morrow. May the God of Battles crown my endeavours with success; at all events, I will take care that my name shall ever be most dear to you and Horatia, both of whom I love as much as my own life. And as my last writing before the Battle will be to you, so I hope in God that I will live to finish my letter after the Battle. May Heaven bless you, prays your

NELSON AND BRONTÉ

My dearest angel, — I was made happy by the pleasure of receiving your letter of September 19th, and I rejoice to hear you are so very good a girl, and love my dear Lady Hamilton, who most dearly loves you. Give her a kiss for me. The Combined Fleets of the Enemy are now reported to be coming out of Cadiz; and therefore I answer your letter, my dearest Horatia, to mark to you that you are ever uppermost in my thoughts. I shall be sure of your prayers for my safety, conquest and speedy return to dear Merton, and our dearest good Lady Hamilton. Be a good girl, mind what Miss Connor says to you. Receive, my dearest Horatia, the affectionate parental blessing of your father,

NELSON AND BRONTÉ

To the first of these two letters he added a few lines on the following day, saying that the action could not be long delayed; and after his death it was found lying, still open on his desk, waiting for the last few words of reassurance which he was never to write.

All through the night of the 19th Blackwood's frigates were in touch with the fleet. In the morning he reported that "near forty sail of ships of war" were out of Cadiz, but, the wind being in the south, they could not get to the mouth of the Straits, where Nelson waited for them. About the middle of the day there were "fresh gales and heavy rain," as Nelson notes in his diary. In the evening the wind dropped again. Special signals were arranged with Blackwood: if the enemy stood to the southward he was to burn two blue lights every hour, if to the westward, he was to fire "two guns, quick." Blackwood had two frigates between him and the French, and Nelson threw out three of his fastest line-of-battle ships between himself and Blackwood. So another night passed.

It should be remembered that Nelson was still keeping carefully out of sight, so that Villeneuve might not know his strength, and perhaps lose his nerve and refuse battle after all. But the wind — what there was of it — had now swung round to the north-west, which was favourable to the Frenchman's purpose, and during the night he made sail southwards for the Straits. Blackwood's frigates could see the lights of his fleet strung out in the darkness to the east near the coast, while a faint glow on the skyline to the south-west indicated the position of the British out at sea. Only ten miles separated the rival fleets. Nelson was to the windward, and could close when he liked. He was now, at 4 A.M., standing to the north-east, so that he must meet Villeneuve soon after daylight, if the wind held. And when dawn broke behind Cape Trafalgar on October 21 the hostile fleets were at last in sight.

He made this entry in his diary:

At daylight saw the enemy's combined fleet from east to E.S.E.; bore away; made the signal for order of sailing, and to prepare for battle; the enemy with their heads to the southward; at seven the enemy wearing in succession.

And then, without pause or break of any kind, he went on:

May the Great God, whom I worship, grant to my country, and for the benefit of Europe in general, a great and glorious
U

victory; and may no misconduct in anyone tarnish it; and may humanity after victory be the predominant feature in the British fleet. For myself, individually, I commit my life to Him who made me, and may his blessings light upon my endeavours for serving my country faithfully. To Him I resign myself and the just Cause which is entrusted to me to defend. Amen, Amen, Amen.

The signal lieutenant, coming down to his cabin for instructions, while the carpenters were already pulling down the bulkheads to clear the decks for action, found him on his knees writing these words. They were the last he ever wrote. But he also got Hardy and Blackwood (who had come on board to report) to witness the famous codicil to his will, in which he formally left Lady Hamilton as "a legacy to my King and Country, that they will give her an ample provision to maintain her rank in life." Having made a similar request in regard to Horatia, he added simply: "These are the only favours I ask of my King and country at this moment when I am going to fight their battle." No man ever had a clearer presentiment of death.

Nelson rose from his knees and received the young signal officer's report. The bulkheads were all gone now. The cabin, where he had lived for so many years, had disappeared so that the deck was cleared from end to end. Even his furniture was moved, and, as they carried off the portrait of Lady Hamilton, it is said that he cried out to them to be careful of his "guardian angel." Then he mounted to the quarterdeck, wearing his full uniform and orders, as his custom was.* It was now broad daylight and the fleets only a few miles apart. Villeneuve, seeing that a battle was inevitable, and knowing in his bones that he must be beaten in spite of a superiority of thirty-three to twenty-seven, had decided that it would be more prudent to head north-east for Cadiz again, in the hope that he might be able to fight a rearguard action, as he had against Calder, and at any rate get away with most of his ships. He

---

* There is evidence that he wore his orders on all sorts of occasions—at dinner in his cabin, for instance—so that it would almost seem that he seldom took them off.

therefore made the signal to wear in succession, and stand away on the port tack — that is to the north and north-east towards Cadiz. And this the allied fleet did, but so slowly and clumsily that the manœuvre was not completed till ten o'clock.

The British fleet had borne up to intercept the enemy in two columns, that on the southern, or starboard and leeward side, headed by Collingwood, in the *Royal Sovereign*, that on the northern or weather side by Nelson, in the *Victory*, and they were now creeping slowly forward in the light wind, about a mile apart, like two spears directed against the writhing body of a pithon. Progress was desperately slow. Nelson, standing on the quarterdeck, saw that all his elaborate plans must be abandoned. It had been the original intention that the lee squadron (in this case Collingwood's) should range up alongside, and envelop the enemy's rear, while the weather squadron cut into the line farther up, separating the van from the remainder of the fleet, and assisting in the annihilation of the latter, as described on p. 291, before the van could come to its rescue. It was never intended that the British columns should advance slowly head on, and at right angles, so that their leading ships could be raked by every enemy within range for some twenty minutes or more before they could break the hostile line. Yet this was what was going to happen now, in this miserable apology for a wind, unless he was prepared to leave Villeneuve a good sporting chance of getting away with most of his fleet to Cadiz. Nelson had made three signals in rapid succession — to form order of sailing in two columns, to prepare for battle, and to bear up in succession on the course steered by the Admiral. And at eleven o'clock (the fleets being then only three miles apart) he signalled again to Collingwood, as if to explain his improvised method of attack, with its inevitable heavy casualties: "I intend to push through the enemy's line to prevent them from getting into Cadiz."

The wind was light and the air clear, but the wooden ships rose and fell in a heavy swell from the Atlantic, so that at one moment a seaman on the *Victory's* gun-deck, looking through the port hole, could see the straggling line of the hostile fleet and the dark coast behind them, and at the next moment only the sky. Nelson knew the signs of the weather in those latitudes, and he made the signal that all his ships were to anchor after the action, in order that they might not be lost in the storm that he knew was coming. Blackwood, the frigate captain, walked beside him on the quarterdeck. He had hoped that when Nelson signalled him to come on board it meant that he was to be given command of one of the seventy-fours whose captains had gone to England to give evidence for Sir Robert Calder. But Nelson made it clear that he was to remain with his frigates, though, "I shall keep you on board till the very last moment."

And now, as the rival fleets drew slowly together, it was Blackwood who, seeing the appalling slaughter that must be wrought upon the decks of the leading English ships — the *Victory* and the *Royal Sovereign,* and the *Téméraire* and *Belleisle* next behind them respectively — began to suggest to Nelson, first, that he should go on board one of the frigates, or, secondly, that he should allow the *Téméraire,* and perhaps the *Neptune,* to go ahead of him in the line. To the first suggestion he made no answer; to the second he agreed grudgingly that they might go ahead if they could. But the *Victory,* like all Nelson's flagships, was a fast sailer (he saw to that) and the *Téméraire,* with all sail set, was not able to pass him, though she managed to get alongside.

Nelson sufficiently indicated his frame of mind by fiercely rating an unfortunate lieutenant who had allowed one of the lower studding sails to be taken in. And now, as the *Téméraire* drew level, he ran to the bulwarks and hailed her. "I'll thank you, Captain Harvey, to keep in your proper station, which is astern of the *Victory,*" came that crisp clear voice. There was no holding him now. The joy of battle was upon him. "It was a treat," says Lieutenant Layman, "to see his animated and collected countenance in the heat of action." To Blackwood he said, looking towards the enemy, "I'll give them such a dressing as they never had before." Yet he knew — that is the extraordinary thing! — he knew all the time. As he saw Blackwood over the side, the latter wished him good-bye, and a glorious victory with twenty prizes. Nelson replied with sudden gravity: "God bless you, Blackwood, I shall never speak to you again."

In the meantime he had been up to the poop, where were the marines in their scarlet coats drawn up in their ranks, and Captain Hardy, and the signal officer, Lieutenant Pasco, whom we have met before. Nelson beamed on them. "I will now amuse the fleet with a signal," he said; and, after thinking for a moment, "Suppose we telegraph, 'Nelson confides that every man will do his duty.'" That would have been like him, that personal appeal. And to his men, after all, "Nelson" and "England" meant the same thing. But the signal officer pointed out that "confides," not being in the signal book vocabulary, would have to be spelled out in full; whereas there was a signal for the word "expects," which seemed to mean very much the same. He also, according to his own account, suggested the substitution of "England" for "Nelson." So the famous signal ran up.

Collingwood, that cold efficient person, was even closer to the enemy line than Nelson was. Within a few minutes they would be raking him, killing and wounding nearly six hundred of his crew. Seeing the new signal fluttering at the *Victory's* mast-head, he turned irascibly to his flag lieutenant — "I wish Nelson would make no more signals; we all understand what we have to do." But when he heard what the signal said, he was touched by that fire that only Nelson could light in him, and immediately had the words announced to his whole ship's company, who greeted it with such a round of cheers that even the French and Spaniards could hear.

Now the British ships engaged in this memorable sea-fight were as follows:

In the weather line: *Victory, Téméraire, Neptune, Leviathan, Conqueror, Britannia, Agamemnon, Ajax, Orient, Minotaur, Spartiate, Africa.*

In the lee line: *Royal Sovereign, Belleisle, Mars, Tonnant, Bellerophon, Colossus, Achille, Dreadnought, Polyphemus, Revenge, Swiftsure, Defiance, Thunderer, Prince, Defence.*

It was just about noon when the French ship the *Fougueux,* lying second astern of the Spanish flagship the *Santa Ana,* fired the first shot at the *Royal Sovereign,* which was now almost on top of the enemy's line. The scanty wind had dropped to almost nothing, so that the English ships crawled up at a snail's pace, presenting their bows, a perfect target, to the French and Spanish gunners. But such was the inefficiency of the enemy's gunnery that every one of the leading English ships, though shot almost to pieces, managed to reach the line and engage at close quarters. "See how that noble fellow Collingood carries his ship into action," exclaimed Nelson, watching from the Victory's quarterdeck about two miles away. At half-past twelve the *Royal Sovereign* passed between the stern of the *Santa Ana* and the bows of the *Fougueux,* firing into them each of her guns as it bore, at a range of a few yards. Then she put her helm over and came alongside the *Santa Ana,* engaging her broadside for broadside at short range. She was also under fire from at least four other French or Spanish ships, and ought, of course, to have been sunk. But the *Belleisle,* following her closely, relieved the pressure by engaging four French ships at the same time (having all her masts shot away in the process and a hundred and twenty-six of her crew wounded). And the other English ships, coming slowly up in succession, completed the envelopment and destruction of the Franco-Spanish rear.

Meantime the *Victory's* ordeal had begun. The *Bucentaure,* Villeneuve's flagship, the big Spaniard the *Santissima Trinidad,* and several other ships in the enemy line, had begun to shoot at her, deliberately as though at target practice. Still she came on slowly, without reply. For forty minutes this went on; her mizzen topmast was shot away, but otherwise the damage to the rigging was surprisingly slight. Fifty men were killed or wounded. Eight marines, drawn up upon the poop in the rigid manner of those days, were swept away by a chain shot;

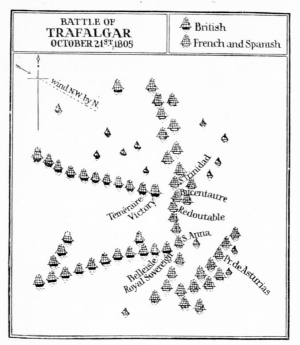

BATTLE OF
TRAFALGAR
OCTOBER 21ST, 1805

British
French and Spanish

wind NW by N.

Trinidad
Bucentaure
Téméraire
Victory
Redoutable
S. Anna
Belleisle
Royal Sovereign
Pr. de Asturias

whereupon Nelson ordered the survivors to be dispersed about the bulwarks. The steering-wheel was smashed, so that ship had now to be steered from the lower gun-deck. A round shot passed between Nelson and Hardy as they paced the quarter-deck. Another killed John Scott, Nelson's public secretary. (In regard to this incident Captain Hardy made a curious mistake of memory in later years. It appears that Scott was talking to him at the moment that he was hit; but Hardy afterwards stated that "good Dr Scott," by which he must have meant the private secretary, "was shot and cast into the sea, and that in falling his body was caught by the tackle of the ship, and his bowels torn out," a sight which he said he could never forget.) They tried to remove John Scott's remains without attracting Nelson's attention; but he paused in his walk, and asked, "Is that poor Scott?" He had a great respect for the secretary.

It was, indeed, a suicidal way of going into battle. Apart from the *Téméraire* next astern, the losses of the ships following the *Victory* in the weather line were almost ludicrously low by comparison. For instance, Sir Edward Berry, commanding Nelson's old flagship the *Agamemnon,* and placed seventh in the line, had only two men killed and eight wounded in the whole action. At the same time it is fairly certain that if the ships opposing her had been British, the *Victory,* instead of losing fifty men and her mizzen topmast, would have been dismasted and sunk with all hands before she ever reached the opposing line.

At last, just before one o'clock, she crawled up under the stern of Villeneuve's flagship, the *Bucentaure,* so close that the ships actually grazed. And immediately her guns, double shotted, began to blaze through the windows of Villeneuve's cabin, and through the whole length of his ship, each as it came to bear, just as the guns of the *Royal Sovereign* had done to the *Santa Ana.* Dust from the shattered woodwork rose in clouds; splinters flew in every direction. It has been estimated that the French flagship lost four hundred men in those few minutes while the *Victory* passed. The French and Spanish

ships, as we have seen, were untidily arrayed, hanging together
in bunches rather than in line, and one of those following the
Bucentaure (the *Redoutable*) was so close up that the *Victory* ran on board of her, and the two ships became locked together.

The Captain of the *Redoutable* was a man of original and
enterprising mind. Knowing that the French ships were unequal to the English both in gunnery and seamanship, he had
made his plans accordingly. His only hope, he decided, lay
in boarding — or, to put it another way, in action from the
upper decks. As soon as he found himself grappled by an English ship (as it happened, the *Victory*), and one of superior
metal to his own, he withdrew all his men from the lower
decks, even shutting the gun-ports behind them, and formed
them up in boarding parties on the fo'c'sle and in the waist.
The English, pumping broadside after broadside into the *Redoutable's* unresisting hull, had to station men with buckets of
water at the port holes to keep off the flames from the blazing
woodwork of the French ship. Up above, the boatswain of the
Victory, seeing the French boarding parties assembled, fired
the fo'c'sle cannonade into the middle of them, doing terrible
execution. That put an end to the threat of boarding, at any
rate for the moment. But it was part of the plan of the *Redoutable's* captain first to clear his enemy's upper decks, so that
his boarding parties might start with an open field. For this
purpose his fighting tops were crowded with marksmen, and
bullets were pattering down upon the *Victory's* poop and
quarterdeck, literally like hail.

Nelson and Hardy paced up and down the quarterdeck on
the larboard side, Nelson on the left, Hardy on the right, trying to interpose his great bulk between his companion and the
French sharp-shooters. The range from the French mizzen
top was absurdly short — perhaps twenty or thirty yards; but
the tossing of the ships in the swell made accurate aim difficult,
otherwise the British marines, shooting from behind their bulwarks, would soon have cleared these dangerous snipers' nests.
Casualties increased every moment (in the final result the *Vic-*

tory had fifty-seven killed and over a hundred wounded). A splinter of wood struck Hardy on the foot, and made him limp. Nelson looked at him with a smile. "This is too warm work, Hardy, to last long."

They continued to walk up and down. They had just reached the gangway and were about to turn and walk aft again when Hardy missed Nelson, swung round, and saw him sinking slowly to his knees. He reached out his left hand to the deck, but the bullet coming from above (from the *Redoutable's* mizzen top) had shattered his shoulder; the arm gave way and he rolled helpless on his back. "They have done for me at last," he said, as Hardy tried to raise him. And again — "My backbone is shot through." The bullet had indeed passed through his lung and his spine from left to right, and there was no hope for him.

They lifted him tenderly and carried him across those red decks; he, even in his agony, thinking to spread a handkerchief over his face, so that his men might not see who had fallen and lose heart. And somehow they got him down the ladders and into the horrible cockpit, below the water-line, where the dead and wounded lay, and the surgeons were working with their sleeves turned up and their wrists and arms red with blood. And they laid him down gently against the "knee" of the ship's side, just beside the midshipmen's berth. In the midshipmen's berth he had begun, and here was to be the end. The doctors examined him. If there was any doubt in his mind (and most certainly there was not) it was only necessary to glance at their faces. A hurricane lantern, swinging above him, gave fitful light to the scene.

At every broadside the ship seemed to stagger, shaking the sawdust from her sides in clouds. Blood ran in the scuppers. Through the hatchway came the sound of English voices, raising cheer after cheer. How was the battle going? Hardy! He sent up message after message. But Hardy was on the quarterdeck, for the moment in command of the fleet, and he could not leave his post. "Will nobody bring Hardy to me?" "He must be killed." A midshipman came down with a message to the effect that the Captain was just then much occupied, but that "he would take the first favourable moment to visit his Lordship."

In that fateful half hour, as Nelson lay a-dying, the destiny of Europe was decided — and by him. The boarding parties from the *Redoutable* had been repulsed, one after another; and the *Téméraire,* following the *Victory,* had fallen aboard the French ship on her starboard quarter and sent in such a broadside that she presently hauled down her flag. At the same time the *Fougueux,* much battered by the *Royal Sovereign,* came drifting down from the southern end of the fighting line and fell on board the *Téméraire,* on her starboard side. She was promptly boarded and taken. The *Bucentaure* surrendered; but before she did so Villeneuve signalled to his van to tack, and come into the battle. It was too late; the ships composing the rear of the combined fleet were striking their flags one after another. The plan had succeeded. The last two ships in Nelson's line, the *Spartiate* and the *Minotaur* (his old friend) had come in slowly with that feeble wind and now lay between the *Victory* and any possible attack from the French van.

Hardy took the opportunity and hurried below to see his friend. They clasped hands. "Well, Hardy, how goes the battle?" Hardy, shaken with emotion, answered huskily that we had taken twelve or fourteen of the enemy's ships. Our victory was complete. And a little later he came back again and said the total number was eighteen. "I bargained for twenty," said Nelson. He was now sinking fast. He whispered to Hardy that Lady Hamilton was to have his hair. "Take care of my dear Lady Hamilton, Hardy." And then, suddenly, "Kiss me, Hardy." And the big man knelt and kissed his forehead.

Dr Scott stood weeping beside him. "Doctor, I have not been a *great* sinner," said Nelson, turning to him. And he repeated that he had left Lady Hamilton and Horatia as a legacy to his country. The sands were running out. He knew that his work was done, his destiny fulfilled. With a last effort he

managed to whisper, "Thank God I have done my duty!" That
was the end.

They stood round him, white and speechless, stunned by
their loss. Did any of them think of Milton's lines?

Nothing is here for tears, nothing to wail
Or knock the breast, no weakness, no contempt,
Dispraise or blame, nothing but well and fair,
And what may quiet us in a death so noble.

CHAPTER XXI

ST PAUL'S CATHEDRAL

THE BATTLE had lasted two hours, from the moment when the *Fougueux* tried her first ranging shot at the *Royal Sovereign*. Collingwood's flagship, as we have seen, as soon as she broke the French line, ranged up on the starboard, or inner, side of the Spanish flagship, the *Santa Ana,* and engaged her broadside to broadside. The other English ships of the lee line, following Collingwood in due order, each of them poured a raking broadside into the *Santa Ana* as they passed on their way to take up their positions. The really critical moment of the battle was already over — the twenty minutes or more when the advancing English ships were raked by the whole enemy line. That line was now broken in two places, and the first ten French and Spanish ships were entirely cut off from the conflict, until they could come about in that faint breath of a wind and return on another tack. Local superiority had been established just as Nelson meant it to be. For all practical purposes the French were now twenty-three ships against twenty-seven. Their rear was enveloped, outnumbered, and outfought by Collingwood's squadron, their centre by Nelson's.

The *Santa Ana,* unable to bear this repeated punishment, with all her masts gone, and her admiral wounded, struck her flag at 2.15 (or, according to the log-book of the *Orion,* at 1.30). The *Royal Sovereign* lay under her lee with only her foremast standing. The *Fougueux,* which, in the same manner, had received the starboard broadside of each English ship, drifted northward, a helpless wreck, and, as we have seen, fell aboard the *Téméraire* and was carried by boarding. Of the next six ships in the enemy's rear five were captured by the

Belleisle, Mars, Tonnant, and *Colossus,* and one bore away
and escaped to Cadiz. And as the remainder came up they
also were engaged by the gathering group of British ships,
firing into them at close range, and five out of eight of them
surrendered.

In almost every case the enemy, in spite of the inferiority
of their gunnery, put up a gallant resistance. There is the
well-known story of the *Achille,* the French seventy-four
which caught fire and sank, but with her flag still flying. As
a matter of fact, as has often been pointed out, her resistance
had ceased long before this, and if the flag was still flying it
was by pure accident. The boats of the *Prince* and the *Swiftsure* were actually engaged in rescuing her crew from the burning decks at the moment when she sank. It is impossible to
describe the proceedings of each ship in detail; for though the
battle was fought strictly according to plan, as Nelson had
devised it, a thick pall of smoke hung over the surface of the
water, and visibility was so bad that you might fight a duel at
close quarters for half an hour or more without discovering
your adversary's name. Or some other ship, with her masts
trailing over her side, would drift suddenly into view and out
again. We have seen how the *Fougueux,* from the rear of the
enemy's line, appeared unexpectedly through the smoke of
battle in the centre of the line, at the moment when the *Téméraire* was avenging Nelson's death upon the *Redoutable* (it
is worth noting, by the way, that it was the marines of the
Victory who cleared the *Redoutable's* mizzen top, so that not
a man came down from it alive). The smoke became so thick
that no signals could be seen; every captain acted on his initiative, and the battle resolved itself into a series of separate actions, between small groups of ships, in which the British
always had the upper hand. As the firing died down and the
smoke lifted, it was seen that eighteen of the enemy's ships
had been captured or burned, and the rest had fled, some
towards Cadiz, and some to the south-west. "Partial firing
continued until 4.30," says the log-book of the *Victory*, "when

a victory being reported to Lord Nelson, he then died of his wounds."

That evening the gale which he had foreseen sprang up. One of his last orders had been to anchor after the action. "Anchor, Hardy, anchor," he had gasped, as he lay dying. But Collingwood thought otherwise, and, in the result, the fleet was caught while still collecting its prizes, and many of the latter, inadequately manned, were driven ashore and lost, or recaptured by their French or Spanish crews and carried into Cadiz. It had been one of Nelson's last requests that he should not be buried at sea; so they put his pathetically small and battered body into a barrel of brandy and sent it home on the *Victory,* his own ship. She reached Spithead on December 5, and was sent round to Sheerness.

England had heard the news of the victory, and of her deliverance for ever from the menace of a French invasion, early in the morning of November 6. But on the same day were published Collingwood's dispatches in which Nelson's death was announced. Instantly joy turned to sorrow: it was as if the whole nation had caught its breath, interrupted itself in the middle of a cheer. From Sheerness Nelson's body was taken up the river to Greenwich, and there lay in state for three days in the Painted Hall, where thousands came to visit it. Poor Dr Scott of the *Victory* sat up with it day and night, mourning over all that was left of his "fascinating little fellow." "Here lies Bayard," he wrote to Emma (herself prostrate with sorrow), "but Bayard victorious . . . so help me God, I think he was a true knight and worthy the age of chivalry." No truer word was ever written of Nelson.

They did his funeral really well. The body was removed from beneath its high canopy of black and gold, and was carried in procession to the riverside with "drums and trumpets" playing. It was placed on the State Barge, and the Lord Mayor of London and others in the procession — including Sir Peter Parker, the chief mourner, Lord Hood, Lord Radstock, Captain Rotherham of the *Royal Sovereign,* and many others — took their places in their barges, every one of which was covered

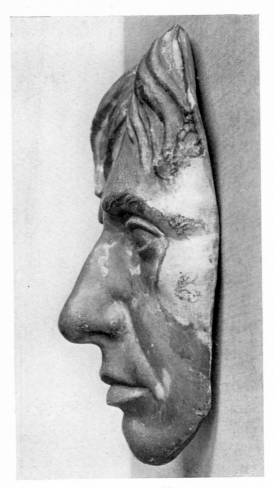

DEATH-MASK OF NELSON

This mask, showing the eyes open, is the property of Hugh Nelson-Ward, Esq. It was almost certainly taken when the body arrived at Portsmouth, and at about the same time as the other mask. See Appendix II.

308

with black cloth, and the whole long procession in order, with the flood tide in their favour though the wind was against them, proceeded slowly up the river toward Whitehall Stairs, while minute guns were fired all the way. At Whitehall the coffin was received with military honours, and conveyed through the streets to the Admiralty, where it was solemnly placed in the Captains' Room, with fifty-two candles round it.

On the next day, which was fixed for the interment, the troops who were to head the procession were drawn up on the Horseguards' Parade at 8.30 A.M. The march began at noon. After the soldiers came forty-eight pensioners from Greenwich Hospital, and after them "forty-eight seamen and marines from H.M.S. *Victory*, two and two, in their ordinary dress with black neck handkerchiefs and stockings, and crape in their hats." Then followed a long train of members of the aristocracy, beginning with the younger sons of barons, and ending with the Prince of Wales himself, who was immediately followed by Nelson's coffin on a funeral car, decorated with a carved imitation of the head and stern of the *Victory*. His brothers and sisters and the chief mourners brought up the rear. And so through the streets to the Temple Bar (where the Lord Mayor joined the procession) and up Ludgate Hill to St Paul's Cathedral, where the church received the body and laid him to rest at last, in a magnificent sarcophagus, originally designed by Cardinal Wolsey.

Emma was not at the funeral. It was not simply that she guessed she might not be wanted, that there was no place for her. She could not face the ordeal. At the news of his death she had taken to her bed, and lay there reading his letters and giving herself up to passionate grief. Across the last of them, which had been found on the desk in his cabin, she scrawled,

> O miserable, wretched Emma!
> O glorious and happy Nelson!

Miserable Emma, indeed! For the first time in her life there was no one to look after her. And though, with her usual resilience, she was soon out of bed, and going to see people, and even visiting the theatre (where she fainted every time Nelson's name was mentioned, as it often was, in some patriotic "turn") yet the evil and inevitable day eventually arrived when she found herself again in money difficulties. She had a handsome enough income from one source or another; but whatever her income had been she would always have exceeded it. Her type was common at the close of the eighteenth century, and is not unknown today.

It was at this point that she, whom Nelson had left so touchingly as a legacy to his King and country, not unnaturally turned to the Government for help. She got none. Even the Duke of Clarence, who had been Nelson's friend, did nothing. Pitt, who was at any rate a gentleman, died soon after Trafalgar. Nelson's fat clergyman brother, who had not only succeeded him in the viscounty, but had been made an earl into the bargain, and was now a rich man through no effort of his own, acted honourably according to his lights. He submitted the famous codicil to the Government (surely Nelson must have anticipated the meanness of English officialdom when he had advanced those almost pathetically groundless claims on Emma's behalf) and the British Government rejected this, his dying request.

The rest of the miserable story is quickly told. The new Lord Nelson did nothing more; his sisters remained friendly with her (after her death the Matchams gave Horatia a home) but neither of them had much money to spare. Merton was sold. She moved restlessly from one place to another, always living in her usual extravagant style, and at last the crash came. She was arrested for debt. There was a last burst of her old spirit when, on August 1, the anniversary of the battle of the Nile, she invited a number of people to come and have dinner with her, within the rules of the King's Bench prison, to drink to the "immortal memory" of the hero. "He cou'd never have thought," she wrote, "that his Child and myself shou'd pass the anniversary of that victorious day where we shall pass it, but I shall be with a few sincere and valuable friends, all Hearts of Gold, not Pincheback." Friends came to her aid, but in 1813 she was in trouble again, and a certain Alderman Josiah Smith (whose undistinguished name deserves to be held eternally in honour) bailed her out, and later helped her to get away to Calais, where she spent the last few years of her life, not very happily "lacking all but the bare necessities of life." And there, obscure and neglected, died Nelson's Emma, in the year of Waterloo.

Still, it was a great funeral.

x

APPENDIX I

THE ATTITUDE OF SIR WILLIAM HAMILTON

Up to comparatively recent times there were two great mysteries associated with the private life of Horatio Nelson, which were the constant subject of controversy and of public curiosity — (1) his relationship with Lady Hamilton, and (2) Sir William Hamilton's attitude in the matter. There has now ceased to be any mystery about the first of these. As to the second, I have not, in this book, attempted to conceal my opinion that Sir William, being a sane, and, indeed, unusually intelligent man, must have known perfectly well what was going on, and only pretended ignorance to save his face. It seemed impossible to take any other view. But recently there has come to light in the British Museum, in the collection bequeathed to the trustees by Lady Capel Cure, a letter addressed by Sir William to his nephew, Charles Greville, which is of quite extraordinary interest for the light it throws on this subject, and on the writer's character in general. As this letter has never been used before, I propose to make some quotations, using for this purpose the excellent summary given in *The Times* of May 12, 1930.

Sir William writes from Naples, under date June 1, 1785. He begins with an account of some of his recent tours in Italy, and then breaks off, with obvious reluctance, to discuss business. Evidently Charles had been pressing him to say something definite as to his (Charles's) prospects as Sir William's heir. "Had I married Lady C.," says Sir William, "as might have happened, it would have been a cruel disappointment to you after having declared you my heir." This had not happened, and Charles might now consider himself reasonably secure. Sir William himself had had (so he suggests) a hard enough time until he was relieved by the generosity of the first Lady Hamilton (who had died three years before), but he will now have enough to live on, even should he be dismissed from his Majesty's service. But he will put nothing out of his power during his lifetime: "to be sure so far I am selfish and I have lived long enough to experience that most people are so . . . Being a younger brother myself and having made my own fortune and being at liberty to dispose of it myself," he will do so. Charles must wait.

Further matters of family business are discussed before Sir William comes to what was evidently the most important proposal in Charles's letter. It is as well to continue the quotation verbatim:

> As to E., was I in England, and you was to bring your present plan to bear, and she would consent to put herself under my protection, I would take her most readily, for I really love her and think better of her than of any one in her Situation, but my Dear Charles, there is a great difference between her being with you or me for she really loves you when she could only esteem and suffer me — I see so many difficulties in her coming here shoud you be under the necessity of parting with her that I can never advise it—tho' a great City Naples has every defect of a Province and nothing you do is secret. It would be fine funn for the young English travellers to endeavour to cuckold the old gentleman, Sig. Ambasciatore, and whether they succeed or not would surely give me uneasiness — my regard for E. is such that if she leaves you and retires in the Country, which I suppose she woud do was you to marry I woud willingly make her an allowance of 50£ a year till your circumstances enable you to provide better for her. I do assure you when I was in England tho' her exquisite beauty had frequently its effect on me it never woud have come into my head to propose a freedom beyond an innocent kiss while she belonged to my friend — and I do assure you I shoud like better to be with you both here and see you happy than to have her all to myself for I am sensible I am not a match for so much wealth and beauty. Now all is out I most sincerely wish you success in any plan that can conduce to your happiness and I do really [?] believe my friendship for you is more sincere than most friendships are in this world. Adieu my Dr Charles.

I do not see how that could leave any doubt in a reasonable person's mind. As the writer in *The Times* well remarked, Sir William, in the last few sentences, deliberately hints at the tripartite establishment which he was to set up some fifteen years hence, not with Greville, but with Nelson.

The letter also affords a remarkable illustration of the contradictory traits in his character—so kindly and even generous, and yet so mercenary; so much dignity and self-indulgence, yet so little real self-respect.

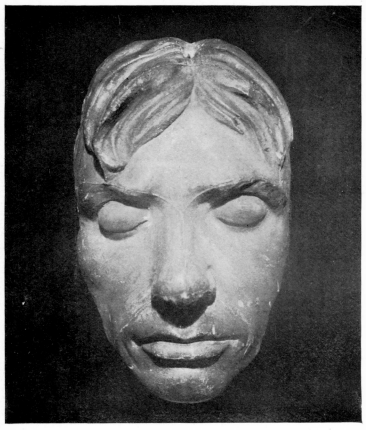

THE DEATH-MASK AT PORTSMOUTH
Photo Stephen Cribb   314

APPENDIX II

NELSON'S DEATH-MASKS

THERE exist two death-masks of Nelson, and both are reproduced in this volume, one at p. 308 and one on the paper cover.* It will be seen at once that they must have been taken at the same time, for they are almost exactly similar — except for the important difference that in one the eyes are open and in the other shut.

Now when Nelson's body was brought home from Trafalgar it was kept in a barrel of brandy, in order to preserve it — a rough-and-ready method which nevertheless succeeded. Upon arrival in port it is known that a death-mask was taken and handed over to his sister, Mrs Matcham. This is the mask with the open eyes shown at p. 308. After Mrs Matcham's death it passed through several hands, and finally became the property of its present owner, Mr Hugh Nelson-Ward. Its history is well authenticated.

The second mask (showing the eyes closed) was the property of Queen Mary until, about a year ago, her Majesty graciously presented it to the *Victory* museum at Portsmouth. Its history is unknown. But it is obviously authentic. If it had been a mere copy, the copyist would have been careful to show the eyes open, as in the Nelson-Ward mask.

The only difficulty about these masks is to explain how one can show the eyes open and the other shut, if they were taken so long after death. Professor G. S. Callender, F.S.A., the great authority on Nelson relics, has suggested that the action of the brandy probably kept the eyelids pliable. He thinks that, in these circumstances, two masks were taken when the ship reached port, one with open eyes and one with shut, and that Mrs Matcham was given her choice and chose the former. It sounds a very reasonable explanation.

It is a remarkable fact that, so far as I know, neither of these impressive and moving reproductions of Nelson's features has ever been used in a life of the hero.

---

* As the paper cover is not permanent I have thought it desirable to supply a copy of the second mask with this Appendix.

INDEX